Prospero's Daughter

The Prose of
Rosario Castellanos

BY

Joanna O'Connell

University of Texas Press
Austin

Copyright © 1995 by the University of Texas Press
All rights reserved
Printed in the United States of America
First edition, 1995

Requests for permission to reproduce material from this work should be sent to
Permissions, University of Texas Press, Box 7819, Austin, TX 78713-7819.

∞ The paper used in this publication meets the minimum requirements of
American National Standard for Information Sciences—
Permanence of Paper for Printed Library Materials,
ANSI Z39.48-1984.

ISBN 0-292-76041-8
ISBN 0-292-76042-6

Library of Congress Cataloging-in-Publication Data

O'Connell, Joanna, date
Prospero's Daughter : the prose of Rosario Castellanos /
by Joanna O'Connell. — 1st ed.
p.   cm.   —   (The Texas Pan American series)
Includes bibliographical references (p.   ) and index.
ISBN 0-292-76041-8 (alk. paper)
ISBN 0-292-76042-6 pbk. (alk. paper)
1. Castellanos, Rosario—Prose. 2. Literature and society—
Mexico. 3. Women in literature. 4. Feminism in literature.
5. Social problems in literature. I. Title. II. Series.
PQ7297.C2596Z76 1995
868—dc20   95-3795

❧ Contents ☙

▓ *Preface* ▓

There is a book on Black women's studies whose beautifully ironic title expresses a challenge: *All the Women Are White, All the Blacks Are Men, but Some of Us Are Brave: Black Women's Studies* (Hull, Scott, and Smith). The challenge is addressed to anyone whose use of categories of race or gender continues to exclude the particular experience of Black women. The authors aim their critique not only at racism and sexism, but also at their companions in critique, at those who are engaged in rewriting what it means to be women or what it means to be African American. These critical efforts, *All the Women Are White* reveals, will only reproduce the logic of exclusion as long as they are formulated in the language of "all."

The authors conjugate the experience of race and gender to assert a collective voice: "but some of us are brave." They must be brave because they will have to confront oppression both as Black people and as women. And they will be confronted by demands for allegiance that may conflict; they may be told sometimes that to speak as women is to be disloyal to men of their community; at other times they will experience alienation or racism in their relations with other women, including feminists.

I am addressed by this observation as well. As a White woman I cannot speak from the position claimed in this instance for "some of us," but I see our common task as the construction of political identities that are both critical and enabling. I am inspired in this effort by the dialogues of bell hooks and Cornel West and their reflections on the tasks facing Black intellectuals, both men and women. Bell hooks speaks to me as well when she proposes these dialogues as a sharing by people of a wider "community of faith . . . a community of comrades who are seeking to deepen our spiritual experience and our political solidarity" (2). And as a White, middle-class intellectual working in the United States in solidarity with the struggles of people in Central America as well as at home, I see that task as inseparable from the liberation struggles of people throughout the hemisphere. Speaking from a similar position, Sharon D. Welch describes this task as the intellectual and moral challenge to "develop a liberating mode . . . within my own situation, where I am both oppressor and oppressed" (13).

This is the challenge that Rosario Castellanos meets in her prose as she confronts formations of social inequality, including the situation of women in a sexist society and that of indigenous peoples in Mexico whose oppression is rooted in the persistence of colonial relations. Castellanos wrote about her contradictory social position as a woman privileged by "race," class origins, and education. Yet beginning with an exploration of her own situation and the naming of her own experiences, she laid the groundwork for the process of shifting allegiances, of constructing a social critique that was radical in its implications if not always without contradictions.

I am fascinated with the trajectory of Rosario Castellanos' writing as it moves through an exploration of this moral challenge. Locating herself deliberately in her contradictory situation as an intellectual Mexican woman, she teaches us about the ways that individuals are called on to identify with or resist competing claims for identity and allegiance. In this book, I read Castellanos' fiction and essays as lessons in how to read with integrity.

Chapter 1 presents a consideration of the Tempest analogy so often used to figure the relations of colonizer and colonized. I reread this tradition by focusing on Prospero's daughter Miranda as figure for the "(ambiguously) non-hegemonic" situation of women writers who are interpellated through their class and racial positioning as owing allegiance to the colonizer, but who, as women, are also positioned in crucial ways as subordinate.[1] Chapter 2 considers Castellanos as "resisting reader" (in Judith Fetterly's terms) of the generally accepted discourse about women and culture in her essay *Sobre cultura femenina* (1950) while Chapter 3 situates Castellanos' narrative in relation to Mexican *indigenismo* considered as ideology, social practice, and aesthetic practice.

In the following chapters, I read Castellanos' *indigenista* fiction as it explores the use of language as an instrument of domination and as a means of resistance, and the ways that different practices of interpretation shape social conflict. Chapter 7 considers the two volumes of short stories that center primarily on women's lives, and in Chapter 8 I examine Castellanos' journalism as a practice of exemplary writing, that is, as the strategic use of the newspaper forum to perform her social critique, and the enactment in a public space of feminist practices of reading.

In her fiction and essays Rosario Castellanos explores Miranda's position as she tries to write her way out of it. I read her prose as a practice of "dangerous memory" (as Welch uses this idea in her feminist thinking about liberation theology) through its naming of the memory of women's suffering and resistances, and also as an enactment of commitment to the struggles of indigenous peoples against dominant forms of knowledge. In her representations of the struggle of indigenous people in Mexico and her attempts to understand her own relation to that struggle, Rosario Castellanos encountered both the failures and the successes of this tremendously difficult task. In this respect I see her writing as an act of faith.

𝕏 *Acknowledgments* 𝕏

Tremendous thanks are due my family, and the friends and colleagues who helped see me through to the end. Francine Masiello's encouragement, her demanding reading of my work, and her example as mentor and scholar got me started and keep me going. Emilie Bergmann, Tony Cascardi, Abdul JanMohamed, David Lloyd, Felicia Miller, and Bill Berges made careful and generous comments on portions of early drafts, while Debbie Ivens' computer support saved me from the despair of endless retyping. Connie Sullivan, Amy Kaminsky, Naomi Scheman, and Cheri Register have been the ideal reading group—challenging and supportive friends—in the last stages.

I especially want to thank José Cerna-Bazán and Silvia López for their careful and insightful comments on the manuscript while acting as my research assistants. Leslie Bary's friendship and intellectual companionship have accompanied this project from the beginning, and Maria Damon helped me recover the joy of writing amid distractions.

I'm grateful to Theresa May at the University of Texas Press for her interest and her calm and cheerful support throughout the process. I also want to thank the two anonymous readers for the Press, whose meticulous, critical, and honest readings inspired my revisions and provided me with a model of professional generosity. And I must thank Maureen Ahern, both for her contributions to the academic study of Castellanos' work and for the role her translations play in bringing Castellanos' writing and ideas to my English-speaking students.

I would like to acknowledge gratefully the support of the University of Minnesota for the single quarter leave in fall 1991 and for grants-in-aid in 1991–1992 and 1993–1994, which enabled me to complete portions of this book.

Prospero's Daughter

THE PROSE OF ROSARIO CASTELLANOS

1

Prospero's Daughter

*Loyalty is an emotion, integrity a conviction
adhered to out of moral values.*

Nadine Gordimer, *The Essential Gesture* (289)

In 1950 Rosario Castellanos published an essay that begins with the question "¿Existe una cultura femenina?" [Does a women's culture/feminine culture exist?] (*Sobre cultura femenina*, 11).[1] At issue is women's cultural competence, defined as the basis for their possible participation in the cultural practices equated with civilization and public life. This question is already a response to the *"ninguneo,"* the "nobodying" or social negation, that Castellanos must overcome in order to write at all.[2]

Throughout her life as a writer, from her earliest student publications in the late 1940s until her death in 1974, Castellanos wrestled with this disabling question, one of the founding assumptions of the intellectual culture in which she participated so actively. As a writer of poetry, fiction, essays, and drama, and as a teacher and public figure, Castellanos asserted her aspirations for full citizenship in the cultural nation along with her critique of the ideas and social structures that devalue, limit, and oppress women. Through her work and public life as an intellectual, Rosario Castellanos became a key figure in the creation of the public space for the feminist discourse that re-emerged in Mexico and Latin America in the 1970s.[3]

What did it mean to speak or write as a woman intellectual in Mexico after the Second World War?[4] Although most Mexican female writers have been women of relative privilege, they could not (and still cannot) share all the privileges available to the men of their families and class, at least not without considerable struggle. In ways that Castellanos was to map in her writing, her place as a woman in Mexico was radically circumscribed, defined for her as marginal: either subordinate or exceptional. In terms of the analogy that has been used so often to characterize relations between colonizer and colonized in Latin America and elsewhere, she is Prospero's daughter; born into the family of the masters, the slaveholders, the landowners, those who hold the magic books, those who represent themselves as the forces of civilization in the face of native barbarism, yet she is not entitled to agency.

The Tempest trope has been used by many intellectuals to enact claims of allegiance and counterallegiance in a kind of metanarrative aimed at authorizing and empowering groups contesting colonial discourses. A few critics (Laura Donaldson, Paul Brown, Sylvia Wynters, Abena P. A. Busia, John Edgar Wideman) have begun to factor in the contradiction of Miranda's position with regard to these claims. Miranda is taught to owe a daughter's allegiance to Prospero; she enjoys the material benefits of Caliban's slavery, participates with Prospero in his rebukes of Caliban's rebelliousness. Yet Miranda's place in this colonialist scheme is, to use a phrase of Rachel Blau du Plessis, "(ambiguously) non-hegemonic."[5] It is as Prospero's daughter that she is located in the sphere of the powerful, that she has access to a place within the culture of the elite, but as a female she does not fully occupy the center of power in a world where female subordination is assumed. And yet, her exclusion or subordination, while real, is ambiguous given the ways her privileges are grounded in the persistence of colonial relations.

How, from this position, did Castellanos set out to claim a voice? She began by questioning her exclusion or subordination as a female writer and thinker. Through the course of her later work she developed a feminist perspective that rendered legible the oppression and suffering, both overt and internalized, of women in Mexico, often through the strategy of debunking the myths, clichés, and pronouncements that act to deny or prohibit the existence or legitimacy of a "cultura femenina."

Another part of her intellectual task is her engagement with the dilemmas of Mexican nationalism. Through her participation in Mexican *indigenismo* (indigenism), a political and intellectual movement concerned with the integration of indigenous people into national life, she tried to delineate the mechanisms of racism and structural inequality that have prolonged oppression of indigenous people despite the promises of the Mexican Revolution (1910–1924).[6] Three of Castellanos' five volumes of fiction can be called *indigenista* (indigenist) writing; that is, they are part of a major current of Latin American literature concerned with the denunciation of oppression and exploitation suffered by people known as Indians. *Indigenismo* poses national questions by linking the colonial past and the enterprise of conquest with present conditions and the need for a program of change. *Indigenismo* signals the persistence of a polarization at the heart of society: "Pone el dedo en la llaga original" [It puts a finger in the original wound] (Lienhard, "Las huellas," 12). Castellanos' original and important contributions as a feminist were formulated to critique and demystify the prevalent images, constructions, and values of her culture, and she was at the same time an active participant in *indigenismo,* a central project of Mexican nationalism after the Revolution.

Despite its profound contradictions, *indigenismo* has been a struggle to imagine and then to realize a more just and equitable form of national identity in a society founded by European domination and continued exploitation of indigenous peoples. As *indigenista* writer and activist, and as vigorous promoter of the writer's vocation as socially responsible critic, Castellanos was a vital part of Mexican intellectual life in its contradictory struggle to redefine the place of indigenous people in national culture. Unlike many other *indigenista* writers, however, in Mexico or elsewhere, Castellanos tried in her writing to understand and represent how gender is at work in the deployment of difference and in the struggle between competing visions of national identity.

Castellanos begins these tasks from her commitment to the moral imperative of addressing human suffering and imagining forms of human freedom, specifically in a Mexico where the disenfranchised might be included as fully human persons, as citizens. These positions lead her to question and reject many of the allegiances of race and class that she learned as a "White" landowner's daughter raised in the still profoundly colonial province of Chiapas. Yet Castellanos consistently rejects the facile equation of (all) women's oppression with that of indigenous people. This analysis is most apparent where she shows how the pain of sexism and racism prevent people from recognizing the suffering of others and from imagining solidarity.

Castellanos' prose wrestles with this contradiction, left unspoken in almost all of the claims of allegiance and counterallegiance made by so many critics and writers through their deployment of the Tempest trope. Because of their "(ambiguously) non-hegemonic" position, privileged women like Miranda, like Castellanos and so many other women writers in her situation, may be complicitous not only in racial and class oppression, but also in their own oppression as women. Miranda's complicity in Caliban's oppression is learned through lessons of love, loyalty, and respect for her father along with lessons in the horror of difference. Margaret Homans signals the dilemma for the woman intellectual from privileged social sectors when she says that, "while victimization takes relatively overt forms with respect to race or nationality, the silencing and oppression experienced by women as women are masked as their own choice" (198). Or, to recall Nadine Gordimer's statement about writers' allegiances, cited in the epigraph to this chapter, Miranda's particular task is to move from the emotional and filial bonds of "loyalty" that she learned as Prospero's daughter to a form of "integrity" defined as a conscious choice of values and action. For Castellanos as intellectual to move from loyalty to integrity, she must come to understand her own contradictory positioning and find a way to choose new allegiances.

In the task of imagining new social relations and contesting old narratives

of identity, Castellanos is in the mainstream of Latin American writing. However, Mary Louise Pratt makes the case in "Women, Literature, and National
Brotherhood" that the paradigms and styles of imagining national communities in Latin America, as elsewhere, are overwhelmingly androcentric; she
spells out explicitly an implication of Benedict Anderson's idea about the imagined community of nationalism as "horizontal comradeship" or "fraternity":
"Gender hierarchy exists as a deep cleavage in the horizontal fraternity, one
that cannot easily be imagined away" (51–52). And through her efforts to account for the effects of gender hierarchy, Castellanos' writing, like that of other
Latin American women writers, both emerges from that androcentric tradition and responds critically to its denial of female subjectivity and agency.[7]

In her fiction and essays, Castellanos writes about the particular history
of the southern province of Chiapas, where she grew up, in order to comment on the Mexican national situation. Violence and social tension are the
legacy of colonialism in Chiapas, despite the transformations of Independence and the Revolution. This fact has been brought to the attention of the
world by the Zapatista uprising of January 1, 1994. In order to rationalize
material oppression, colonialist discourse casts the relation between colonizer
and colonized, or between oppressor and oppressed, into "Manichean allego-
ries," or polarities of self and other (JanMohamed, 1–5). In Chiapas, the Mexican Revolution's nationalist project of unification has disrupted this model
of social relations between the landowning oligarchy and the Maya peasants,
because new national laws and the rhetoric of justice and equality provide
alternative grounds for building social allegiances. At issue in this struggle is
citizenship, understood as the inclusion (or exclusion) of people in certain
social categories (women, the poor, Indians), and their full enfranchisement
as human beings, a status that in colonial society was reserved for the few.

In the essay "Notas al margen: El lenguaje como instrumento de dominio"
[Marginal Notes: Language as Instrument of Domination] (*Mujer que sabe latín*), Castellanos recognizes the crucial importance of language as it has been
used to mark and enforce hierarchy in the history of Mexico. This issue has
important implications for her own critique since she is bound to use the
colonizer's language and assumptions to represent the experience and effects
of colonization. In other regions of the world where political independence
has altered but not eliminated colonial relations, the use of the languages of
the colonizer—for example, in Africa the use of English or French rather than
African languages—as means of cultural critique has been the subject of pas-
sionate debate, but who occupies the places set up by the opposition colonizer/
colonized seems fairly evident to all concerned—at least rhetorically.[8]

In Mexico, however, as in other Latin American countries, the distinction
between colonizer and colonized can no longer be so easily made along

linguistic lines, nor are national boundaries strictly linguistic since Spanish is the official language of many countries. The question of the identity of the colonized in Latin America cannot be reduced to a simple polarization between European and indigenous peoples and their languages, even while such polarizations persist in other forms. Yet the questions of ethnicity and language have informed writing in Mexico in fundamental ways.

The Mexican struggle for independence included a revolt by both the masses and the elite sectors; it led to the ejection of Spaniards from political rule, but did not eliminate colonial structures. These struggles were prolonged as the Creole (*criollo*, those of Spanish descent born in Mexico) and Mestizo (those of mixed European and indigenous descent) contended to establish the form and identity of the new nation and the region and to resist imperialism from other quarters, both military and economic. The identity of the colonized could no longer clearly be conceived in terms of a split between Spaniards and "Indians"; rather, the "colonized" included Creole, Mestizo, Indian, and African.[9] Spanish, as the language of literacy, and thus of political and social hegemony as well, was also the language in which national and regional identity were articulated and debated. The Mexican struggle in the nineteenth century for a national identity in the face of French and North American invasions went hand in hand with the elaboration of an ideology of *mestizaje* (racial/cultural mixture) as national identity. *Mestizaje* was promoted, especially by liberals, as the fusion of Spanish and Indian cultures, but the contradiction of this founding "we" was that it was always the project of Mestizos contesting colonialism. It was not the project of the large numbers of unassimilated indigenous peoples, who continued to resist or revolt; as "Indians" they might be mobilized or invoked to legitimize the interests of one group or another, but they were considered legitimate participants in the nationalist project only if they became assimilated into the interests and culture of non-Indians. The same critique has been leveled at the participation of writers, anthropologists, and other intellectuals like Castellanos in the elaboration and enactment of *indigenista* ideas and politics since the Revolution.

In 1992, the quincentennial of Columbus' first voyage, indigenous peoples from all over the hemisphere participated on the local, national, and international levels in the campaign called "Five Hundred Years of Resistance," a campaign that did not end with 1992. They see their affirmations of cultural identity and autonomy as inseparable from overall strategies of anticolonial political organization. One of the many challenges to a totalizing view of Latin American literature is the new understanding that emerges from indigenous peoples' representations of themselves, their history, and their visions of the future.

It is in this context that I want to reread the trope of Prospero and Caliban, which has been such an effective vehicle for utopian calls for community in the Americas. Many writers in English, French, and Spanish have read Shakespeare's play *The Tempest* as a powerful analogy for the relations between colonizer and colonized, most often to enunciate anticolonialist ideas.[10] The Cuban writer Roberto Fernández Retamar opens his essay *Calibán: Apuntes sobre la cultura en nuestra América* with a question put to him by a European: "¿Existe una cultura latinoamericana?" [Does a Latin American culture exist?] (7). This question arouses the deepest indignation in him for, in his view, it is tantamount to asking "¿Existen Uds?" [Do you exist?]. It is the cultural equivalent of the "nobodying" to which Castellanos responds in *Sobre cultura femenina*. In the history of Latin American literature, such questions have often acted as a "hidden polemic" to shape Latin American writing long after political independence affirmed the official existence of Latin American nation-states.[11] In the battle over political and cultural autonomy, literary production has been a privileged site of ideological struggle as writers grapple with the "hidden polemic," the assertion of what Fernández Retamar calls "Prospero's thesis": the opposition of European Civilization to Latin American Barbarism.[12]

In his own contribution to this vigorous revisionist tradition of rereading Shakespeare's play, Fernández Retamar traces the history of the Prospero/Caliban analogy and of the various roles these figures have played in the service of different ideological positions. All identify Prospero as the European who possesses and controls what is considered high culture. Some have portrayed him as a positive figure representing Civilization; in 1878, the French philologist Ernest Renan gave voice to his reaction against the Paris Commune in *Caliban, suite de la Tempête,* where he identified Caliban with the mob. In response to the bloody anticolonial revolt on Madagascar in 1948, Octave Mannoni expressed a more ambivalent view, using the figures Caliban and Prospero in a psychoanalytic model of paternalistic colonial relations to claim that the colonized rebelled because they were afraid that the colonizer would not live up to the colonial relation, and that they in fact desired a state of dependence.

For writers engaged in anticolonial movements, however, such as the Cuban José Martí at the turn of the century or Caribbean Francophone writers Aimé Césaire and Frantz Fanon after World War II, rereading the play and remobilizing the analogy were acts of resistance to the hegemonic colonialist discourse made concrete in the readings of Renan or Mannoni.[13] Their use of the Caliban analogy was meant to counter negative stereotypes, but it was more than a gesture of negation; it was also a means of affirming a positive cultural position, and of valorizing the African and Creole elements of colonized peoples' cultures. For those educated in the English colonial school system, such as Barbados writer George Lamming, Shakespeare symbolized the culture to which the colonized could aspire but never be admitted. Re-reading *The Tempest* was thus a powerful counterstrategy for contesting colonial discourse; the anticolonial writer engaged with a text from Prospero's canon and then worked to redefine its values, to expand its terms so as to include a new reality and a perspective previously silenced. In this way, the (male) anticolonial intellectual could both claim the European cultural heritage and rewrite it.[14]

José Enrique Rodó wrote his hugely influential essay *Ariel* in the aftermath of the United States' 1898 seizure of Spain's last colonies. Rodó used Ariel to represent the Latin American intellectual, who, in his view, should be mediator between two cultures, while Caliban represented the uncivilized, materialist Yankee. But along with French- and English-speaking writers, Spanish-speaking intellectuals later came to identify with Caliban as a way to position themselves in anticolonialist struggles. Fernández Retamar takes up José Martí's warning from his essay "Nuestra América" [Our America], and defines Caliban as the American Mestizo, of mixed racial and cultural heritage, who embodies the utopian and revolutionary impulses of colonized peoples.

Rob Nixon provides a very thorough review of more recent permutations of the Prospero-Caliban trope. He points out that the counterreadings that denounce racism and colonialism through the figure of Caliban seize on two passages of the play as emblematic of colonial struggle. The first passage, concerning the claims of territory, is Caliban's reproach to Prospero: "This island's mine by Sycorax my mother, / Which thou tak'st from me" (Act I, ii: 331–332). The second passage is one of special importance to writers and intellectuals for it concerns the circumstances in which their own acts of rereading occur: the problematic relation to the language of the colonizer. Caliban says: "You taught me language, and my profit on't / Is, I know how to curse. The red plague rid you / for learning me your language!" (Act I, ii: 362–364). This curse represents the paradoxical situation of the Latin American (or of anyone who identifies with Caliban), who must respond to a colonizing discourse using the language of the colonizer. Fernández Retamar sums up the problem when he asks:

Ahora mismo, que estamos discutiendo con esos colonizadores, ¿de qué otra manera puedo hacerlo sino en una de sus lenguas, que es ya también nuestra lengua, y con tantos de sus instrumentos conceptuales que son ya nuestros instrumentos conceptuales? (12)

Even now as we debate with those colonizers, how else can we do so except in one of their languages, one that is also now *our* language, with their conceptual instruments, which are now *our* conceptual instruments?

It should be evident from this brief overview of some of the uses of the Prospero/Caliban analogy that it has been invoked in an ideological struggle over cultural territories that threatens the boundaries of nationalist literary traditions; the colonized assert their presence and thus challenge their exclusion from nationalist and European canons. They call attention to the institutional uses of literature, in the schools and in traditions of reading taught there, that form and sustain discourses of racism and colonialism. Moreover, writers from different colonial situations claim common cause with the colonized everywhere, proposing their own way of reading and use of literature as distinct from the European (or European-based), often around the common bond of a non-European (whether African or Native American) heritage.[15] New generations of readers, actively reclaiming the play, render legible the protests it tries to contain.

Yet, powerful as this symbol and strategy may be, they still depend on a duality: the polarization between colonizer and colonized, between White and Black, or between Europe/United States and Latin America. This binary opposition can also act to suppress recognition of other differences. In "Three Women's Texts and a Critique of Imperialism," Gayatri Spivak remarks that neither Ariel nor Caliban figures the indigenous cultures of the Americas: it is clear that Fernández Retamar uses Caliban to represent the Mestizo. *Mestizaje,* whether understood as "racial" or as cultural mixture, has its origins in violence. In some areas of Latin America it is an option that has been resisted by indigenous peoples for centuries, even if only partially, and despite tremendous pressure. Indigenous peoples have their own languages and cultural traditions to which they can turn as an alternative to hegemonic culture.[16] However, in the different versions of the Tempest analogy, even those put forth by anticolonialist writers, they are not present as interlocutors. The Ariel-Caliban antitheses to Prospero's thesis are both enunciated in the language of Prospero, but indigenous people and their culture are silenced in this dialogue. In Mexico, as elsewhere in Latin America, the anticolonial critique that motivates *indigenismo* contains the same contradiction, as Castellanos' work makes clear.

Another exclusion is at work in all of the readings and rereadings of the Caliban trope: the exclusion of female subjects. Rob Nixon does note that this configuration has exerted almost no attraction for women writers; this is because the whole complex analogy is so explicitly gendered that it suppresses recognition of the subjectivity and agency of female subjects unless they render absolute allegiance to the forms of their own subordination. Caliban's claim to the island is through his mother Sycorax, yet, as Abena P. A. Busia demonstrates, in both the analogy and its anticolonial rereadings Sycorax is the figure for the colonized woman who is silenced in what Busia calls "a deliberate unvoicing" (87), subsumed as a figure for the land, the territory of struggle but not an agent or a subject.

The other exclusion of female subjectivity and agency reproduced in many of these critical rereadings appears in the very exchange on language that so many writers have used to illustrate the cultural situation of the colonized writer. This exchange is usually quoted as occurring between Prospero and Caliban. Prospero claims to have enslaved Caliban because he tried to rape Miranda, his daughter, and Caliban chortles: "O ho, O ho! Would't had been done! / Thou didst prevent me; I had peopled else / This isle with Calibans" (Act I, ii: 349–351). Critics almost always attribute the reply that follows to Prospero:

[PROSPERO.] Abhorrèd slave,
Which any print of goodness will not take,
Being capable of all ill! I pitied thee,
Took pains to make thee speak, taught thee each hour
One thing or another: when thou didst not, savage,
Know thine own meaning, but wouldst gabble like
A thing most brutish, I endowed thy purposes
With words that made them known. But thy vile race,
Though thou didst learn, had that in't which good natures
Could not abide to be with; therefore wast thou
Deservedly confined into this rock, who hadst
Deserved more than a prison.

CALIBAN. You taught me language, and my profit on't
Is, I know how to curse. The red plague rid you
For learning me your language! (Act I, ii: 352–364)

In fact, it is Miranda, not her father, who delivers the "Abhorrèd slave" speech in the 1623 Folio. This critical misidentification is the result of a silencing that occurred early on in the canonical Shakespearian editorial tradition. In 1667, John Dryden substantially rewrote much of *The Tempest;* one of the changes he made was to put these lines in the mouth of Prospero.[17] Until quite recently, editors have maintained this attribution, justifying the change on the grounds that Miranda is too innocent to have spoken so roughly. The energy she displays in these lines did not accord with their idea of the feminine. The editorial note that typifies this attitude (and that is cited approvingly by later editors) is that of Theobald, who wrote in 1726:

> I am persuaded that the author never design'd this speech for Miranda. In the first place; 'tis probable Prospero taught Caliban to speak, rather than left that office to his daughter. In the next place, as Prospero was here rating Caliban, it would be a great impropriety for her to take the discipline out of his hands; and, indeed, in some sort an indecency in her to reply to what Caliban was last speaking of. (Shakespeare, *New Variorum*, 73)

Some current editions of the play still sustain this variation, despite the scholarship that has since restored Miranda's voice. Given this editorial history, it is no wonder that even critical readers have (unknowingly) perpetuated the false attribution.

And yet, the logic of the play itself has worked to sustain this silencing. Miranda's role is to mediate the desires and power struggles of masculine figures: Caliban attacks her to avenge himself on Prospero, and Prospero manipulates her in his quarrel with his enemies. Miranda's own awakening desires, which might run counter to her father's designs, are properly channeled in the end through marriage and dynastic alliance. Mary Jacobus writes of how this trope—woman as object mediating exchanges between men—operates in and structures texts by male theorists. Miranda can be seen as another example of the woman whose role is that of object mediating between masculine desires, or who serves as the terrain for struggle between masculine subjects.[18]

Miranda represents the situation of a particular kind of woman in the colonial society of which Prospero's isle is the figure, but not that of all women. She is defined through her familial relation to a man, her father, Prospero. But if he is the only man apart from Caliban whom she has ever seen on the island until she sees Fernando, she has seen no other women either. Other women are mentioned, but absent. The princess Claribel, whose marriage was the reason for the sea voyage, has been the means of a dynastic alliance of exactly the kind Miranda will make, passing from the control of one man to another. The purpose of that control—legitimacy—is the uneasy basis for the only mention made of Miranda's mother: "Thy mother was a piece of virtue and / She said thou wast my daughter" (Act I, ii: 56–57). Sycorax, Caliban's mother, was a woman of power and is dangerous precisely because that power was not subordinated to the masculinist structure of power on which Prospero bases his grievance: inheritance that passes through legal paternity and the recognition of the father's name.

Even though it is clear that Shakespeare stages this very trope as a problem by showing Prospero's manipulations and desire for power as dangerous, the resolution of the play works to contain the impulses and the discourses associated with Miranda, Ariel, and Caliban. In "'This Thing of Darkness I Acknowledge Mine': *The Tempest* and the Discourse of Colonialism," Paul Brown provides a thorough and fascinating discussion of *The Tempest* within its own moment of English colonial expansion in the Americas and in Ireland, reading the play through its efforts to register and contain the contradictions of that enterprise at home as well as in the colonies. Brown places the play in the context of English writing in which the colonizer defines and attempts to discipline the "non-civil" subjects through discourses of "savageism" and "masterlessness" as well as through a discourse of dangerous sexuality. Miranda is interpellated as the "civil virgin," and allowed voice only to the extent that she accedes to Prospero's account of history and manipulation of her sexuality.

In the play, Caliban and Ariel speak their own desires and claims for autonomy, and a long line of intellectuals have used these figures to make claims of political independence and to assert the existence of cultural identities for the colonized. The defiant stance of a Caliban is to appropriate Prospero's language, as writers appropriated the trope of Caliban itself, and to turn it to one's own ends. But the exchange about language between Miranda and Caliban shows that Miranda is Caliban's teacher—the schoolmarm, the social worker, the intermediary who is entitled to use the language, but who, in other contexts, is also positioned by that discourse as subaltern. The very real and troublesome question for Miranda as well, then, is whether using the language and concepts that seek to limit her agency to her role as Prospero's daughter (his agent or mouthpiece) does not simply amount to perpetuating the logic of the hegemonic discourse.

We can see that both the canonical tradition and the countertradition of using the Tempest trope are already gendered or gender-inflected. By replacing Sycorax and Miranda in the dialogue, another story becomes legible, another way of reading becomes possible; neither suppresses knowledge of the gendering of imagined communities as fraternities.

As part of a project for rereading the writing of Mexican women intellectuals like Castellanos, we must recognize that Miranda is not and cannot be the figure for all women involved in colonial relations; she cannot stand for women in dominated social groups. Thus, it would be wrong to say Miranda represents Woman, or "the feminine" or "the female." Rather, the figure of Miranda represents a specific contradiction, not because she is a woman but because, as a woman, she is named as Prospero's daughter and identifies herself with him and with his role as bearer of culture. The figure of Miranda renders legible conflicting allegiances, contradictions in the structures of

11

power in terms of relations between women as well as between groups with other forms of corporate identity. Casting either the colonized or the female as "other" is an ideological move that masks particular historical circumstances of oppression. As Busia has pointed out, in this respect the play's figures can be read as metaphors for another crucial aspect of colonialist fictions: "It is important to note that images of all women in colonial fiction run in tandem acting as polar opposites of each other: European women voiced, unsexed, and the focus of much power, the native woman silenced, licentious, and powerless" (86 n8).

Busia is primarily concerned with the necessary work of restoring voice to those who have been positioned historically as "native woman." I see Castellanos' intellectual trajectory as a rich site for understanding how women intellectuals who have been interpellated as Prospero's daughters ("voiced, unsexed, and the focus of much power") learn to reread and remake their own allegiances.

These uses of the Tempest analogy join the vigorous tradition of reconfiguring colonial cultural relations through the figures of Caliban and Prospero, in a process that Adrienne Rich has called "writing as re-vision." She is speaking of women's writing, but her words capture the spirit of the task of any writer engaged in choosing new political allegiances as well:

> Re-vision—the act of looking back, of seeing with fresh eyes, of entering an old text from a new critical direction—is for women more than a chapter in cultural history: it is an act of survival. Until we can understand the assumptions in which we are drenched we cannot know ourselves. And this drive to self-knowledge, for women, is more than a search for identity: it is part of our refusal of the self-destructiveness of male-dominated society. A radical critique of literature, feminist in its impulse, would take the work first of all as a clue to how we live, how we have been living, how we have been led to imagine ourselves, how our language has trapped as well as liberated us, how the very act of naming has been till now a male prerogative, and how we can begin to see and name—and therefore live—afresh. A change in the concept of sexual identity is essential if we are not going to see the old political order reassert itself in every new revolution. We need to know the writing of the past, and know it differently than we have ever known it; not to pass on a tradition but to break its hold over us. (35)

Rich describes the task of both the writer and the critic as a new kind of reading, one motivated by a consciousness of community, and moving toward a reconstitution of community through a new relation to language and to the past. The act of writing can be said to require here, as for writers in any colonial context, a prior task, in Myra Jehlen's words, "the construction of an enabling relation with language that itself would deny them the ability to use it creatively" (77). The new versions of Caliban's story describe a discursive practice that has worked as such an enabling strategy.

My own strategy for reading Castellanos' prose takes her writing as such an act of re-vision, of rereading old "texts" from a critical perspective, whether those texts be the maxims and myths that structure the lives of women like her or the historical discourses of ethnic conflict in which *indigenismo* intervenes. Yet, as the Miranda analogy makes clear, to even begin such a critical reading means working toward an understanding of her own situation as "(ambiguously) non-hegemonic."[19]

Judith Fetterly describes this process as the move from "immasculation" to becoming "the resisting reader." Through the social practices and institutions of literature and reading, women (and especially women intellectuals) learn how to read the texts of the hegemonic androcentric culture properly; that is, they learn to read as men: "the cultural reality is not the emasculation of men by women but the *immasculation* of women by men. As readers and teachers and scholars, women are taught to think as men, to identify with a male point of view, and to accept as normal and legitimate a male system of values, one of whose central principles is misogyny" (xx). What Fetterly is describing is how female readers are interpellated into an androcentric system of values and are expected to function as ventriloquists.[20] The response of the resisting reader, whose reading may be enacted as writing or scholarship, is to question those loyalties and read against the grain.

Castellanos' place as a female intellectual in Mexico means that she is supposed to read not only from a male point of view but specifically from Prospero's point of view, from within the framework of a colonizing mentality. There is safety for Miranda if she remains complicit in the oppression of subaltern groups, including women. To question, to talk back, to be "disloyal to civilization" means, as Adrienne Rich reminds us in the essay of that title, dealing directly with sexism and racism; the "resisting reader" runs the risk of being cast out of the subordinate safety available to the "civil virgin." Within the symbolic economy of Prospero's civilization, the only alternative to Miranda's position seems to be the one defined for Sycorax (Sphinx, Medusa); in Mexico, historically and mythically, one figure of the woman who speaks and acts for herself is Malinche, a popular symbol of victimization and treachery.[21] How, then, to imagine a way out of these stories? Through her performance of critical rereadings, Castellanos creates a space in which readers can imagine their social relations in new ways, not by suppressing knowledge of gender hierarchy in the service of the national fraternity, but in ways that incorporate a critical consciousness.

What I want to explore is the ways that an explicit analysis of gender relations transforms the *indigenista* project of Rosario Castellanos and the extent to which her analysis of class and ethnic conflict contributes to her evolving feminism. Castellanos performs critical rereadings and then turns each act of rereading into a new point of departure. These in turn suggest new grounds of authority (new kinds of truth claims) and potential spaces of creating bonds of community with readers.

In a country with a high rate of illiteracy, where education is still a privilege, where access to publication and circulation of books is still limited to a small group, and where women writers are still regarded as exceptional figures, who are the women who become writers? Most of them, like Rosario Castellanos, have been women of relative privilege; they are most often from middle-class or upper-class families (in a country where those two groups are in the distinct minority); certainly they are of the few with access to a university education. Women writers in Mexico, as elsewhere in Latin America, are most often women of greater material privilege than the majority of women in their countries. This was the case for Castellanos, daughter of a family from the landowning oligarchy of the southern state of Chiapas, a part of the country where the majority of the population is still Maya-speaking indigenous people.

Castellanos was, by birth and by education, a member of the most privileged sectors of Mexico. Her family was part of the old elite that derived its status in Chiapas from its Spanish conquistador ancestors. Their local domination was built on the exploitation of indigenous labor and buttressed by a racist ideology that dictated the cultural and racial superiority of their class. This elite's local power was not seriously disturbed by Independence, although some left Mexico for Guatemala, but it was challenged by the Mexican Revolution and by the consolidation of the state's control over the provinces.

Castellanos was born in Mexico City on May 25, 1925. The family returned almost immediately to their home in Chiapas, where they were to live until Rosario was sixteen, dividing their time between the family ranch and the small town of Comitán de las Flores near the Guatemalan border. When tensions between landowners and the Maya who worked their land increased, the family moved permanently to Comitán. Although not wealthy, the family occupied an elite position in the rigidly hierarchical provincial society.[22] Castellanos and her younger brother, Mario Benjamín, were kept isolated from the rest of the world by their parents, who made no secret of their preference for the male heir. When the boy died, Rosario was more isolated than before; she was to recall her childhood as a time of great loneliness.

During the thirties, the Mexican state justified its redistribution of power and resources with a rhetoric of social justice for the poor as it extended modernization efforts begun by Liberals before the Revolution. While these efforts often favored the middle or upper sectors rather than poor or indigenous peoples, the latter were now recognized as legitimate participants in national life. When Castellanos' family moved to Mexico City in 1941 as a result of Lázaro Cárdenas' agrarian reforms, they moved to the anonymity of middle-class life, without the household of servants and the assumption of social status they had enjoyed in Chiapas. This move also gave Castellanos access to an education she probably would never otherwise have had. In Mexico City, she was able to go to the best preparatory school, and then to the National Autonomous University of Mexico (UNAM). She began her university studies in law, but soon disappointed her parents by switching to literature and then to philosophy in an effort, as she said, to find answers to some of the questions of values that the move from Chiapas to Mexico City had made urgent for her.[23] She wrote poetry and collaborated on literary magazines as part of a group of young writers later called the "Generation of '50."[24]

In a candid and often bitter interview, Castellanos called her parents' marriage a disaster.[25] There was little communication between them, never a physical gesture of affection, and her father slept in the same room as the two children, Rosario and her younger brother, Mario Benjamín (Poniatowska, ¡Ay vida, 116). Rosario's father, César Castellanos, was a person of considerable importance in their town. From a prominent landholding family, he had been educated in the United States as an engineer, and was involved in local politics and in running the local school. All of these things made him an attractive marriage prospect, but he remained unmarried until the age of forty. Castellanos' mother, Adriana, was from a poor family and had little education. What is more, she was still unmarried at twenty-two, almost an old maid by the standards of a small Mexican town in the twenties. When César decided to marry her, he had not yet ever spoken to her; he asked her mother for permission.

Rosario was brought up in intimate contact with indigenous people, especially women, but like all children of her class, she was taught to consider herself superior. The two children were cared for by "la nana Rufina" and they also had a *cargadora*, an Indian girl their own age who lived with the family and whose "job" it was to serve as playmate and toy. In the Castellanos family, this girl, María Escandón, was paid seven centavos a day. Castellanos was to say later,

> Yo no creo haber sido excepcionalmente caprichosa, arbitraria y cruel. Pero
> ninguno me había enseñado a respetar más que a mis iguales y desde luego
> mucho más a mis mayores. Así que me dejaba llevar por la corriente. El día en
> que, de una manera fulminante, se me reveló que esa cosa de la que yo hacía uso

era una persona, tomé una decisión instantánea; pedir perdón a quien había yo ofendido. Y otro para el resto de la vida: no aprovechar mi posición de privilegio para humillar a otro. ("Herlinda se va," El uso de la palabra, 262)

I don't think I was exceptionally capricious, arbitrary, and cruel. But nobody had taught me to respect any but my equals and especially my elders. So I let myself be carried by the current. The day that it was revealed to me, in a flash, that this thing that I was using was a person, I made an instantaneous decision: to ask the pardon of the person I had offended. And another decision for the rest of my life: never to take advantage of my position of privilege to humiliate another.

Castellanos does not say exactly when this revelation occurred, but it could have happened at any time over a period of years, for María Escandón was to remain in service with the family even after their move to Mexico City; after the death of Castellanos' parents in 1948, María Escandón stayed with Castellanos until her employer married at the age of thirty-two: "Ya vas a estar bajo mano de hombre" (literally, "Now you'll be under a man's hand") was how María put it (*El uso de la palabra,* 263).

From her dependence on her parents and on her servant, a decent woman was supposed to pass into a relation of dependence and indeed subordination to a man. María's dependence was of a different order. When she returned to Chiapas and went to work for Gertrudis Duby de Blom, her new employer was shocked to learn that Rosario had never taught María to read or write. Castellanos was socialized into the caste and class privileges of her society, and the process of becoming conscious of these structures and of rejecting them was a long one.[26] She was to spend years working with the Instituto Nacional Indigenista (INI) working for social change in her home in Chiapas and attempted in all her writing to analyze and denounce the sexism, racism, and multiple forms of oppression of the society in which she grew up, but as she acknowledged in an essay published in 1973, she was still blind to many of the forms of her own privilege: "Yo andaba de Quetzalcóatl por montes y collados mientras junto a mí alguien se consumía de ignorancia" [I was running over hill and dale playing Quetzalcóatl (an ancient Mesoamerican redeemer/cultural hero) while next to me someone was consumed by ignorance] (*El uso de la palabra,* 263).

As well as the rigid structures of relations between Ladinos, as non-Indians are called in this region, and Indian, master, and servant, Castellanos learned early the hierarchy of male and female in her world. Both children were overprotected, and neighbors recalled how the parents kept them from playing with other children. Benjamín, however, was sent to a good school while Rosario was sent to a girls' school that was decidedly inferior; it served as the model for the girls' school in her first novel, *Balún Canán*. When this school was closed by the government as part of the antichurch measures in the thirties, Rosario was kept at home with her mother and the indigenous servants. Of her brother she said,

> *Nació dueño de un privilegio que nadie le disputaría: ser varón. Mas para mantener cierto equilibrio en nuestras relaciones nuestros padres recordaban que la primogenitura había recaído sobre mí. Y que si él se ganaba las voluntades por su simpatía, por el despejo de su inteligencia y por la docilidad de su carácter, yo, en cambio, tenía la piel más blanca. (Solana, 89).*

He was born owner of a privilege that none would ever dispute: being male. But to maintain a certain equilibrium in our relations our parents reminded us that primogeniture had fallen to me. And that if he won people over by his congeniality, by the clarity of his intelligence, and by the docility of his character, I, on the other hand, had whiter skin.

The three important factors whose conjugation structured life in the provinces and conferred status or value were gender, property (primogeniture), and skin color. But Castellanos was to absorb the bitter lesson of the absolute value of the male when her brother died.

When Rosario was eight, a cousin of her mother's who was involved in spiritualism told Adriana that she had dreamed that one of the children would die. Adriana's immediate reaction, overheard by both children, was "¡Pero no el varón!" [But not the male!]. Their mother's choice was clear, but the children were afraid. When the boy died of appendicitis only a few weeks later, the family was devastated. Castellanos told Samuel Gordon that she overheard again, "¿Por qué murió el varón y no la mujercita?" [Why was it the male who died and not the little girl?] (Poniatowska, *¡Ay vida*, 91). It was evident to the child that her parents would willingly have sacrificed her for her brother, yet she suffered tremendous guilt because in her fear she had wished that her brother would die instead of her. These guilty memories were the germ of *Balún Canán*.

With the death of the male heir, her parents placed all their hopes in Rosario. This meant sending her back to school, but she was both smothered by their fears for her safety and acutely aware that, in some sense, her parents resented that her existence forced them to continue living:

> *Yo me sentía al mismo tiempo muy superflua pero también muy frágil . . .
> Recuerdo que tenía 22 años cuando murió mi mamá; yo no sabía prender una*

cerilla a esa edad. Nunca me habían dejado hacer nada. *"No; te va a dar
catarro." "No; lo vas a quebrar." No. No. No. ¿Qué puede hacer una mujer
así . . . sentarse a escribir . . . ¿no?* (Poniatowska, ¡Ay vida, 119)

I felt myself at once very superfluous and also very fragile . . . I remember
that I was twenty-two when my mother died; I didn't know how to light a
match at that age. They had never let me do *anything.* "No, you'll catch a
cold." "No, you'll break it." No. No. No. What can a woman like that do . . .
sit down and write, no?

A woman of her class was expected to be dependent, but, unlike María Escandón, Rosario had access to education. Reading and, later, writing were to
provide Castellanos with a refuge from the loneliness and isolation of her
childhood, a means for rejecting a world hostile to her as a female and also a
way for her to attempt contact with other worlds. Yet if reading was a form
of escape, and later of empowerment, it was also a site of struggle. In a number of autobiographical texts, Castellanos figures scenes of a girl's reading as
traumatic inductions into gender prescriptions.

The essay "Lecturas tempranas" [Early readings] (*Mujer que sabe latín*)
stages the process of learning to read as one that involves a frightening inscription into gender roles and structures of power. Castellanos claims that
reading was a refuge, a door into another world because the real world gave
her a sense of "vertigo." Her description of her first attempts to write make it
clear that her verses were also meant to act as a kind of charm against that
solitude.

Reading did not always mean pleasure and safety, however. Embedded
in these reflections on the act of reading is a disturbing drama of how her
own literary competence came to be painfully marked by her interpellation
through gender. She says she discovered the existence of evil by reading
Perrault's fairy tales. Reading one tale in particular, "Piel de asno" [Donkey
Skin], produced a crisis. In this story, the princess tries to escape the amo-
rous attentions of her stepfather by running away covered with the skin of
an ass. Castellanos recounts that she was horrified that anyone would use
such an obviously noticeable costume as a disguise:

*Nunca averigüé el final de la aventura porque, naturalmente, caí enferma. Los
médicos diagnosticaron lo que es ortodoxo que padezca una niña: resfrío,
indigestión. Pero yo sé que mi fiebre tenía otro origen: el miedo. Y que el miedo
(que aún hoy me estremece, que aún hoy me hace subir la fiebre) se originaba en
el descubrimiento del mal del que yo no sólo tendría que ser la víctima—tarde o*

temprano—sino también el instrumento, el vehículo, la personificación. (Mujer que sabe latín, 188)

I never found out the end of the adventure because, naturally, I fell ill. The doctors diagnosed what was orthodox for a girl to suffer: chills, indigestion. But I know that my fever had another origin: fear. And that the fear (that even today makes me shudder, that even today makes a fever rise in me) originated in the discovery of an evil of which I would be not only the victim—sooner or later—but also the instrument, the vehicle, the personification.

It was not only the discovery of evil itself that horrified her. The girl Rosario was reading herself into an incest story. Her own child's experience and logic seemed to tell her that wearing the skin of an ass would not be a very effective disguise, that the princess wanted to get caught. As a reader she identified with the female character, the daughter, and saw that to be female in the eyes of others meant accepting female sexuality as victimization. She was learning to read a system of gender. Second, through this positioning as female there also occurred a seeming complicity with the system of signification that also threatened her: she read the daughter's means of escape as a sign that she wanted to get caught. In both ways, she was an "instrument of evil." To be interpellated as female according to this story involved both victimization and guilt. The position from which she might read was here a site of struggle over meaning, one that she lived in her body's feverish refusal of that interpellation. The authorities, the doctors, read her bodily symptoms in the orthodox manner, one that had nothing to do with her own consciousness, with what she "knew" was happening to her. To be positioned as female means here to be threatened; to learn to circulate in this system at all means to be a victim. Yet the disguise, the means she might try to use to escape—reading itself and intellectual activity—will mark her difference and her revolt and make her somehow responsible for her dis-ease.

The end of her first novel, *Balún Canán*, also links becoming a writer with a guilt structured by the demands of gender interpellations. The circumstances surrounding her brother's death as explored in this novel involve a reading similar to the one described in "Lecturas tempranas." The guilt she felt over her imaginary complicity in that death was that of a female trying to escape the control of a patriarchal discourse in which the female could and should be sacrificed to save the male (see Chapter 4 here).

The 1966 essay "Historia mexicana" (*El uso de la palabra*) gives another example of Castellanos' reflection on the consequences for the adolescent

Rosario of reading and speaking as a woman. In form, this essay is like a parable, almost a fairy tale, that parallels her own history. It relates the fate of an intelligent girl growing up in the Mexican provinces as an ugly duckling; the first sentence pronounces the judgment of her community: "Era anormal" [She was abnormal]. That she should read and write were bad enough, but that she should also speak! "Era que hablaba" [It was because she talked] (48). Intelligence in a girl is such a curse that her parents decide to leave town, and her intention to study at the university is considered the height of absurdity.

The title "Historia mexicana" extends the irony of the essay from the individual case to the situation of women in Mexico in general: conformity or isolation. In her poetry and prose Castellanos dissects the mechanisms of socialization that place women in the kind of impossible situation she describes in "Lecturas tempranas," of complicity in victimization and the kind of painful visceral resistance that precedes the "toma de conciencia" [moment of coming to consciousness] that she considered so vital. These dramas about the consequences of reading as female in this social world prepare our understanding of Castellanos' insistent return to this theme in her fiction and essays.

In 1941, at the age of sixteen, Castellanos moved with her family from the sheltered provincial life she evokes in "Historia mexicana" and in the stories of *Ciudad Real* to the capital of Mexico. In Chiapas the world revolved around her family's class. Every aspect of life was colored by the distinctions between Ladino and Indian. But, as Castellanos pointed out later, the agrarian reforms did not necessarily impoverish the landowners. It was, rather, the loss of their social status, the damage to their self-conception that they found so terrifying:

> . . . el aniquilamiento del símbolo que ellos habían encarnado. Allá en sus tierras, en sus propiedades, en sus dominios, eran señores de abolengo y sus antepasados habían hecho la historia y sus descendientes conservarían los privilegios. ("El hombre del destino," El uso de la palabra, 205)

> . . . the annihilation of the symbol they had incarnated. There on their lands, on their property, in their domains, they were lords of high lineage whose ancestors had made history and whose descendants would retain their privilege.

In this same essay, Castellanos declares that it was the fact that Cárdenas' land reforms wrenched apart her family's world that made it possible for her to escape the stifling and limited options laid out for her as female.

Because of her drastic lessons in gender hierarchy and her anomalous situation as a female intellectual, Castellanos was already somewhat disaffected from the norms of her childhood world, but she would be able to articulate an understanding only much later. The highly autobiographical story "Three Knots in a Net" (translated by Maureen Ahern) continues where "Historia mexicana" leaves off, after the family has arrived in the capital. In place of the essay's mockingly humorous tone, this story communicates an appalling family dynamic of frozen rage and displaced emotional violence. The young girl's own acts of cruelty (torturing lizards, shutting her mother out of her success in school) are presented as acts of survival uninformed by the clearer understanding available to the adult looking back on her past.

In 1948 both her parents died, her mother of cancer and her father of a heart attack. In that year, influenced by her discovery of José Gorostiza's *Muerte sin fin,* Castellanos wrote and published two long poems—*Trayectoria del polvo* and *Apuntes para una declaración de fé*—works that she later rejected as too abstract but that attracted some recognition.[27] Her third book of poetry, *De la vigilia estéril,* was published in 1950. That same year she finished *Sobre cultura femenina.* While she would change many of her ideas in years to come, as a sustained examination of women and writing this last essay stands as an important document in Latin American feminism.

After completing her thesis, Castellanos received a scholarship to study in Spain for a year. With her friend the writer Dolores Castro, she traveled through Europe, an experience both said made them more conscious of what it meant to be Mexican. Back in Mexico, she returned to Chiapas, where she got her first job in Tuxtla Gutiérrez as a cultural organizer. She went to work with great enthusiasm, but came down with tuberculosis after a year and had to go back to Mexico City, where she spent a year in bed recovering. While she did research on Mexican women and culture with a Rockefeller grant, she continued to write and publish poetry, including some poems with indigenous themes in *El rescate del mundo* (1952). She also tried her hand at writing dramatic pieces from 1953 to 1955 and began to write her first novel and some short stories based on her memories of Chiapas.[28]

The years 1956–1957 were important ones for Castellanos. Impelled by a sense of the debt her family owed the Maya who worked their land, she returned once more to Chiapas, this time to her home, to work for the Instituto Nacional Indigenista. At first she worked without pay, and she also gave away what land she had inherited (Poniatowska, *¡Ay vida,* 112). She was put in charge of the traveling puppet theater called Teatro Petul and went about on horseback with six Maya men, speakers of both Tzeltal and Tzotzil, presenting didactic puppet shows that promoted indigenous assimilation through notions of Mexican citizenship (see Chapter 3 here). At the same time, she was finishing *Balún Canán* and working on her second novel, *Oficio de tinieblas,* and the stories of *Ciudad Real.*

When she was thirty-two, Castellanos returned once more to Mexico City where she married UNAM professor of philosophy Ricardo Guerra, a late marriage by Mexican standards of the time. In the next three years she was pregnant three times, but only the last child, her son, Gabriel, survived at birth; he was born in 1961. In the years after leaving Chiapas, Castellanos kept up an extraordinary pace of activity both as a writer and as an intellectual working in various institutions of Mexican culture. She published *Balún Canán* in 1957, the poetry collection *Al pie de la letra* and two dramatic poems, *Salomé* and *Judith,* in 1959, the short story collection *Ciudad Real* and the poetry volume *Lívida luz* in 1960, *Oficio de tinieblas* in 1962, and more short stories in *Los convidados de agosto* in 1964. At the same time, she continued to work for the INI editing school materials, and then was director of public relations for the UNAM where, throughout the sixties, she also gave classes in comparative literature. On top of all this, she wrote a weekly column for the major newspaper *Excélsior.*

Castellanos enjoyed great success as a teacher, poet, and novelist, but her journalism brought her a new, wider, and more popular audience. In her columns she wrote in a direct and personal voice about a variety of topics, especially the literature and history of Mexico; in particular she wrote often about women. These essays were collected and published in *Juicios sumarios* [Summary Judgments] (1966) and *Mujer que sabe latín* [A Woman Who Knows Latin] (1973). Two other collections of essays, *El mar y sus pescaditos* [The Sea and Its Little Fishes] and *El uso de la palabra* [The Use of the Word], were published posthumously, and over ninety more essays remain unanthologized (Ahern, *Homenaje,* 134–143). The essays in *Mujer que sabe latín* show the range of Castellanos' feminist ideas and concerns; it is this book and not *Sobre cultura femenina* that has had an impact on women readers seeking affirmation of their own concerns and insights. These essays are themselves her ironic counterpoint to the fate dictated by the second half of that traditional saying, "ni tiene marido ni buen fin" [will have no husband and come to a bad end].

Castellanos and her husband were divorced in 1971, and when she was offered the post of ambassador to Israel, she accepted it. Her characteristically ironic and self-deprecating newspaper articles recounting her experiences there show her initial insecurity over this new role rapidly turning into a great joy. In addition to her work teaching and promoting Mexican trade and culture, in 1972 she published *Poesía no eres tú* [You Are Not Poetry], a volume collecting all of her previously published poetry as well as some new material. She returned to dramatic writing with *El eterno femenino: Farsa* [The

Eternal Feminine: A Farce], a corrosively feminist piece that takes on the gender myths of Mexican history and contemporary life with the tremendous humor and irony that had come to characterize her later writing.

Rosario Castellanos died in 1974 at the age of forty-nine, accidentally electrocuted by a lamp at the Mexican Embassy in Tel Aviv. Her burial in La Rotunda de Hombres Ilustres [The Rotunda of Illustrious Men] in Mexico City was the occasion of many personal expressions of love and grief. It was also the occasion for what Elena Poniatowska terms the "beatification" of Castellanos by the state:

> Mito o no, institucionalizada en los sesentas como una segunda Virgen de
> Guadalupe, adulada, condecorada y reconocida por los grupos de poder,
> Rosario Castellanos fue una figura bien ajena a los que pretendían beatificarla.
> (¡Ay vida, 45)

> Myth or not, institutionalized in the seventies as a second Virgin of
> Guadalupe, adulated, decorated, and recognized by the groups in power,
> Rosario Castellanos was a figure very different from those who proposed to
> beatify her.

Despite her public career as a feminist, Castellanos is often treated, like Sor Juana Inés de la Cruz, as one of the "great exceptions"—a woman who was a great writer in spite of her gender.

Castellanos' writing examines the responses of individuals as they try to negotiate between competing and contradictory loyalties and constructions of identity. In her first published prose, the essay Sobre cultura femenina (1950), she tried to work through the conflict she experienced as a female intellectual seeking a place within the cultural sphere as one of the Prosperos, an impossible enterprise that moves her in the direction of a feminist position not yet clearly articulated. In her fiction of the fifties and sixties, she continues her critique from a position as an indigenista writer and participant in the politics of indigenista action. Her books of that period, Balún Canán and Oficio de Tinieblas and the short stories of Ciudad Real and (to a lesser extent) Los convidados de agosto, map the complex intersections of two kinds of inequality: the situation of women in sexist societies and that of indigenous peoples in the Americas, through the example of the Maya in Mexico, whose oppression is rooted in colonialism and the persistence of colonial relations. Her last collection of short stories, Album de familia [Family Album] (1971), while no longer thematically oriented by overt ethnic conflict and more centered on the lives of middle- and upper-class women in Mexico City, continues her exploration of the social dynamics of oppression, resistance, and consciousness. And throughout the sixties and seventies, in hundreds of newspapers essays, Castellanos created a public space as a woman intellectual engaged in redefining the national community.

In Castellanos' two novels, where we can recognize the situations of women like Miranda, it will be through the figures of other women, especially mothers, that the problem of contradictory social allegiances for "Prospero's daughters" will be posed. Solidarity or positive bonds between women are either frustrated or absent in Castellanos' fiction until her very last story, in contrast to her essays, where such bonds are enacted through Castellanos' remembering and praise of other women.

The question of the existence of a "cultura femenina" is the starting point for Castellanos' self-definition as an intellectual. If it can be read as a skeptical question that Castellanos must answer, it can also be read as Miranda's question to Prospero about the possibility of speaking or writing, of claiming a voice as a woman when she has been taught to read from Prospero's books. In this context her *indigenista* writing constitutes a further refusal to swear allegiance to her father's world. Her fiction addresses the issue of the responsibility of the writer in Mexico as social critic: to name reality, to denounce injustice.

We can read her work as a consistent attempt to answer the question of where she stands. What is her place if she refuses to be Prospero's obedient daughter? From what standpoint can she re-vision her world? How does she find another place from which to speak that is not Miranda's? All of us who read Castellanos are compelled to return to the last lines of the poem "Meditación en el umbral" (*Poesía no eres tú*, 316):

> Otro modo de ser humano y libre
> Otro modo de ser.

> Another way to be human and free
> Another way to be.

The words *human* and *free* are key in her intellectual engagement with the problems of place and voice in her essays, beginning with *Sobre cultura femenina*.

In *Sobre cultura femenina* Castellanos tries to come to terms with the powerful interdictions aimed at women writers. Although these first efforts were rather abstract, later she was to become more conscious of how women shared certain situations as women, but were divided by class and ethnicity in ways that made it almost impossible to communicate or to unite. In her poetry, drama, and prose writing she was to denounce the forms of injustice she saw, and in her newspaper columns she was to advocate that Mexican women and men become conscious of that injustice and work for change.[29]

Through her dramatization of the conflicts and consequences of ways of reading, Castellanos calls on her audience to learn a new way of reading the history of Mexico and the experiences of women. Many readers of Castellanos' work return to the words of her friend José Emilio Pacheco, in his prologue to *El uso de la palabra*:

> *Cuando se relean sus libros se verá que nadie en este país tuvo, en su momento, una conciencia tan clara de lo que significa la doble condición de mujer y de mexicana, ni hizo de esta conciencia la materia misma de su obra, la línea central de su trabajo. Naturalmente, no supimos leerla.* (8)

> When we reread her books we will see that nobody in this country had, at the time, so clear an awareness of the meaning of the double condition of woman and Mexican, or made of this consciousness the very stuff of her writing, the central line of her work. Naturally, we didn't know how to read her.

Years after her death, a community of readers is beginning to try to learn to read along with her.

2

Castellanos as Resisting Reader: Sobre cultura femenina

Suppose we were to ask the question: what became of the Sphynx after the encounter with Oedipus on his way to Thebes? Or, how did Medusa feel seeing herself in Perseus' mirror just before being slain?

Teresa de Lauretis, *Alice Doesn't* (109)

Rosario Castellanos was born into the most privileged class in her family's social world. Yet, as a Mexican woman who was also an intellectual she had to contend with a society that regarded these two as incompatible. She was to make this dilemma the subject of her master's thesis in philosophy, "Sobre cultura femenina." Published as a book in 1950, a year after Simone de Beauvoir's *Le deuxième sexe*, this essay questions the Western philosophical categories and values that define women as inferior and limit their possibilities for intellectual and literary activity.[1] *Sobre cultura femenina* deserves to be read as a courageous attempt by Castellanos to challenge deeply rooted assumptions about women's capacity to act as cultural subjects, especially as it was written three years before Mexican women won the right to vote, and at the end of almost a decade of silence and disarray from a previously vigorous women's movement.[2] This project was vital to her if she were to be able to write at all.

Sobre cultura femenina is significant as an early consideration of women's participation in cultural production, especially writing, in Latin America. Written without the benefit of the decades of sustained feminist inquiry that have provided us with a critical vocabulary and a wide audience for such ideas, the essay raises many of the questions about women as cultural subjects that still motivate such discussions: Does a women's culture exist? How has Western philosophical discourse defined women's capacity as cultural agents? What has been the impact of such negative notions on women's creativity? What is the relationship for women between creativity and motherhood?

But while *Sobre cultura femenina* anticipated the resurgence of feminism in Mexico and Latin America in the seventies, it did not reach a wide public when it appeared, before Castellanos had achieved celebrity as a writer and widely read journalist. Reread in the light of her later work, *Sobre cultura femenina* is a text marked by profound ambivalence, motivated by a powerful but never clearly articulated rejection of the misogynist tradition of Western European thought, yet still closely bound up in the concepts and values of that tradition. At stake is whether or not women can be accorded full status as knowers and subjects, whether they will be granted the citizenship conferred by cultural literacy. But the fact that the question is posed in fairly abstract, idealistic terms with no direct reference to Castellanos' own historical context is a measure of how much her discussion is determined by the terms of the discourse she questions.

Sobre cultura femenina represents the first step in the trajectory of Castellanos' feminist thought as it developed over the next twenty-five years in her fiction, poetry, drama, and journalism. She begins the essay with a question that must have been urgent for the young writer who had just published her first two books of poetry: "¿Existe una cultura femenina?" (11). This question can be translated into English in two ways: "Does a culture of women/made by women exist?" or "Does a feminine culture exist?" In the first case, *femenina* is synonymous with *de mujeres*—of or by women—and posits women as producers of culture. Translating *femenina* as feminine, however, shifts the focus of the question from whether or not women can be artists to the possibility of difference in women's cultural activity and the related question of the cultural construction of the feminine.[3] The problem Castellanos must resolve is the negative prescriptive force that definitions of the feminine have on women like herself who are, or want to be, subjects of cultural production.

We have seen how Roberto Fernández Retamar begins his essay *Calibán* by responding to a very similar question: "¿Existe una cultura latinoamericana?" (7). He makes clear that the assumption motivating such a question arises from "Prospero's thesis" that European culture acts as the universal standard for Civilization, and that this thesis historically has worked as a euphemism for assertions of racial superiority over non-White peoples; to question the existence of a group's culture is to refuse to recognize in that group the capacity for human agency.[4] *Sobre cultura femenina*, like *Calibán*, is a response to the negation and silencing that such questions enact.

Fernández Retamar attacks Prospero's thesis directly; the historical successes of the Cuban Revolution in 1959 and of other anticolonial struggles lend authority to his claim that Caliban's position is a Latin American revolutionary subject. And a growing international dialogue and textual tradition of anticolonial cultural critiques that use the Prospero-Caliban analogy also provide resonance for his use of these figures. In *Sobre cultura femenina* Castellanos attempts a similar revisionary and critical project in that she tries to imagine women as cultural subjects by working through some of the disabling historical constructions of the feminine. However, she was not writing in the

27

context of a collective experience of successful political struggle by Mexican women, but, rather, at a moment when public awareness of the rich and substantial history of women's political activism in Mexico had been contained and suppressed; Castellanos was to go on to investigate women's writing later, in the years following her studies.[5] And, as she herself acknowledges in the essay, there was for her no culturally or historically sanctioned place from which to speak as a female producer of culture within the terms of European philosophy. Instead, the figures available for her to imagine herself as an intellectual woman are images of impossibility and monstrosity:

la imposibilidad absoluta de que monstruos tan extraordinarios como las serpientes marinas y las mujeres cultas o creadoras de cultura, sean algo más que una alucinación, un espejismo, una morbosa pesadilla. (11)

the absolute impossibility that monsters as extraordinary as sea serpents or learned women, women who create culture, could be more than a hallucination, a mirage, a morbid nightmare.

The *Tempest* analogy that works so powerfully for anticolonial writers could not provide Castellanos with an enabling metaphor; the dilemma for Castellanos in *Sobre cultura femenina* is that to speak as a woman intellectual means an oscillation between speaking as Miranda, the dutiful daughter of the ruling class whose role it is to act as the bearer of Prospero's word, or as a female monster, a "sea serpent" or a "morbid nightmare."

As she was grappling with the conflict between being a woman and being a writer as those two terms were defined for her, there was almost no public space for a feminist discourse in Mexico that would lend authority to her efforts. When she wrote this work she was not connected to an organized women's movement or engaged in dialogue with feminist thinkers in her country. Like Simone de Beauvoir, Castellanos chose to write in an authoritative academic mode, yet, more like Virginia Woolf in *A Room of One's Own*, at times she displays a great deal of ambivalence about her excursions into such frankly hostile territory. In parts of *Sobre cultura femenina* she uses an elaborate irony and some rather slippery rhetorical strategies to camouflage her critique.

Unlike Woolf and de Beauvoir, however, she wrote *Sobre cultura femenina* before achieving her public success as a writer, and without the encouragement of an entourage of (sometimes) supportive, successful (male) intellectuals. This comparative isolation shows in the uneven results; the text is painfully contradictory and seems divided from itself. At times her splendid irony leaves little doubt that she rejects the misogynist categories she examines, while at others, her status as student and her own internalization of misogynist discourse seem to sweep away her confidence; she appears to accept without question the very concepts she mocks elsewhere. In this first step toward a feminist critique Castellanos only partially succeeds in challenging the authority of a philosophical tradition that denies women a capacity for creativity outside of biological reproduction. The ambivalence that is staged in the text opens up a space for critique, but it also escapes her control. Despite this division, the essay has some powerful moments when another voice resonates through the masters' voices.

Castellanos avoids overtly assuming the label of feminist, although her subject is the participation of women in culture. Indeed, in part of the essay she seems to accept the definitions of "feminine" and "culture" as handed down to her by a virulently misogynist philosophical tradition. This posture corresponds to Judith Fetterly's idea of "immasculation" (see Chapter 1), whereby female readers are interpellated into a system of values that equates male experience with personhood. Castellanos here is deliberately adopting immasculation as a strategy of enunciation.

And yet, at the same time, *Sobre cultura femenina* is also clearly a feminist essay if we take feminism to suppose a consciousness of a situation of inequality and oppression for women, an opposition to this state of affairs, and a commitment to change. Without this dimension of opposition or advocacy, an interest in women can just as easily be antifeminist as feminist. A feminist consciousness does shape *Sobre cultura femenina* by marking rhetorically within the text a place for an impertinent female reader who resists her positioning as feminine, and, by so doing, denaturalizes her immasculation. Through a strategy of ironic double-voiced discourse, Castellanos questions the litany of voices that would deny women agency and personhood. The resisting reading staged in the text conveys an acute longing for "otro modo de ser" [another way to be] ("Meditación en el umbral," *Poesía no eres tú*, 316).[6]

The seven chapters of *Sobre cultura femenina* fall into three parts, marked by shifts in rhetorical strategies. The first two chapters pose the question "¿Existe una cultura femenina?" and the problem of how Castellanos as a woman can answer it. Parallel to the question with which Roberto Fernández Retamar begins *Calibán* ("¿Existe una cultura latinoamericana?"), this question poses Prospero's thesis of the civilized male through the negation of female creativity and cultural agency. In this opening section Castellanos' tone is ironic and playfully subversive, but in the middle part of the essay, Chapters 3, 4, and 5, the irony all but disappears as Castellanos struggles with some of the prevailing negative definitions of the feminine. She adopts a masterful tone, combining the logical progression of her argument with a grand display of erudition, but not questioning the concepts she presents. In the last two chapters, the ironic distancing returns as she tries, unsuccessfully, to resolve for women writers the dilemma of their relationship to prescriptive notions of womanhood.

Even as she poses the question of the existence of *cultura femenina* Castellanos ridicules a previous tradition of answers; she compares her question to the one about the possible existence of sea serpents and qualifies both questions as superfluous and stupid. In its day, she says, the question of the existence of sea serpents generated much learned opinion and heated argument; like the question of *cultura femenina*, it also arose from a "rumor" about the existence of such astonishing creatures. The rumor has generated books and heated pronouncements both for and against; some adventurers claim to have seen the fabled monster,

> *Pero hay también, al lado de estos generosos y frecuentemente exagerados visionarios, un coro de hombres cuerdos que permanecen en las playas y que desde allí sentencian la imposibilidad absoluta de que monstruos tan extraordinarios como las serpientes marinas y las mujeres cultas o creadoras de cultura, sean algo mas que una alucinación, un espejismo, una morbosa pesadilla. (11)*

> But there are also, next to these generous and often exaggerated visionaries, a chorus of sensible men who remain on the shore and from there make pronouncements about the absolute impossibility that monsters as extraordinary as sea serpents or learned women, women who create culture, could be more than a hallucination, a mirage, a morbid nightmare.

Her irony is specifically directed at the authority of those who claim to know, those "sensible men" who have never left the shore yet profess to know what lies out there in the ocean depths.

If common sense today holds that such creatures as sea serpents are imaginary, then extending the comparison would seem to imply that the *mujer culta,* the learned woman, is imaginary as well, although Castellanos' own enunciation of her text suggests that common sense should tell us the opposite. Unlike sea serpents, women exist, but the question "What is a woman?" (as Simone de Beauvoir pointed out) is really about the social category "woman" and had not generally been elaborated out of the experience of being a woman at all; historically, most of those who have pronounced opinions have been "sensible men" for whom women's experience is an uncharted ocean. Castellanos announces that her goal is to account for that "chimera"

(11), the intellectual woman, but her underlying anxiety is that the intellectual woman is not a "real" woman at all.

The elaborate irony of this opening paragraph, with its extended image of voyages into perilous waters in search of a creature that strikes terror into men's hearts, invites us to read what follows from a skeptical position. For most of the rest of the chapter, Castellanos simply quotes long passages by philosophers who state flatly that women are incapable of reason or of participation in cultural activity. She reports the discourse of a few of the more virulently misogynist "sensible men"—Schopenhauer, Weininger, and Simmel—and the chorus of voices that tell her she must not, cannot speak.[7]

This chapter seems to me an enactment of Teresa de Lauretis' image of Medusa looking at herself in the mirror before she is slain, a chilling representation of the bifurcated consciousness of the female intellectual trying to read her way out of such a monstrous fate. The answer that the men give to Castellanos' question as to whether or not a *cultura femenina* exists is, unsurprisingly, "No." Woman has no "I," says Weininger (*Sobre cultura femenina,* 14), and woman receives her consciousness from man, says Schopenhauer: "Tomadas en conjunto las mujeres son y serán las nulidades más cabales e incurables" [Taken altogether women are and will be the most perfect and incurable incompetents] (*Sobre cultura femenina,* 12). Simmel claims that women are amoral and that their being is entirely in their sex (*Sobre cultura femenina,* 19). While Castellanos quotes most extensively from three men in a specific philosophical tradition, she is careful to place their words at the end of a long history of similar statements by other men, from Aristotle to Nietzsche, who have been "unable to resist the temptation" (24), as she puts it, of such mockery and insults. She maintains her distance from these pronouncements from the shore by interjecting ironic asides between the long quotations, as, for example, in her characterization of Simmel's notion of the relation of women to culture:

> *Muchos autores han querido hacer de la mujer una especie de poder tras del trono o de diablo tras de la cruz, y de la cultura una especie de enfermedad que, como la hemofilia, las mujeres no padecen pero transmiten. (19)*

> Many authors have tried to portray women as a kind of power behind the throne or devil behind the cross, and culture as a kind of illness that, like hemophilia, women transmit but do not suffer.

The last paragraph in Chapter 1 states the problem for the woman reader of such authoritative statements on women, but retreats from an explicitly confrontational posture, tempting though that might be:

Mucho quisiéramos, como las inconfundibles feministas, protestar airadamente
contra un destino tan monótono, tan arbitrariamente asignado y tan modesto.
Pero la fidelidad a la convicción íntima nos lo impide. En efecto. Atentas
observaciones de nuestras semejantes presentes y pasadas, de próximas o ajenas
latitudes, despiadada introspección, nos convencen de que las teorías que hemos
expuesto son verdaderas, que las aseveraciones, por ofensivas que parezcan,
son justas. Y sin embargo . . . Aceptemos las experiencias de quienes nos
antecedieron y sus conclusiones. Pero no confiemos ciegamente en ellas. Acaso
no se ha llegado al punto que se debía porque no se escogió bien el camino; tal
vez el deseo preconcebido—el prejuicio—era tan fuerte que aunque hayan
tocado puntos distintos de los que se propusieron, persistieron en considerarlos
como si fueran aquellos que habían planeado y en vez de regocijarse y
enorgullecerse por el descubrimiento de fértiles Américas continuaron creyendo
haber alcanzado legendarias Indias. La crítica, no obstante, es impracticable si
no se tiene una base sólida, un punto seguro desde el cual partir. Y para
establecer este punto no queda más remedio que recurrir a la propia tentativa, a
la propia labor, al propio hallazgo. (28)

We would so like, as unmistakable feminists, to protest angrily
against a destiny so monotonous, so arbitrarily assigned, so modest. But
faithfulness to intimate conviction prevents us from doing so. Indeed.
Attentive observations of other women, past and present, from latitudes
near and far, a pitiless introspection convinces us that the theories we have
presented are true, that these assertions, however offensive they may seem,
are right. And yet . . . Let us accept the experiences and the conclusions of
those who have preceded us. But let us not confide blindly in them. Perhaps
they did not arrive at the point they should have because the path was not
well chosen; maybe preconceived desire—prejudice—was so strong that
although they arrived at points that were not the ones they proposed to
reach, they persisted in considering them as if they were the ones they had
planned and, instead of rejoicing and taking pride in the discovery of fertile
Americas they continued to believe that they had reached the legendary
Indies. A critique, nevertheless, cannot be practiced without a solid base, a
sure point from which to depart. And to establish that point there is nothing
left to us but to fall back on our own endeavors, our own work, our own
discoveries.

To accept but not to trust will be her rhetorical strategy: the subjective "Aceptemos . . ." [Let us accept . . .] announces the hypothetical nature of what
follows; it keeps open a space for doubt. Castellanos is not ready yet to identify herself overtly with feminists and, indeed, distances herself from them in

this passage, either because it is not safe or because she really is not sure of her ground. But the phrase "Y sin embargo . . ." [And yet . . .] widens the doubt into a protest, a space that is as yet in the form of an ellipsis. The doubt is reinforced in the ironic metaphor of Columbian "discovery" that parallels her sea serpent analogy; those who claim to know where they have arrived, who claim authority for their conclusions about women, are in fact lost, mistaken, merely clinging to their prejudices.[8] Both the conclusions of those who preceded her and the path that led to them are questionable; she proposes her own experience and efforts as more proper to the task. To assert a woman's experience as the proper basis for a philosophical inquiry into *cultura femenina* means to speak from the yearning that is as yet uncharted territory ("And yet . . .").

Even as she quotes these male philosophers she carefully distinguishes her own enunciation from theirs and constructs a gendered speaking voice that identifies her, as female, with the object of their prescriptive discourse. To start with, Castellanos uses a series of verbs with the subject "we" and includes the pronoun *nosotros* (the masculine form that can also stand for any group in which there is at least one male). This positions her (along with her readers) as reader of these men's words about women: "Nosotros vamos en persecución de otra quimera (11) . . . Vayamos ahora (15) . . . Ahora dirigiremos nuestra atención (17) . . . Vayamos más adelante (19) . . ." [We are off in pursuit of a different chimera . . . Let us go now . . . Now let us turn our attention . . . Let us continue . . .]. However, in the last paragraph of the chapter (quoted above) the verbs are still conjugated in the first person plural but there is a shift in positioning that marks the speaking voice as female: "Atentas observaciones de *nuestras semejantes* . . ." [Attentive observations of those like us / our fellow women . . .] (28; emphasis added). *Semejante* can be translated as "fellow man" but *nuestras* [our], is in the feminine plural form. Castellanos thus identifies herself here as speaker with women as the object of all of the observations she has quoted. The elaborate irony with which she frames her citations of the "sensible men" clearly invites us to read them with the greatest skepticism. She thus shifts the ground of the reader's understanding to one that lies outside the assumptions of that discourse; by locating herself as female and ironic reader in the text, she engenders a privileged space for a resisting reader.

In the second chapter of the essay Castellanos abandons the first person plural *nosotros* and speaks for the first time in the first person singular as a woman, reminding us that her text is being written by an intellectual woman (one of those hallucinated creatures), and even more clearly identifying herself with women as the object of the philosophical discourse that denies the existence or possibility of this text's enunciation. The chapter, called

"Intermedio a propósito del método" [Interlude on the Subject of Method], is itself not on the map of her text; it is the only chapter that is not summarized in the table of contents that follows the essay. Whereas every other chapter receives a long outline of its logical progression, the second chapter is like those blank spots on explorers' maps labeled "here lie monsters."

This interlude, treated as an aside, is only three and a half pages long, but it is here that she addresses squarely the problem she raises at the end of the first chapter, that of the ground or territory from which she might speak. She tells the reader that here lies the heart of the matter, the point of departure that she must create for herself, and that will in turn depend on her goal: discovering *cultura femenina*. She knows what *"femenina"* is because she has been informed by the experts that the feminine is what cannot do culture. Women are defined by what they lack in relation to men. She declines to argue with this definition, she says, because, according to men, women are inferior, and "desde mi punto de vista, *conformado tradicionalmente a través del suyo*, también lo soy" [from my point of view, *shaped traditionally through theirs*, so am I] (32; emphasis added). The qualifying phrase lets the reader know that if she accepts this definition of the feminine it is because she is reading "as a man," in conformity with the tradition through which men and women have been taught to read.

By calling attention to the mechanisms of immasculation that oblige her to enunciate her own inferiority, yet deliberately locating herself as immasculated reader, the first two chapters of Castellanos' essay produce a difference of intonation, an emphasis that might make it possible for us to hear a double-voiced discourse. Nancy K. Miller uses the example of *La princesse de Clèves* to develop this idea in "Emphasis Added." Referring ironically to T. S. Eliot's remark about English and American writing as "two literatures in the same language," Miller speaks of a difference in women's writing that would stem, in part, from the irreducibly complicated relationship women have historically had with the language of the dominant culture, and that is manifested in their writing as an emphasis, an intonation, or a certain quality of voice. Mme. de Clèves' dreams and actions refuse a certain masculine logic of desire and her story gestures to and demands "something else" outside the conventional plots of fiction: a story that would turn out differently. The doubleness imagined here as emphasis or intonation is not the superposition of two codes, but, rather, a quality of voice that tells the resisting reader to take these plots in a different way. Some readers will not hear this difference of intonation. Miller explains that the legibility of this difference is a problem of "plots and plausibilities"; the refusal of most critics to find *La princesse de Clèves* "plausible" is a posture that can be understood as their adherence to a set of conventions for plots of desire. The resisting reader, like Castellanos, will question these conventional maps and might turn to her own experiences and efforts for direction as she reads.[9]

Castellanos' careful statement about her point of view as it is shaped by the convention of female inferiority calls our attention to the process of immasculation; after reading what the philosophers have to say, she knows her place. If we read this as not ironic, it sounds like internalized misogyny. But by this time, the text has given us enough instruction in resisting reading that this positioning process is made visible.

Castellanos' deliberate move to identify herself with the "monotonous" destiny assigned to her would appear to suspend her own experience. But she then goes on to say that if one foot rests on the definition of woman as inferior, the other foot "gravita en el vacío" [hangs in the void], the void, that is, of what is meant by "culture" (31). Her irony becomes even more elaborate at this point: men, she says, define themselves as human because they inhabit a world of culture and produce art, but they deny entrance to women. What, then, is one to make of those women who do create culture and produce art?

> ¿Cómo lograron introducir su contrabando en fronteras tan celosamente vigiladas? Pero sobre todo ¿Qué fue lo que las impulsó de modo tan irresistible a arriesgarse a ser contrabandistas? (32)

> How did they succeed in bringing their contraband across such jealously guarded borders? But above all, what was it that pushed them in such an irresistible fashion to risk becoming smugglers?

It is these women in particular (women like herself) and their motivations that she is concerned with: What drove them to break the law? She's asking Freud's question—What do women want?—as if it mattered what women might answer (de Lauretis, 111). Castellanos outlines the magic circle, the territory of culture as defined by masculinist discourse, and then rather than attacking from the outside she walks in and says "Yes, but . . ." She figures her own activity when she speaks of these women as *contrabandistas*, as smugglers. What she smuggles into the magic circle of misogyny dressed up as philosophy is her own body: her gendered gaze and voice. The self-deprecating tone of the obedient daughter is invaded by skepticism and an awareness of injustice.

This second chapter about method is "off the map" because Castellanos insists that, because of her gender, she will have a different approach. Of course, this is what the experts would have told her to begin with, as she ironically acknowledges when she says parenthetically "(ni siquiera estoy acostumbrada a pensar)" [I am not even accustomed to thinking] (33). She calls on the old standby, her intuition; after all, is it not the reliable feminine mode of comprehension? Castellanos is walking a fine line here. Her irony suggests that there is something inadequate about the prevailing logic, and that one's own experience can be a valid measure of ideas. Yet at the same time, her challenge is left unspoken, is so covert that it risks not being heard at all.

Her counterproposition to "women cannot do culture" is "women are not attracted to cultural production," thus rejecting the equation of women with a particular, disabling definition of the feminine. It would seem that she is going to attempt something along the lines of Virginia Woolf's project in *A Room of One's Own* by addressing some of the material conditions that affect women as writers and artists; but although she will raise this issue tentatively at the end, in the next three chapters she abandons irony in order to construct her argument in a traditional academic philosophical mode, using idealist concepts of "culture," "spirit," and "the feminine."

In the middle section Castellanos plays the conventional game of philosophical mastery, spending many pages defining terms and working through her logical propositions. Although she has just questioned characterizations of women, she has not yet arrived at the point of entirely asserting an alternative. In the appendix of "concluding points" she summarizes her argument as a set of rational propositions. The first of these points restates her opening question (Does *cultura femenina* exist?), indicates the traditional answer (No), and summarizes the definitions that she works through in the middle section of her essay:

> 1.—*A la pregunta de si existe la cultura femenina (concibiendo la cultura como realización de los valores, los valores como cualidades en las que se reconoce un conferidor de eternidad, cualidades susceptibles de ser conocidas y realizadas por el espíritu, forma de conocimiento y modo de conducta específicamente masculinas) los especialistas del tema y los no especialistas, es decir, todos, responden negativamente. (101)*

> To the question of whether there exists a feminine/women's culture (conceiving culture as the realization of values, values as the qualities through which is recognized a means to eternity, qualities that can be known and realized by the spirit, a form of knowledge and mode of conduct specifically masculine) the specialists on the topic and the nonspecialists, that is, everybody, respond negatively.

The long string of parenthetical qualifiers following *cultura femenina* suggests that the negative answer given by "everybody" to the question is an inevitable product of very narrowly defined concepts such as value, eternity, spirit, and their denomination as masculine. Castellanos does not overtly question the appropriateness of these terms for her purposes, but their containment within parentheses sets them in opposition to the question and response that frames them. The authority of these definitions is cast into doubt by her ironic qualification of those who answer the question as "the specialists on the topic and the nonspecialists, that is, everybody." The suggestion is that the specialized arguments are in fact a rationalization of the common wisdom that sea serpents do not write books.

But if this brief summary contains elements of irony, the extended discussion in the essay does not. The three middle chapters develop the formula of "culture as the realization of values, values as the qualities through which is recognized a means to eternity, qualities that can be known and realized by the spirit, a form of knowledge and mode of conduct specifically masculine." Castellanos sets aside irony for erudition and authoritative elegance. In her discussion of definitions of culture her references range from Heraclitus, Kant, and Sartre to Shakespeare, Gracián, Bacon, Dante, and Huxley. Instead of citing the authorities only to distance herself from them through ironic framing, now her mode is the sweeping synthesis and the aphoristic pronouncement, as she performs the kind of judgment and selection that is expected of the intellectual. Castellanos' enunciation here, unlike in Chapter 1, marks no distance between her own position as female speaker and that of the authorities to whom she refers when she makes such declarations as "Resulta pues que el artista es un solitario" [The result is therefore that the artist is a solitary being] (47), and "La función de toda cultura, creativa o receptiva, colectiva o individual es ésta" [This is the function of all culture, creative or receptive, collective or individual] (47). Cultural creation, she concludes, is the means of achieving the transcendence to which the spirit aspires.

In the last two chapters of her essay Castellanos returns to her irony and the mode of "emphasis added" as she zeroes in on the category that is the crux of her equation: the "feminine spirit." She reminds us that the conclusions so firmly advanced in the preceding pages really apply only to men. Again, she claims to "accept" the equation of man as creator, all the while with an edge that highlights the fact that these are terms men have set up for themselves:

El hombre (y esta afirmación es un axioma que no necesita demostrarse) es el rey de la creación. Sobre sus hombros está su cabeza que, a juzgar por la cantidad y la solidez de sus contenidos, debe pesarle tanto como el mundo. El es quien inventa los aparatos para dominar a la naturaleza y para hacer el tránsito

*humano sobre la tierra más cómodo, más fácil, más agradable. El es quien lleva
a cabo las empresas comerciales, las conquistas, las exploraciones y las guerras.
El es quien dice los discursos, organiza la política y dicta las leyes. El es quien
escribe los libros y quien los lee, quien modela las estatuas y el que las admira.
El descubre las verdades y las cree y las expresa. Es el que tiene los medios de
comunicación con Dios, el que oficia en sus altares, el que interpreta la voluntad
divina y el que la ejecuta. El es el que diseña los vestidos que usarán las mujeres
y el que aprueba el diseño de vestidos. El es . . . y no vamos a caer en el
lamentable lugar común de los feministas de suplir el presente del verbo por un
pretérito tan optimista como falso. Repitamos con mayor énfasis y con una
sencillez que abarque todas las actividades del hombre: él es. Todo lo demás está
sujeto a su dominio y depende de su habilidad: las cosas, los animales, las
mujeres. (79)*

Man (and this affirmation is an axiom that needs no proof) is the king of
creation. On his shoulders rests his head, which, judging by the quantity
and solidity of its contents, must weigh on him like the world. He is the one
who invents the machines for dominating nature and for making human
passage through the world more comfortable, easier, more pleasant. He is
the one who carries out commercial enterprises, conquests, explorations,
wars. He is the one who makes the speeches, organizes politics, and dictates
the laws. He is the one who writes the books and reads them, who sculpts
the statues and admires them. He discovers the truths and believes them and
expresses them. He is the one who has the means of communication with
God, who officiates at his altars, who interprets divine will and executes it.
He it is who designs the dresses that women will wear and who approves the
designs. He is . . . and let's not fall into the lamentable feminist cliché of
replacing the present tense with a past tense that is as optimistic as it is
false. Let us repeat with greater emphasis and a simplicity that encompasses
all the activities of man: he is. All the rest is subject to his dominion and
dependent on his ability: things, animals, women.

By the last mocking repetition of "El es . . ." Castellanos has demolished
the axiomatic force of her previous pronouncements about culture, values,
eternity, the spirit, all concepts now suspect because they are so clearly in
the service of upholding men's power over "things, animals, women." Given
this reality, she remarks, women have had little choice but to "hide their claws
like cats," find a man who will think for them, fatten him up and domesticate
him so that he will give them what they really want: children (79). If creativity requires the desire and the means for transcendence, women have the
same desire as men, but have in their bodies a means that men do not. Women

have children instead of making works of art (84) and men have made of women's sexuality and reproductive capacity a sin, a danger, and an obstacle (85). Cultural production is best seen then as a form of compensation: "la cultura es . . . el refugio de quienes han sido exiliados de la maternidad. En los hombres eso es natural, claro. Pero ¿en las mujeres?" [Culture is . . . the refuge of those who have been exiled from maternity. In men this is natural, of course. But in women?] (89). Although she echoes Freud's ideas about women and civilization, she also cites Karen Horney as an example of someone who spoke from within Freudian discourse, using its categories—"empleando las mismas armas" [using its own weapons], in order to revise it (83). This reference to Horney figures to a certain extent her own intention and strategy.

Even as she asserts the importance of women's reproductive capacity, Castellanos anticipates later feminist thought by raising the problems of motherhood as an institution. Women turn to cultural activity out of frustration, she claims, the frustration of childlessness but also the frustration of having children in a society that devalues motherhood and femininity.[10] She thus points to the cultural construction of motherhood as contradictory. Women turn to that activity that is valued: cultural creation; in particular, writing attracts women because the means and training for other forms of cultural activity have been denied them (and here she cites Virginia Woolf's *Three Guineas*).

But what about the results? Castellanos now feels obliged, as did Woolf and de Beauvoir, for that matter, to judge women's writing by the criteria and values put forth by a misogynist literary canon, which claims that most women's writing is flawed by narcissism:

> *como cuando las mujeres no se atreven a mirarse . . . ni a hablar, sin rodeos, de lo que más les interesa y les apasiona que es su propia personalidad y afectan estar hablando de otras cosas al través de las cuales no dejan de insinuarse ellas mismas. (96–97)*

as when women don't dare to look at themselves . . . or to speak, without being roundabout, about what most interests and excites them, their own personalities, and they pretend to be talking about other things through which they still insinuate themselves.

This describes her own strategy of indirectness; she is talking about herself in this essay, after all. The question becomes: When does she mean what she says? Does she really think women's writing is no good? When it comes time to judge the writing of women, Castellanos once more seems to speak as an "immasculated" reader, without challenging the standards or values she has received. The power that authorizes the discourses that claim that women are either incapable of cultural creativity or neurotic and frustrated when they attempt it can also render her irony ineffective if not illegible.

Yet if her judgment of women's writing is harsh, it also contains the possibility of an alternative: women writers, she says, are not using language to transcend their own limits but, rather, to mark them, to affirm their individuality: "Yo soy mi cuerpo" [I am my body] (96). Were she to value this rather than reject it, she would be pointing in the direction taken by many feminist literary critics in later years.

In the last paragraph of the essay, where Castellanos puts forth her idea of the kind of writing women should aim for, she does something other than simply recommend an objectivity she has criticized women for lacking:

Si es imprescindible que las mujeres escriban, cabe esperar, al menos, que lo hagan buceando cada vez más hondo en su propio ser en vez de efectuar tentativas lamentablemente fallidas de evasión de sí mismas (ya la misma profesión literaria es una tentativa de evasión) que no la llevan tan lejos como se quisiera pero sí lo suficiente como para colocarla en un terreno falso que ni conoce ni domina. Lo que cabe desear es que invierta la dirección de ese movimiento (ya que no invierte la dirección del movimiento que la aparta de su feminidad confinándola a una mimetización del varón) volviéndolo hacia su propio ser pero con tal ímpetu que sobrepase la inmediata y deleznable periferia apariencial y se hunda tan profundamente que alcance su verdadera, su hasta ahora inviolada raíz, haciendo a un lado las imágenes convencionales que de la feminidad le presenta el varón para formarse su imagen propia, su imagen basada en la personal, intrasferible experiencia, imagen que puede coincidir con aquella pero que puede discrepar. Y que una vez tocado ese fondo (que la tradición desconoce o falsea, que los conceptos usuales no revelan) lo haga emerger a la superficie consciente y lo liberte en la expresión. (97)

If it is imperative that women write, let us hope that, at least, they will do it by diving ever deeper into their own selves instead of making lamentably frustrated attempts at self-evasion (the literary profession itself is an attempt at evasion) that don't bring them as far as they'd wish, but only far enough so as to place them in a false terrain that they neither know nor dominate. What we have to hope for is that she will reverse the direction of that movement (when she no longer reverses the direction of the movement that separates her from her femininity, confining her to an imitation of males), turning it back toward her own being but with such impetus that she goes beyond the immediate and negligible periphery of appearance and sinks as deep as she can until she reaches the truest, and until now inviolate, root, putting to one side the conventional images of femininity with which men present her so that she can form her own image, an image based on a personal, untransferable experience, an image that might coincide with that conventional one but that might also differ. And once she has reached those depths (unknown or falsified by tradition, and that the usual concepts do not reveal) that she bring them to the conscious surface and liberate them in expression.

Once one untangles the long tortuous sentence that is most of this paragraph, setting aside the tentative initial "If . . . ," there emerges a call for women to create a more authentic representation of themselves based on their own experiences. Women are to explore and then to represent "su propio ser" [their own selves] rather than rely on the images men have dictated. This desire brings the reader back to the critical spirit with which Castellanos began the essay. By diving deep into themselves, women might achieve a new self-knowledge and a new consciousness; this type of exploration is offered as an alternative to the traditional modes of knowing women's experience.

This final exhortation to women writers comes close to speaking directly to women rather than to a hostile audience of male philosophers determined to silence her. Castellanos is wary of her reception by male readers. In *A Room of One's Own*, Virginia Woolf jokes about Sir Archibald Bodkin, who might be hiding in the linen cupboard, eavesdropping as she talks to other women (115); he is the figure standing in for all the male authorities whose presence would try to dictate not only the conventions of her speech, such as the proper form of a peroration, but the content as well: women dislike women. Woolf's own irony and her doubled voice, as it emerges from her play with shifts of personae, audiences, and pronouns, work to prevent the collapse of her speaking voice into the object of the discourse she is contesting.

Castellanos gestures toward rhetorical positionings for the female reader/ intellectual, as Miranda or as sea serpent. But the result is a text divided against itself. Her imagined and actual audience is not a room full of sympathetic women, but a panel of male philosophy professors. Because she concedes too much, at times the difference of intonation disappears: there is no longer tension between two perspectives. When Castellanos emerges at the other end of her masterful performance in Chapter 5, having followed her own advice of accepting the conclusions of her predecessors, she finds herself in the extremely awkward position of having to conclude that she is indeed inferior to men and that women's cultural production is neurotic. But her frustration with this conclusion is clear when she implies that tradition's "usual concepts" misrecognize or falsify her self: "those depths (unknown or falsified by tradition, and that the usual concepts do not reveal)" (97).

In this contradictory and confused conclusion we see one of the dangers of the strategy of double-voiced discourse, of a simple "emphasis added." For this mode to operate effectively, the speaker must maintain the distance or gap between her presence as speaking subject and her presence as object of a discourse, which would deny her the authority to speak on her own terms. If this gap disappears, through her own lack of confidence or the sheer difficulty of the enterprise or, more crucially, because there is not yet a community of readers capable of recognizing the differences of intonation, then the speaker is reduced to the image she receives of herself from that prescriptive and censoring discourse; the mask becomes her face.[11]

If the stereotypes about women and culture constructed and brandished by the "sensible men" are supposed to discipline and silence the female knower, their very production also produces the possibility of disruption through a powerful rereading. In *Sobre cultura femenina* Rosario Castellanos is not yet able to spell out new concepts of culture and the feminine that would enable her to assert the value of her own intellectual and creative activity, but she does set out deliberately to speak as a woman-knower, she does try to refigure women as more than reproductive beings mired in contingency. Her own text suggests a reading lesson that would show us how to read it against the grain, and whose deep yearning in the end projects a new form of imagining women's subjectivity and agency: the sea monster that will know itself by diving deep into itself.

Patrocinio Schweickart elucidates the reading lesson I have taken from *Sobre cultura femenina* in her call for a new way of reading:

> Recall that a crucial feature of the process of immasculation is the woman reader's bifurcated response. She reads the text both as a man and as a woman. But in either case, the result is the same: she confirms her position as other. Taking control of the reading experience means reading the text as it was *not* meant to be read, in fact, reading it against itself. Specifically, one must identify the nature of the choices proffered by the text and, equally important, what the text precludes—namely the possibility of reading as a woman *without* putting one's self in the position of the other, of reading so as to affirm womanhood as another, equally valid, paradigm of human existence. (50)

Rosario Castellanos opens up a place for the reader to resist immasculation and thus makes it possible for us to read her own text against itself. If, in the end, the essay is too profoundly contradictory to satisfy us as a coherent feminist critique, it does present for the first time one of the questions that will motivate Castellanos' writing until the end of her life: What does it mean to read and write as a woman in Mexican society? One way that Castellanos was to continue to address this question was through the practice of writing out of her own experience and resurrecting a "dangerous memory" of women's suffering.[12] She tried out this strategy in a somewhat tentative form in *Sobre cultura femenina* by marking her voice and subjectivity as female in the text. She would go on to expand this technique in her poetry, fiction, and essays by using an autobiographical mode to scrutinize the forces that construct women's lives and roles, and by making of women's daily lives and experiences the point of departure for her analysis of Mexican society (Rivero). In later years Castellanos came to assume a more public role as example for women; in her many essays on the roles and responsibilities of writers and intellectuals she returned often to the idea of a writer's life and work as exemplary. By the time the collection of essays *Mujer que sabe latín* was published in 1973, there existed a community of readers for whom her lessons in a feminist rereading of Mexican culture were legible without ambiguity. And her play *El eterno femenino: farsa* addresses itself to a female public and uses its irony and humor with confidence to critique the construction of gender norms in Mexican history and culture.

We must not lose sight of the fact that the "culture" at stake in *Sobre cultura femenina,* both for the philosopher-authorities she cites and critiques and for herself, is understood as Western European high culture. The question is whether or not women—of the privileged classes—will be accorded full status as knowers of and actors on the terms of that culture, whether they will be able to function as part of the intelligentsia, what Angel Rama has called "la ciudad letrada" [the lettered city]. The dilemma is that full access is predicated on mastery of a cultural literacy that seems to require for women their "immasculation," that they position themselves as masculine subjects precisely through the exclusion of their own subjectivity or agency. But at no point in this early academic essay does Castellanos display a consciousness of her own situation as a Mexican, or of the fact that she was brought up in a household and a region in which a Manichean polarization between Indians and non-Indians regulated social relations. Nowhere does she acknowledge that in Mexico other peoples and cultures continue to exist in conflict with the "universal" culture she has studied at the university. At this point Castellanos has begun a feminist critique of the misogynist discourse that constitutes its power through the silencing of women, but the form of her critique does not register (and is complicit in) the historical grounding of that same discourse in the oppression and exclusion of non-European populations and cultures. But, like Alejo Carpentier, who said that he came to consciousness about the African part of Cuban identity only when he went to Paris, Castellanos was to return from her year in Europe to plunge into an intense exploration of the place of indigenous peoples and culture in Mexico, and to make of these experiences the foundation of her critique of Mexican society.

⛭ 3 ⛭

Castellanos and Indigenismo *in Mexico*

Lo que ocurre es que yo tuve un tránsito muy lento de la más
cerrada de las subjetividades al turbador descubrimiento
de la existencia del otro, y, por último, a la ruptura del esquema
de la pareja para integrarme a lo social, que es el ámbito en
que el poeta se define, se comprende y se expresa.

Rosario Castellanos, *Mujer que sabe latín* (203)

What happened is that I made a very slow transition from the most
closed of subjectivities to the disturbing discovery of the existence
of the other, and, finally, to a rupture with the model of the couple
in order to integrate myself with the social, the orbit in which the
poet defines, understands, and expresses himself or herself.

In *Sobre cultura femenina* Rosario Castellanos writes as a *contrabandista*, a
smuggler. By speaking from the position of "woman" as the term excluded
from cultural production, she challenges misogynist assumptions concerning women and writing. As a woman writer and intellectual in 1950 Mexico
she must struggle to claim a place from which to speak. When she smuggles
her ironic voice into the territory of authorized discourse, she succeeds to
some degree in revealing some of its mechanisms of power and exclusion
but faces the difficulty inherent in trying to revise the terms of an argument
from within. Yet the entire polemic of the essay is conducted as if "culture"
in Mexico were simply European high culture; Mexico's own history of conquest, colonization, cultural conflict, and syncretism is absent from her frame
of reference. In this respect her essay is blind to the "euphemisation" by which
a historically colonialist discourse has constructed itself as universal (Brown,
66). In her Afterword to *Out of the Kumbla: Caribbean Women and Literature*,
Sylvia Wynters sums up this situation wherein White or Western/European
women seek to claim a voice for themselves but in a manner that perpetuates
the silencing of women of color or colonized peoples:

> In consequence if, before the sixteenth century, what Irigaray terms as
> "*patriarchal discourse*" had erected itself on the "silenced ground" of women,

from then on, the new primarily silenced ground (which at the same time now enables the partial liberation of Miranda's hitherto stifled speech), would be that of the majority population-groups of the globe—all signified now as the "natives" (Calibans) to the "men" of Prospero and Ferdinand, with Miranda becoming both a co-participant, if to a lesser *derived* extent, in the power and privileges generated by the empirical supremacy of her own population; and as well, the beneficiary of a mode of privilege unique to her, that of being the metaphysically invested and "idealized" object of desire for all classes (Stephano and Trinculo) and all population-groups (Caliban). (363, emphasis in the original)

This characterization aptly describes the situation of *Sobre cultura femenina*. While that situation itself persisted, in the fiction and essays Castellanos wrote over the next twenty-four years, she began to address more critically her own location within it. By making Mexico's history of ethnic conflict and the persistence of colonial relations the focus of her fiction, Castellanos had the possibility of exploring these dynamics: the feminist mode of inquiry she explored in *Sobre cultura femenina* is brought together with another powerful mode of social critique, Mexican *indigenismo*. As *indigenista* writer she joined other Mexican intellectuals of the fifties and sixties in their attempts to redefine a national identity through a more responsible engagement with Mexican reality. In her *indigenista* writing Castellanos confronts the construction of her own privilege as well as her oppression.

Because Castellanos' early fiction addresses the oppression of indigenous people in Mexico it is usually labeled *indigenista* writing. Her first three books of fiction— *Balún Canán* (1957), *Ciudad Real* (1960), and *Oficio de tinieblas* (1962)—pose the question of imagining community, or national identity in Mexico, as predicated on the problem of "civility"; she examines the postrevolutionary attempt to redistribute power and land and that attempt's rhetoric of social justice and inclusion as these efforts clash with the interests of a firmly entrenched social sector whose identity and hegemony derive from its enforced exclusion of women, indigenous people, and other subordinates from the category of personhood. Castellanos continues to focus on the subordination and oppression of women, now in the specific context of her childhood home in the state of Chiapas. What her fiction attempts is the reimagination of her society's "conflictive heterogeneity" (Antonio Cornejo Polar's term) in terms of possible new relations of community, motivated by a commitment to the recognition of the humanity of the oppressed. This is the radical premise of *indigenismo*, too often contained or channeled into new forms of subordination rather than equality.

At the same time, Castellanos faces a problem very similar to the one that stymied her in *Sobre cultura femenina:* the concepts and assumptions of *indigenismo* provide her with a vehicle for social critique and yet limit what she can say and imagine in the process, as I will explore in this chapter. This dilemma is one dimension of a broader context: through her position as a member of a privileged class and ethnic group she has inherited the possibility of access to the literate Western European culture she displays in *Sobre cultura femenina,* but with respect to the indigenous people of Chiapas about whom she writes, she is located in what Cornejo Polar has termed "the hegemonic pole" ("El indigenismo y las literaturas heterogéneas," 11). That is, the repertoire of representational means available to her, including alphabetic literacy, has historically emerged in Mexico from its exclusion and suppression of indigenous means of representation and knowledge.

To situate Castellanos' practice as *indigenista* writer and activist, I will examine some of the uses of the term *indigenismo* as it encompasses a set of concepts and practices that have shaped much of the discussion about ethnic conflict in Mexico, and as it is used to categorize Castellanos' earlier fiction. To better understand how *indigenismo* came to be so important in Mexican social policy of this century, it will be useful to review the history of some of the ethnic categories on which it relies.

In his introduction to *Keywords* Raymond Williams tells how he came to write the histories of words. When he returned to the university in England after the Second World War, he found that he shared with others the experience that he and his colleagues were not speaking the same language:

> When we come to say "we just don't speak the same language" we mean
> something more general: that we have different immediate values or
> different kinds of valuation, or that we are aware, often intangibly, of
> different formations and distributions of energy and interest. In such a case,
> each group is speaking its native language, but its uses are significantly
> different, and especially when strong feelings and important ideas are in
> question. (11)

Williams' project involves bringing to the fore memories of "subjugated knowledges," in Michel Foucault's terms, and the histories of conflicts and struggles enacted in the use of language. The terms *indigenismo* (indigenism) and *indio* (Indian) are just such "keywords" in Mexico, ones with very different meanings—often bitterly contested—for different groups. They bear the histories of conflict over the production of knowledge entailed by European colonization and indigenous resistance in the Americas, and the national rearticulations of that conflict. *Indigenismo* refers to various efforts that take as their object "Indians" (often beginning with the attempt to identify or constitute such an object) and to restructure the relations between them and non-Indians.[1] At stake are issues of language, education, land distribution, and national identity as they are mediated by ethnic categories. The word *indígena* means native or indigenous person and has been taken up in the twentieth century as an alternative to the word *indio,* or Indian, quite often used pejoratively in Latin America. Some indigenous political groups and intellectuals have reappropriated the label *indio,* asserting their right to define their own identity, reclaim their history, and articulate their own political projects. My own use of the term "Indian" in this chapter refers to the category as socially constructed by colonialism.

Ethnic categories in Mexico have their roots in Spanish colonization and the colonial rule that structured an ethnic hierarchy. Social stratification by ethnicity has persisted, but the initial pair of terms "colonizer" and "colonized" underwent a series of changes.

Spanish invaders subjugated and colonized the many indigenous peoples they named Indians, enslaving and subsequently administering them through this category. However, toward the end of three centuries of colonial rule and by the time of the wars of independence from Spain, we see that if the Spaniard can still be identified as the colonizer, the colonial subjects now include many groups besides the so-called Indians, as new categories of identity were produced through a discourse of social hierarchy: *criollos,* or Creoles (American-born of Spanish or European ancestors); Mestizos (of mixed European-indigenous ancestry); African and American-born Blacks, both enslaved and free; and other *castas* (people of mixed ancestry).

When Spanish control over its colonial empire fell apart, the stakes in allegiance were different for the different groups. The Creole elites were split; some remained loyal to the Crown while others became republicans. Either way they were in a position to control wealth, power, and status in the new republics. But with independence, that control was challenged by Mestizos and others. In the long power struggles over who would define national interests, intellectuals began to speak from the rhetorical position of "the colonized" by virtue of their opposition to the colonizer. They could enact this positioning through their access to and control of literacy, print, and public discourse—academic, political, and literary.

This rhetorical strategy is possible because of the way we articulate "the colonizer" as subject and "the colonized" as object of an action. But the pair of terms sets up an opposition that does not entirely account for the particular case of Spanish colonialism. Because Creoles and Mestizos were subjected to colonial administration and excluded from power we cannot call them the colonizers; in fact, Mestizos were to lay claim to an indigenous status because of their mixed heritage, their *mestizaje.* Mestizo efforts to elevate *mestizaje* to the status of official national ideology in Mexico have made the Mestizo the new protagonist of Mexican history and literature, equating *mestizaje* with being Mexican. And yet, this process has rhetorically displaced the original colonization and oppression of indigenous people whose exploitation continues to be linked to their ethnic identification, for in Mexico and other regions of Latin America with large indigenous populations, the very real cleavage along ethnic lines built into colonial society has remained in place since independence. This division continues to operate in Mexico both structurally and discursively, even as ideological concepts of the "Indian" have mutated.

During the colonial period, ethnic categories were determined to a large degree by legal status and social position within a hierarchical system of social stratification that was known as the Régimen de Castas (Mörner, 201–202). Wealth, place of birth, patronage, gender, and other factors all interacted in a complex hierarchy that, while not absolutely rigid, still powerfully determined most aspects of an individual's life.[2] Spaniards born in Spain occupied the chief ranks in the colonial hierarchy in order to maintain Crown control over colonial affairs, although in fact strict enforcement was not always possible. Those of Spanish descent born in the colonies, the Creoles, formed the second rank of colonial society, the colonial oligarchy. From the unions between Spaniards, indigenous people, and Africans came the Mestizos, *mulatos,* and other mixed-race *castas.* According to Moisés González Navarro, "the term 'mestizo' became synonymous with bastard, a stigma that was to disappear only after the Revolution of 1910 rehabilitated Indian culture" (145).

The use of the word *indio,* or Indian, arose, as we know, from a case of mistaken identity. Columbus went looking for a route to Asia and was convinced, even on his fourth voyage, that he had arrived in the Indies somewhere south of Japan or China rather than in some part of the world previously unknown to Europeans.[3] The name was applied to all indigenous inhabitants despite their myriad languages and forms of social organization; they were united in conquest as "Indians."

Américo Ferrari notes that the name "Indian" in the early writings of the Spanish colonizers referred to a native of the Indies, and that the word "Indian" was not used in opposition to "White": early usage posited Indians as a people or a nation in the sense that the Spaniards were a people or a nation.[4] In 1492, the year of the so-called Discovery, Spain was in fact many kingdoms and peoples united politically by the final phase of the Reconquest and the expulsion of the Moors and the Jews. The colony of New Spain owed allegiance to the Crown as one of those kingdoms.

But the existence of previously unknown lands and peoples challenged the European vision of the universe centered around Christianity, and the nature of indigenous people was the subject of much discussion, including the extraordinary confrontation between Fray Bartolomé de las Casas and Juan Ginés de Sepúlveda before the court of Carlos V, staged to decide how the Crown should deal with its new subjects. Ginés de Sepúlveda condemned Indians for being in the grip of Satan while Las Casas tried to defend them from the depredations of their conquerors. But both shared the teleological framework that held that the New World and its inhabitants was there *for* the European, whose gaze revealed the true nature of this world.

Partly as a result of this debate, the New Laws were passed in 1542, granting Indians special rights and privileges. Under the law, their labor was not to be coerced, yet in practice the Crown's protective measures were most often ignored. For the Spaniard, the colonies' purpose was to extract wealth for the Crown and for the settlers, and the means to this end was the labor of indigenous people or enslaved Africans. For three centuries in New Spain, Indians were compelled to supply labor in one form or another as tribute or to pay off debts. After 1822, racial designations were not permitted officially and the term "*indígena*" was substituted for the legal caste term of the colonies, but the concept "Indian" persisted and continued to function. In some regions indigenous people still had to pay special taxes or tributes, and their recognition through this form of social identity was still used to decide land distribution and to enforce debt peonage. Ethnicity was not only a mark of cultural difference, it signified and structured economic relations as well.

By the eighteenth century, there were a variety of people who could be considered native to New Spain. However, indigenous people were still called Indians; it was the Creoles who were known as Americans. A new consciousness of a Creole identity emerged, promoted through the writings of Jesuits expelled from the Americas, such as Francisco Clavijero, who portrayed indigenous cultures as part of an earlier stage of history. History's new narrative was cast as Civilization overcoming Barbarism, and in order not to be cast as the Barbarians themselves, it was important to the Creoles that they distinguish themselves from the "Indian."

The wars of independence from Spain (spanning the period 1810 to 1825) were fought by people from all ranks of society, but while the participation of the *castas* was great on both sides, the leadership was largely from the elite. Although nationalist history has not always acknowledged that fact, ethnic conflict has always been part of Latin American history and was also a factor in these wars of emancipation. In nineteenth-century Mexico, the fear of "caste war" became a reality in many areas.[5]

In the Maya regions of Mesoamerica, Creoles maintained power and ethnic unity longer than in other areas where *mestizos* were more successful, and here the important social distinction has continued to be between Indians and non-Indians. In Chiapas, non-Indians often call themselves *castellanos* (Castilians) or *gente de razón* (rational people) while the Maya call them *caxlanes* (from *castellano*). Another common term for the non-Indians in this region is "Ladino," a word with its own fascinating history. Ladino is the language of the Sephardic Jews expelled from Spain in 1492; the word was used in a pejorative sense to mean a shifty or marginal character. In the modern regional context of southern Mexico and Central America where it is used today, Ladino is not synonymous with White, although European ancestry and culture—and whiteness by association—operate as privileged terms. Nor is it identical to the term "Mestizo"; whether or not an individual is of mixed European/indigenous ancestry does not in and of itself determine ethnic identity. These two ethnic categories, Indian and Ladino—socially constructed by colonialism and through mutual exclusion—continue to determine most aspects of life in Chiapas and other Mayan regions today. *Indigenismo* is, among other things, the attempt to intervene in these categories and how they structure society.

A useful comparison can be made with another colonial context. In *Orientalism,* Edward Said explores the "European way of dealing with the Orient." Using Michel Foucault's notion of discourse, he examines Orientalism as an ideology, as social practice and institutions, and as a literary "style of thought," all "for dealing with the Orient—dealing with it by making statements about it, authorizing views of it, describing it, by teaching it, settling it, ruling over it: in short, Orientalism as a Western style for dominating, restructuring and having authority over the Orient."(3).

Indigenismo can also be examined in this way—as ideology, an array of social practices, and mode of imagination—but only if we observe important differences as well. Said defines Orientalism as a European (and later North American) way of dealing with an entire geographical area and its inhabitants, the way Europe established and maintained hegemony over another part of the world and other cultures. One can say "Europe" or "the Orient" and signify two opponents in a struggle, even while recognizing that the so-called Orient has its own history, its own self-definitions, and its own resistance to imperialism and the discourse of Orientalism. While *indigenismo* has its roots in European ways of dealing with those it has named Indians and is seen by many as an extension of those ways, it is not itself a European phenomenon; it is not the European way of dealing with Latin America. Instead, "*indigenismo,*" as the term is used today, refers to a Latin American philosophy or ideology that has named and defined itself as such since the beginning of this century. It is also the name given to a set of institutions and social practices, often called *acción indigenista* [indigenist action] in Mexico, whose purpose

51

it is to act on people identified as Indians. Finally, Said marks a territory of imaginative or aesthetic practices that can be called Orientalism (a "style of thought"); *indigenismo* is a literary category critics use for a set of texts and a tradition of writing dating from the nineteenth century whose common denominator is a sympathetic representation of the "Indian" and denunciation of social injustice.

Indigenismo can be seen as the mode by which former colonies attempt to manage an unresolved colonial heritage. Nationalism in the nineteenth century required a unified story of national identity as cultural identity. Writing in Mexico was the forum for the debate over what form this story should take and who should be its protagonist (Martínez). The break with Spain seemed to call for the rejection of historical continuity with the colonizer, yet how could the Creole or Mestizo intellectuals imagine their historical continuity with the conquered, largely unassimilated, indigenous cultures all around them, especially as they were unwilling to relinquish their power over them? The ideological debate that ensued over the nature of the "Indian" echoed that between Las Casas and Ginés de Sepúlveda. Some rejected the Indian as barbaric while others denounced colonial exploitation of indigenous people as a Spanish evil and claimed the indigenous past as part of the new national heritage. Mestizos claimed their mixed ancestry as that which constituted the authentically Mexican identity; elevating the "Indian" was a means for elevating themselves. This new Indianist discourse, emerging in the nineteenth century, represented the "Indian" as an idealized figure inhabiting the past but it largely ignored contemporary indigenous culture.

Beginning in mid-nineteenth-century Mexico, and gathering impetus after the Mexican Revolution, Mestizos claimed the indigenous past as part of their heritage in order to establish their own cultural independence and identity. *Mestizaje,* or racial intermixing, was held up as a model or dream of cultural integration. In the nineteenth century those who regarded indigenous culture in a positive light were called *indianistas* [Indianists]; they engaged in debate with the *hispanistas* [Hispanists], who thought that Mexican culture was properly an outgrowth of Spanish culture and history, and that the indigenous element was backward and degenerate, something to be suppressed for the progress of the nation (Van Zantwijk). Indianist writers glorified the pre-Conquest past and held up the suffering of the Indians under colonial rule as a metaphor for their own situation, part of their own history. This sympathy, however, did not usually extend to the efforts of indigenous peoples of their own day and age to reclaim some autonomy: the Maya in the Yucatán and the Yaquis in the north of Mexico were fighting for their own independence while peoples in other regions made demands for land reform that culminated in the Zapatista movement of the Mexican Revolution (van

Zantwijk, 98). The history of this kind of resistance was feared and suppressed by nineteenth-century writers, who preferred the myths of a long-suffering and passive Indian, fallen from pre-Columbian greatness.

One result of the discursive recuperation of the "Indian" as a part of the new nation was a new scholarly interest in pre-Columbian history. Although neither group paid much attention to their indigenous contemporaries, much less included them as participants in the nationalist debate, the discussion did generate interest and investigation that were to feed into the development of Mexican historiography, anthropology, and literary activity.

The writing of literary histories was one form of intervention in this ideological debate since their overt purpose was nationalist consolidation. The practice of literary history in Mexico derived from two models: the French and German model proposed that the spirit of a people was manifested by the geniuses of that culture in works of literature, while the colonial intellectual tradition of New Spain had elaborated its own histories of textual production in New Spain, culminating in some of the texts of Creole patriotism. Both of these models posit originality as that essential element that makes possible the differentiation of a people. In order to use such models, nineteenth-century Mexican writers and scholars had to constitute the originality and unity of Mexican history, to construct a collective protagonist of the saga of national history.[6]

To this end, the documents and monuments of pre-Conquest indigenous culture and history were studied as part of the national past, but not until the Revolution did scholarly attention turn to the indigenous people whose massive participation in the Revolution could not be ignored. Anthropologist Manuel Gamio's 1916 book *Forjando patria* [Forging the Nation] is a manifesto for the new society to be created; it put forth the assimilation of Indians into national life as an essential step in imagining the new national community (Hewitt de Alcántara, 19). Since the Revolution, *indigenismo* as an official Mexican policy has encompassed a variety of ideologies, institutions, social and imaginative practices that all promote the social assimilation of Indians into national life as a goal. By recognizing the humanity and agency of indigenous peoples, and their right to participate in the polis, *indigenismo* has radical potential. Yet by reproducing the strategy of representing the Indian while excluding indigenous self-representations and actions, *indigenismo* has often colluded in the modernization of colonial relations rather than their elimination.

The primary assumption of *indigenismo* has been that there is a continued split between two cultures, a split that must be resolved in the national interests and in the interests of the Indians themselves. The first step is to ask the question "What is Indian?" in order to be able to figure out who is Indian so they can then be made "Mexican." President Lázaro Cárdenas was to articulate this formula in 1940 as official government policy when he said: "Our native problem does not exist in keeping the Indians as Indians; neither to make Mexico, Indian; but to make the Indian Mexican" (van Zantwijk, 99).

The earliest official efforts of *acción indigenista* in this direction date from 1925 and focused on education and language policy as the means for acculturation. "Casas del pueblo," cultural missions, and a special school for Indians were established, following in the colonial missionary tradition but without the religion. Social anthropology was promoted as the instrument for integrating "underdeveloped" groups, a process described by theorists of *indigenismo* as "progress" and "elevation" (Caso, "Los ideales de la acción indigenista"; Aguirre Beltrán, "Integración regional").

In 1936 the government established the Department of Indigenous Affairs, and in 1940 the first Interamerican Indigenist Congress was held in Pátzcuaro. It laid the bases for an international *indigenista* politics, which Mexico was to pursue most vigorously, and led to the foundation of the National Indigenist Institute in 1948. Alfonso Caso's article "Los ideales de la acción indigenista" [The Ideals of Indigenist Action] could be called the manifesto of the INI. It lays out plainly the goals and justifications of *indigenismo* considered as both "una actitud y una política y la traducción de ambas en acciones concretas" [an attitude and a form of politics and the translation of both into concrete actions] (7). As a later critic of the INI, Margarita Nolasco Armas, put it, *indigenismo* in Mexico must be understood as (1) a theory or a set of ideas, for the most part elaborated by anthropologists, (2) an official attitude or policy ("política indigenista") that takes the form of laws and institutions such as the INI, and (3) *acción indigenista*, or the proposed solutions and their translation into action (68). Caso's "Ideales" shows the official *indigenista* line, which begins with the assumption that there is an "Indian problem."

Indigenista policymakers rejected any thesis of biological inferiority:

El indio en Mexico no es definido racial, sino culturalmente, pero la raza biológica y sociológica aun desempeña un papel en varios casos importantes, en las actitudes y relaciones de indios y no-indios. (de la Fuente, 69)

The Indian in Mexico is defined not racially but culturally; however, biological and sociological race still play a role in many important cases in the attitudes and relations between Indians and non-Indians.

This view assumes that the source of problems was unequal conditions that could be subject to change. But it is revealing that Caso, when speaking of this proposed change, goes on to say that the Indians must change themselves. Although theorists recognized unequal conditions, they then set these conditions aside as a proposed object of change in favor of the Indians as object. In practice, the government rather than indigenous people themselves defined and directed these actions whose purpose was to change Indians into Mexicans. This meant deciding who, for official purposes, were the Indians.

What makes someone an Indian in Mexico? In daily life, communities identify individuals as either *indio* or Ladino without any difficulty. The question did not really arise until anthropologists and social policymakers realized that defining the object of their intentions was not as straightforward as they thought; their considerations of this question over the years often reveal the contradictions in their methods and goals.

The focus of official *indigenismo* after the 1940 Congreso was to be the indigenous community and not the individual. This resulted in part from the recognition that individuals can cross ethnic boundaries. By changing clothing, language, job, residence, and customs, someone identified as an Indian can "pass" over into the non-Indian community and be recognized as a Mestizo, although this process is very difficult. Usually it means that an individual has to leave the community and go elsewhere; in fact, passing usually occurred when a person left to work in another region, through proletarianization, or in the next generation. Usually, as long as the individual remained in the community, he or she was considered Indian.[7]

The heart of the INI's program was the regional coordinating centers. The first such center was set up in Chiapas, where Castellanos would come to work fewer than ten years later. In theory, these centers were supposed to effect change on the entire community of non-Indians and Indians, but in reality only those defined as Indian were the object of the centers' efforts. There were different areas of intervention: in the agrarian sector, INI centers dealt with land and *ejido* problems; in the agricultural sector, new seeds and technology were to be introduced, but economic action was limited, primarily for lack of credit; education in the form of literacy campaigns and hygiene programs continued to be a cornerstone of INI activity. The Chiapas center, called the Tzeltal-Tzotzil Center after the two major Maya language groups of the region, had jurisdiction over only fifteen of the forty-two indigenous communities, those of the highlands. Changes were to be accomplished without force. Those elements such as dress, art, and communal ownership of some land that did not "interfere" with improvement were not targeted for change. The changes in cultural patterns were also to take place on the ideological level: "no podemos simplemente modificar la tecnología que corresponde a un estado cultural, sin cambiar también la ideología que corresponde a este mismo estado" [We cannot simply modify the technology that corresponds to a cultural state, without also changing the ideology that corresponds to that same state] (Caso, "Los ideales," 11). Thus the INI was to educate, effect change, and then withdraw.

This social experiment has not produced the expected results; to a great extent the INI has failed in its objectives.[8] Part of the INI's failure to achieve its goals of modernization and assimilation of indigenous peoples has to do with the choice of means: "agents of acculturation," also called "*promotores culturales*" [cultural promoters], people chosen to be trained and then sent back to their communities to work for the INI. Because indigenous people have quite often seen outsiders, with reason, as agents of domination, and thus have rejected them, it was felt that change would be more easily accepted coming from members of the community. These agents were to be catalysts for a systemic change, or a kind of chain reaction. Agents were trained at a school in the center, but the problem arose that they often did not want to return, or adopted the majority view that their culture was inferior. Another problem was that they were sometimes rejected by their communities precisely because of their assimilation.

Intermediaries between Ladino and indigenous communities have always existed—priests, teachers, and political bosses—but they have most often been Ladinos. The *promotores culturales* were not independent agents, responding to the needs or desires of their communities; they were supposed to follow the directives of the Ladinos who ran the INI center. Anthropologists were supposed to run the centers according to criteria that would ensure understanding and prevent discrimination and exploitation. In reality, bureaucrats often had more control. In any case, anthropology as an academic discipline was in the service of the government as applied anthropology. The study of the dominated was applied to the dominated, but this knowledge was not shared with them, nor was it developed on their terms, and there was no corresponding study of the so-called national culture or society.[9] The basic premise of this colonialist anthropology, up until the 1960s, when critics within the discipline challenged these intellectual foundations, was to "westernize" the "Indians" in order to assimilate them into an industrializing nation. While the methodology became more sophisticated, this goal was not really challenged until critics pointed out that the elimination of a culture at the hands of a class of technicians amounted to ethnocide, the maintenance and rationalization of colonial relations without the use of force:

La antropología aplicada—indigenismo—ha sido siempre una antropología colonialista, destinada al conocimiento—y en consecuencia al uso—del dominado. (Nolasco Armas, 72)

Applied anthropology—indigenism—has always been colonialist anthropology, intended for knowledge of—and subsequently the use of—the dominated.

The INI was trying to cultivate agents of change from within the social group it wanted to change, agents who would understand the culture on its own terms, people who could articulate change from within indigenous culture.[10] What makes the INI's project unworkable is precisely that such agents might end up articulating a program of change on cultural terms and from a perspective that the INI's goal of assimilation could not admit.[11]

The INI program fits in with a long history of efforts to domesticate this indigenous labor force from colonial times through the nineteenth century. INI policies are formulated in the language of solving the "Indian problem" and helping the Indians, but those policies can be seen as part of the process of modernizing a semifeudal economy while avoiding armed conflict.

It is no accident that the first INI center is in Chiapas, close to the Yucatán, where for many years the Maya fought off federal troops and maintained a pocket of independence. Since the sixties, the INI approach has been criticized both for failing to take on the caste structure and the values of racial and cultural superiority, and for failing to consider ethnic relations in terms of class.[12]

Said's intention in *Orientalism* is to demonstrate the hegemonic function of Orientalist discourse. *Indigenismo,* too, has clearly had a hegemonic function—the administration of an indigenous population by a government—a function carried over from three centuries of colonial administration. But because *indigenismo* is not the ideology and practice of colonial administrators on a territory, but rather an internal practice growing out of Latin American struggles to constitute integrated national societies, it has also had a counterhegemonic component when it has been used to serve groups struggling to redefine their societies in a radical way.

At once an administrative mode growing out of colonialism and a contestatory mode used by one group of non-Indians to dispute the power of another group to define and control their emergent society, one thing *indigenismo* is not is indigenous. Indigenous people themselves have never been its principal promoters or practitioners. They have their own modes of self-representation, their own history of resistance and action. Whether overtly hegemonic or counterhegemonic, *indigenismo* is always bound up in projects of nationalism enunciated by non-Indians, and it always has as its first move the constitution of the category "Indian" as its object. In recent years, indigenous people have organized themselves politically on a more than local level and elaborated their own political discourses and agenda (Bonfil Batalla).

57

Indigenismo is also the name for the kind of imaginative practice with which Castellanos' novels have been identified. As a literary category, *indigenismo* describes a current of Latin American writing recognizable for its thematics and for particular ideological stances. The word has been used since the twenties and thirties as an overarching label to characterize writing that shares the theme of the suffering and oppression of indigenous people in Latin America. Jean Franco distinguishes three general approaches, roughly corresponding (but not limited) to three periods: the exoticizing *indianista* [Indianist] period in the late nineteenth century; social realist *indigenismo* up to 1950; and *nuevo* [new] *indigenismo* after 1950 (*The Modern Culture of Latin America*, 162–166). The chronological division should not obscure the fact that the earlier approaches continued to produce texts even after they were no longer dominant. The literary category could emerge because it was the imaginative terrain of a wider political struggle that had begun to constitute itself as a discourse.

In 1934, Concha Meléndez identified a series of texts written between 1832 and 1899 as *indianista* because they exhibited sympathy for indigenous people or, rather, for the Indian in the abstract. The Indian was portrayed as an exotic, idealized figure with a mythical past and was in part received from European romantic Indianist texts such as Chateaubriand's *Atalá*. But along with using the European literary cliché, these nineteenth-century Andean and Mexican writers also adopted a stance in defense of the Indian, which was their own intellectual heritage from Las Casas, Sahagún, Clavijero, and other colonial thinkers who constituted a tradition advocating better treatment for indigenous people and considered their cultures in a positive light. Unlike their colonial predecessors, however, these writers did not live and work with indigenous people, or have much firsthand knowledge of their culture and history, and their sympathy, real though it was, was also part of their overall rejection of their own recent colonial past and their desire to stake out a cultural territory in opposition to Spanish colonial heritage. The role of the Indian in this writing was to stand for Spanish injustice toward Spain's colonial subjects, to mark the position of the oppressed. The Creoles and the Mestizos could then claim this position, that of the colonized, for themselves. The duality of colonizer-colonized was thus maintained, but in the process the real divisions between indigenous people and colonial settlers were suppressed. The "Indian" was the spoken, not the speaker, as a slogan in the struggle among the grandsons of the settlers.[13]

This social contradiction is central to the emergence of literature in Latin America. Latin American literature as an institution constituted itself in large part by differentiating itself from the colonial and neocolonial centers of power in Europe and North America and by rejecting its naming as derivative or inferior; the utopian and liberational force of this movement continues to find expression in resistance literature (Harlow; Beverly and Zimmerman). Yet the institutionalization of literature in Latin America must also be understood as prolonging and reenacting the colonial hegemonic project in its relation to the cultural world of indigenous peoples.

In the twenties in Mexico, *indigenismo* was getting its start as official government policy. In Peru in the late twenties and the thirties *indigenismo* was also part of a political process, and *indigenista* writing was identified in a series of polemical articles as a literature of struggle. José Carlos Mariátegui's *Siete ensayos de interpretación de la realidad peruana* rallied this trend and remains important because the situation it addressed in 1929 remains critical. He called literary *indigenismo* the "reivindicación de lo autóctono" (reclaiming of the autochthonous) as opposed to an exoticist interest and argued for the role of this writing in the larger political context: *indigenismo* was a necessary element of a nationalist project in Peru as understood through the historical circumstances of Latin American colonialism. Mariátegui also made the crucial observation that *indigenismo* is still a literature of Mestizos and not the writing of indigenous people themselves. Another of his important contributions to the international discussion was the redefinition of the situation of indigenous people in economic terms that located their oppression as part of a larger process rather than seeing them as artificially isolated victims whose "redemption" had to be undertaken in spite of them.

The desire to resolve the social split between "Indian" and non-Indian informs Angel Rama's discussion of form and ideology in *indigenista* writing as a space for transculturation, as does Antonio Cornejo Polar's framing of *indigenismo* in terms of "conflictive heterogeneity."[14] Using Peru as an example, Cornejo Polar claims that

> lo que es esencial en el indigenismo es su heterogeneidad conflictiva, que es el resultado inevitable de una operación literaria que pone en relación asimétrica dos universos socioculturales distintos y opuestos, uno de los cuales es el indígena, (al que corresponde la instancia referencial), mientras que el otro (del que dependen las instancias productivas, textuales y de recepción) está situado en el sector más moderno y occidentalizado de la sociedad [peruana]. Esta contradicción interna reproduce la contradicción básica [de los países andinos]. ("Sobre el 'neoindigenismo' de Manuel Scorza," 550)

> What is essential in indigenism is its conflictive heterogeneity, which is the inevitable result of a literary operation that puts two different and opposing sociocultural universes into an asymmetrical relationship: one of these is the indigenous (corresponding to the referential instance) while the

other (on which depend the productive, textual, and receptive instances) is situated in the most modern and westernized sector of Peruvian society. This internal contradiction reproduces the basic contradiction of Andean countries.

In his account of this asymmetrical relationship, the issue for Cornejo Polar is not how to make *indigenista* writing "an inside view" of indigenous culture, but, rather, whether and how the desire on the part of *indigenista* writers to represent (a truth of) indigenous people appropriates their experiences and situation in the service of political projects that are not theirs, or continues to silence their voices. Martin Lienhard points out that these are two somewhat different visions; Rama posits the relation between cultural modes of discourse as fusion while Cornejo Polar sees it as one of conflict. Both, however, try to account for relations between discourses as unequal relations of power.

In their representations of the "basic contradiction" of their countries, *indigenista* writers, many of them anthropologists, have enacted in specifically nationalist terms the same kinds of dilemmas of "writing culture" (Clifford) or ethnography that challenge anthropologists today. While *indigenista* intellectuals postulate national integration, the "style" in which they imagine it (to follow Benedict Anderson's idea) seems to derive from the desire to present knowledge of indigenous culture as if "from the inside," having somehow transcended social divisions. But Mariátegui recognized early on that *indigenismo* "es obra de mestizos" (is the work of Mestizos) and not the writing of indigenous people themselves. If the social basis for *indigenismo* can be seen as the existence of hegemonic and dependent poles in society structured in alignment with ethnicity, then *indigenista* writers have historically been from the hegemonic pole in their origins and social position as well as in the language and literary forms they use.

The *indigenista* novelist may produce discursively heterogeneous texts, but this heterogeneity is not of the same order as the kinds of "double-voiced discourse" proposed elsewhere to explain African American or women's writing (Gates, *Black Literature and Literary Theory;* Showalter). We cannot cite the *non*-hegemonic position of the author as the factor that originates this double-voicedness. Rather, if we think of the novel in Bakhtin's terms as the genre of "heteroglossia"—characterized by the presence of multiple social discourses—what is at issue in the *indigenista* novel is how those heterogeneous discourses are ordered, what circumstances are seen to confer more legitimacy, or more "naturalness," to one discourse than to another. The question of double-voiced discourses is not, then, one of the writer's origin or social positioning per se, but, rather, how some (but not all) discursive acts are authorized: how the performance of writing from that situation can be read, how it may also teach us ways in which it can be read at all.

Marta Portal sums up the situation and mission of *indigenista* writers as follows:

> *El escritor indigenista es un ser que trata de asumir sus reponsabilidades respecto a la raza oprimida y trata igualmente, de suscitar la indignación y el remordimiento entre los de mejor voluntad de su raza. La literatura indigenista es una literatura restringida, el horizonte de lectores es reducido, y el ser humano que pudiera encontrar en esta literatura el reflejo de su propia situación existencial generalmente no sabe leer.* (Proceso narrativo de la revolución mexicana, 213)

> The *indigenista* writer is one who tries to assume his or her responsibilities with respect to the oppressed race and tries as well to arouse indignation and remorse among those of goodwill in his or her own race. *Indigenista* literature is a restricted literature, its horizon of readers is limited, and the human being who might find the reflection of his or her own existential situation in this literature does not know how to read.

It is in light of the cultural separation of *indigenista* writer from indigenous people themselves that critics speak of a "new *indigenismo*" when they talk about certain novels written after Ciro Alegría's *El mundo es ancho y ajeno* (1941), citing as examples José María Arguedas, Miguel Angel Asturias, and Rosario Castellanos. What distinguishes the works of these writers from earlier efforts, critics claim, is the authors' more intimate knowledge of indigenous cultures and their incorporation of myth and literary tradition (both written and oral) into their narratives along with the observations they made by living or working in indigenous communities, often as anthropologists. In addition, critics point with relief to the high aesthetic quality of these novels in comparison with their social-realist predecessors of the thirties whose efforts appear earnest but crude by comparison. The "new" *indigenista* writers use such literary techniques as interior monologue or a contrapuntal presentation of time. According to this critical view, a greater technical literary sophistication, part of the wider pattern of innovation in the novel in Latin America, enabled these writers to communicate a more authentic (or at least less distorted) sense of indigenous cultural experience. In these novels, indigenous characters are presented as individuals rather than as mass protagonists or as the generic Indian, and, rather than relying on a Manichean identification of Whites as evil exploiters and Indians as innocent victims, indigenous characters are allowed to emerge as "human beings"—that is, as "round"

61

characters. In fact, it is often because characters in these works are more convincing according to literary standards of character development that the vision of their lives as presented in these novels is felt to be more authentic. The "new" *indigenistas* by no means abandon the denunciation of social injustice that is the major identifying characteristic of *indigenista* writing of the thirties, but they are more conscious of the problems inherent in their efforts. They continue to expose the economic and social nature of the exploitation of indigenous peoples, but rather than presenting this as only a situation of class struggle, they also pose the problem in terms of the ethnic cultural formations that mediate social relations. They attempt to represent the possibility that alternative cultural practices, or subjugated knowledges, might potentially produce political subjects within the nationalist context, subjects whose history of resistance might enable counterhegemonic projects.

Castellanos' two novels are set in Chiapas, where she spent the first fifteen years of her life. Chiapas is the southernmost state in Mexico, bordered to the south and west by the Pacific and Oaxaca, to the south and east by Guatemala, and to the north and east by Veracruz, Tabasco, and the Yucatán peninsula. Isolated from the more northern provinces both physically and historically, Chiapas is part of what was formerly the Maya domain and shares much culturally and historically with the Yucatán peninsula and neighboring Guatemala. It is also one of the areas of Mexico where large numbers of indigenous people remain relatively unassimilated into the hegemonic culture that evolved out of the Conquest and that today calls itself the "national" or "Mestizo" culture. The history of relations between indigenous peoples and the descendants of their conquerors is one in which the dynamic of violence put in motion by the Conquest continues to play itself out.

In an interview with Emmanuel Carballo in 1964 Castellanos spoke of why she chose to write about Chiapas and its people:

> La gente que en mis escritos pugnaba por surgir era la de Chiapas. En los tres libros no creo haber agotado el tema: es una realidad compleja, rica, sugerente, y hasta ahora, prácticamente intacta. Me interesa conocer, en esas tierras, los mecanismos de las relaciones humanas. Para entenderlos, cuando trabajé allí para el INI, me auxilió la lectura de Simone Weil—digo Simone Weil porque no conocía otros autores que me hubieran sido más útiles. Ella ofrece, dentro de la vida social, una serie de constantes que determina la actitud de los sometidos frente a los sometedores, el trato que los poderosos dan a los débiles, el cuadro de reacciones de los sojuzgados, la corriente del mal que va de los fuertes a los débiles, y que regresa otra vez a los fuertes. Esta especie de contagio me parece dolorosa y fascinante. (420)

The people that in my writing struggle to emerge are the people of Chiapas. In my three books I don't think I've used up the theme; it's a complex reality, rich, suggestive, and until now practically untouched. I'm interested in knowing, in these lands, the mechanisms of human relations. To understand them, when I was working there for the INI, I was aided by my reading of Simone Weil—I say Simone Weil because I didn't know any other authors that could have been more useful to me. She offers, in social life, a series of constants that determine the attitude of the subjugated before those who have subjugated them, the treatment that the powerful give the weak, the picture of the reactions of the oppressed, the current of evil that goes from the strong to the weak and returns once more to the strong. This kind of contagion seems to me both painful and fascinating.

Which groups the reader chooses to identify as the strong and the weak in these novels determines a great deal about how one reads them. Clearly, in the first instance the "subjugated" are the descendants of the original Maya inhabitants of Chiapas, the Tzeltal and Tzotzil peoples among whom Castellanos was reared. Both of Castellanos' novels tell the stories of indigenous rebellions against Ladino authority and oppression. *Balún Canán,* based on Castellanos' own family experiences, focuses on the family of one landholder. The novel is set in the thirties, when the agrarian reforms passed by President Cárdenas brought tensions between Ladino landowners and the Maya to the point of violent confrontation. Castellanos examines how relations of oppression and resistance both structure and are structured by the institutions of family and inheritance. In particular, she shows the ideological continuity between the economic exploitation of indigenous labor, racism, and the oppression of women.

Her second novel, *Oficio de tinieblas,* treats the same questions on a wider historical scale. Its account moves between indigenous and Ladino communities, detailing the social structure of each and their close interdependence. Although *Oficio de tinieblas* is also set in the Cárdenas era, it narrates the rebellion of the entire region, and the story is based on a rebellion that actually took place in Chiapas from 1867 and 1870. This "caste war," also called the War of Saint Rose of Chamula, is transposed in the novel to a postrevolutionary setting in order to demonstrate the historical continuity of relations of oppression in Chiapas and, by implication, in Mexico and Central America as a whole. These relations persisted long past the end of the Revolution and are present to a great extent today.

The short stories of *Ciudad Real* detail interaction between Ladino and Maya, each story focusing on a particular aspect of those relations. In most of the stories, the tremendous abuse and exploitation of indigenous people by Ladinos are shown to be the fabric of daily life. Some of the stories also show the efforts of outsiders to help change the situation of the Indians, efforts whose failure forces the outsiders to struggle painfully with their own motives and assumptions.

At the same time, both of the novels and *Ciudad Real* are concerned with how women, both Maya and Ladina, find their lives shaped by ethnic conflict and by patriarchy. Castellanos wrote two other short-story collections in which Maya are not the protagonists: *Los convidados de agosto* details life in the Ladino communities of Chiapas while *Album de familia* is set in Mexico City. In both, women and the ways their lives are shaped—warped and twisted—by male domination are the focus.

Because *Balún Canán, Ciudad Real,* and *Oficio de tinieblas* are "about" indigenous people, they are accordingly classified by literary critics as *indigenista* writing. Yet Castellanos herself stated that the focus of her work was women and their experience:

> *Y que si hay un hilo que corra a través de las páginas de* Balún Canán, *de*
> Oficio de tinieblas, *de* Ciudad Real *y de* Los convidados de agosto *no son las*
> *tierras altas de Chiapas, en las que se desarrolla la anécdota ni la inconformi-*
> *dad y rebeldía de un grupo contra sus opresores ni, menos aún esos opresores*
> *encerrados en una cárcel de prejuicios que no son capaces de abandonar porque*
> *fuera de ella su vida carece de sustento y sus acciones de justificación.*
>
> *No, la unidad de esos libros la constituye la persistencia recurrente de ciertas*
> *figuras: la niña desvalida, la adolescente encerrada, la solterona vencida, la*
> *casada defraudada. ¿No hay otra opción? Dentro de estos marcos establecidos,*
> *sí. La fuga, la locura, la muerte. La diferencia entre un cauce y otro de vida es*
> *únicamente de grado. Porque si lo consideramos bien, tanto las primeras como*
> *las otras alternativas no son propiamente cauces de vida, sino formas de muerte.*
> (El uso de la palabra, 229)

If there is a thread that runs through the pages of *Balún Canán, Oficio de tinieblas, Ciudad Real,* and *Los convidados de agosto,* it is not the highlands of Chiapas where the anecdote unfolds, nor is it the defiance and rebelliousness of one group against its oppressors, nor—least of all—those oppressors shut up in the prison of prejudices that they are incapable of abandoning because without them their lives would have no support and their actions no justification.

No, the unity of those books is constituted by the persistent recurrence of certain figures: the helpless girl, the locked-up adolescent, the defeated old maid, the disappointed wife. Is there no other option? Within the established framework, yes. flight, madness, death. The difference between one course and another is only one of degree. Because if we think about it closely, both the first and the second alternatives are not courses for life, but forms of death.

Although her novels and some of her stories clearly share the thematics and a sense of mission with *indigenista* writing, she disapproved of the exoticizing tendency, the Manichean vision, and the neglect of form and style that she associated with the label (Carballo, 422–423). In the speech she gave when awarded the "Chiapas" prize for *Balún Canán,* she clarified her ideas on the responsibility of the writer in Mexico, rejecting both the art-for-art's-sake and the *"comprometida"* [engagé] stance as too limited—the first because it is concerned with the "how" but not the "what" or the "for whom" of writing, and the second because it puts the work in the service of a theory. She defines the office of the writer as an engagement that requires autonomy: "El escritor no lo es si no pone en entredicho lo que ha heredado" [A writer is not a writer unless he or she can excommunicate what she or he has inherited] (*Juicios sumarios,* 406).[15]

In her novels, one of the ways in which Castellanos rejects oppressive inherited values is by showing how individuals are called on to give allegiance to their communities through engendered ethnic identity. The way that an individual knows how to "read" the ethnic categories of Chiapas society is structured by the interaction of competing stories about identity. The colonial legacy survives in the patriarchal landowner ideology with its static, Manichean divisions of race and gender. Outsiders attempt to redistribute allegiances around a new, national identity. And an embattled indigenous community fights for survival, sometimes by adopting elements of the conquerors' culture. These processes are represented by Castellanos as strategies for rereading that mobilize subjugated knowledges. Inflecting the interaction of these discursive systems, at times in a critical fashion, is the way each of them defines and constrains the female.

Clearly, it is not enough merely to point out that Castellanos shows that women and indigenous people are oppressed in Mexico. She does not present their oppression as identical: in her fiction she stages situations that demonstrate that, while Ladina women may suffer as women, they may also participate in the oppression of indigenous people. And while all indigenous people are oppressed as "Indians," indigenous women also suffer as women at the hands of Ladinos and their own people alike. In the three books Castellanos delineates these mechanisms of privilege and oppression, their interaction and reinforcement, and their connections to other factors such as class as it revolves around the ownership of land and competing nationalist programs for Mexican society. She moves beyond the tentative feminist critique of *Sobre cultura femenina* by taking the step of writing as *indigenista*, out of a commitment to the perspective of the oppressed. The risk involved in this step is that a solidarity with the oppressed, the commitment to speak with them, becomes so easily another form of silencing when it is confused with identification, speaking as or for them.

As was the case in *Sobre cultura femenina*, Castellanos' critique in her *indigenista* fiction is enacted around issues of reading and revisioning cultural discourses, but here she faces her social reality more directly, examining Mexican history and social relations along with the possibilities and contradictions of *indigenista* action. As I read *Balún Canán*, *Oficio de tinieblas*, and *Ciudad Real*, I want to look at how Castellanos represents the ways that individual subjectivities are constructed and negotiated through narratives of identity and conflict, enforced and resisted through "reading lessons." The resisting reader as female intellectual must now also understand her positioning in a context of other histories of resistance, and her own inscription into relations of privilege, violence, and oppression.

❊ 4 ❊

Balún Canán *as Palimpsest*

Esta tierra, lo mismo que la otra de mi infancia,
tiene aún en su rostro,
marcada a fuego y a injusticia y crimen,
su cicatriz de esclava.

Rosario Castellanos, "Monólogo de la extranjera," *Poesía no eres tú* (112)

This land, like that other one of my childhood,
still bears on her face a slave's brand,
burned in by fire, injustice, and murder.

Trans. Maureen Ahern, *A Rosario Castellanos Reader* (112)

Castellanos' first novel, *Balún Canán,* is another story of how Miranda, the girl-child of the oligarchy, learns to read; but the history lessons, the words and remembering are not Prospero's alone, are not the words of men only. The historical presence of a cultural alternative to the heritage of the conquerors is affirmed in this novel even as Castellanos works through a painful understanding of the limits of her own position in relation to it. Her attempt to read her way out of an unbearable situation as a woman is here situated in the context of the wider social conflict over national identity and the legacy of colonialism in Mexico. Words, storytelling, and the use of language itself are the grounds of struggles over meaning and interpretation, action and responsibility (Harrison-MacDonald).

In writing *Sobre cultura femenina* Castellanos staged herself as a reader of the hegemonic academic and philosophical Western discourse on the participation of women in culture. She enacted two ways of reading from within the dominant cultural paradigms, ways whose incompatibility with each other hinges on the fact that each involves different definitions of the feminine and of culture; one way has the weight and power of tradition and institutions behind it while the other comes from Castellanos' own experience as a woman and her still-tentative consciousness of the validity of that perspective. When she reads "as a woman" Castellanos' text is ironic, subversive, and the text that emerges from her reading is productive of a "double-voiced discourse." However, as she is still respectful of the conventions of her genre and of the categories of the discourse she questions, we also see her read "as a man," attempting to read as a philosopher, or as a student of philosophy, on the terms recognized by the academic institution. She tries to take on the masculine subject position, through participation in conventions recognized by the men who enunciate, read, and judge that discourse. The inevitable conclusion of that discourse is that *cultura femenina* is a chimera or an aberration, a painful conclusion for the woman reader and artist.

From this contradictory positioning as Miranda, Castellanos moved, in her poetry and, later, in her novels and drama, to a clearer recognition of the necessity and power of rereading and of reading as a woman. Poems such as "Lamentación de Dido," in which she rereads the story of Dido and Aeneas from Dido's perspective, or the dramatic poems *Judith* and *Salomé*, which recast these female biblical figures in the dramas of Chiapas' history, focus this way of reading both on the author's inherited literary tradition and on the social and political inheritance of her class.

Dido not only represents a woman's perspective in a love story, she also is one of many women in Virgil's poem who represent a threat to the foundation of the nation. The two dramatic poems *Judith* and *Salomé* approach the theme of a daughter's sexuality as an issue of racial and national loyalties within the context of ethnic conflict and the Mexican Revolution in Chiapas. What is so striking about these two pieces is that in both of them the mother is the figure who mediates the daughter's allegiance to the father and to a position in a racial hierarchy. While the daughter is repelled by the mother's suffering at the hands of the father, the mother's enforcement of race and class loyalties entraps the daughter. This complex entanglement is displayed and worked out in both of Castellanos' novels as well.

Castellanos began writing *Balún Canán* to recount a crucial and painful incident in her childhood, the death of her younger brother. It is an act of memory that is both deeply personal and a form of "dangerous memory" grounded in her own suffering. The circumstances surrounding this event connected being female with the experience of injustice and showed clearly the power of speech acts in the general subordination of women. Her return to Chiapas, where she completed the book, widened her consciousness of social injustice in her world as the basis for her family's position in relation to indigenous people. In the novel, Castellanos focuses on the experience of a girl, of her family, and of the Tzeltal Maya community whose existence has been dominated by that family for generations, to lay bare the connections between these two kinds of injustice: the injustice governing the lives of the women of her class, and the cumulative history of injustices governing the lives of Maya men and women. Through the story of the Argüello family we see how the institution of family in Chiapas is predicated on possession: senior male possession of female family members; Ladino possession of indigenous people and their labor; and above all, Ladino possession of the land.

This system of possession and control works through the enforced recognition (enforced reading) of the patriarchal name; legitimacy of landownership and legitimacy of birthright assure the continuity of the family and its dominance in the region. These in turn are maintained by control of female sexuality through economic dependence and fear. The allegiance of elite Ladina women to the roles defined for them in the reproduction of the family and its values depends on the constitution of a Ladino community that defines itself around racial superiority and fear of retribution by the oppressed. When the agrarian reform laws pose a challenge to the landowners' almost complete economic and social hegemony, those laws catalyze a social drama and widen the lines of cleavage that separate indigenous and Ladino communities.[1]

Balún Canán also shows how social inequality is manifested and maintained through the use of language.[2] In the novel few Maya speak Spanish, the medium of commerce, education, and the law, and so they continue to be exploited at the hands of those who control both the institutions and public discourse. Individuals are called on to recognize themselves in terms of their positions in communities through discursive categories of gender and culture; this recognition is carried out as a kind of reading of different sets of shared conventions, including those of the oral and literate modes of storytelling. The same event, experience, or speech act can mean different things for different people depending on how it is "taken," that is, on what conventions are recognized by both speaker and listener as being in force. In *Balún Canán*, a series of narrative acts and documents are "read" in different ways by different characters, and the conflicts generated by reading from different positions and different conventions are played out through violence as Castellanos explores the politics of memory and the grounding of alternative claims to truth.

Rosario Castellanos was haunted by the death of her younger brother, Mario Benjamín.[3] When he was seven and she was eight, he died of appendicitis. But is was not just the death itself that marked her by leaving her an only child; the events surrounding it were to remain painful for many years. She described the situation in an interview with Samuel Gordon while in Israel:

Mi mamá se dedicó a hacer jueguitos de espiritismo con una amiga suya; en uno de esos juegos, la amiga tuvo una visión y recuerdo, yo tenía ocho años y es una memoria muy viva porque fue para mí determinante, que estábamos descansando en el comedor, mi hermano de 7 años, mamá y yo cuando entró

despavorida una prima con el pelo blanco, todo parado y sin peinar, como una
especie de medusa, y le dijo a mi mamá que acababa de aparecérsele alguien que
le avisó que uno de sus dos hijos iba a morir. Entonces mi mamá se levantó como
resorte y gritó ¡Pero no el varón! (Gordon, cited in Poniatowska, 113–114)

My mother passed the time playing little psychic games with a friend of
hers; in one of those games, her friend had a vision and I remember, I was
about eight and it's a very vivid memory because for me it was decisive, that
we were resting in the dining room, my seven-year-old brother, mom and I,
when in came a cousin, terrified, with her white hair uncombed and
standing on end like a kind of Medusa, and she told my mother that
someone had just appeared to her who warned her that one of the two
children was going to die. Then my mother jumped up as if on springs and
cried out, "But not the male!"

In the weeks that followed, the children were silent witnesses to family arguments over whether the male or female child should be the one to die. Both
children were terrified and each "dreamed" that it would be the other. So
when only a few weeks later the boy did die, the girl was left with the awful
guilt of having wanted to survive when her family had made it clear that they
would have readily seen her sacrificed to save the male heir. Even at the fu-
neral, the parents repeated "Pero ¿Por qué el varón?" [But why the male?]
(Poniatowska, ¡Ay vida, 113–114), a question with the force of a curse.[4]

Castellanos tried to write about these memories first in the short story
"Primera revelación," published in 1950 in *América: Revista Antológica,* but
she was not satisfied with the results. A few years later, as she was recounting her childhood to her friend, the writer Emilio Carballido, he urged her to
write it down, so she tried again. Over the next two years (1953–1955) she
worked on what was to become her first novel, *Balún Canán,* writing parts
one and three, the parts narrated by the unnamed girl, who clearly represents the author as a child.

While she was writing this novel, she took a job with the Instituto Nacional
Indigenista (the INI) in 1955 at the Centro Coordinador Tzeltal-Tzotzil in
San Cristóbal de las Casas, the former colonial capital of Chiapas. Friends
remember her at this time as intensely devout, even ascetic (Poniatowska,
¡Ay, vida, 64). She herself places this sojourn in Chiapas under the spiritual
aegis of Simone Weil, whom she quoted often in her essays.[5] Like Weil, she
was driven by a sense of debt; in her case it was to those exploited at the
hands of her family. This return to Chiapas meant confronting her childhood
memories and learning more about the situation of her class and the world
she had escaped when her family moved to Mexico City. At first she worked

for the INI without pay. In this expiatory attitude, she joins many of the scholars who were the driving force behind the INI at this time and who also saw their work as a mission to redeem and uplift the Indians.[6]

Castellanos characterizes the motivations of her *indigenista* colleagues and herself in the essay "Discriminación en Chiapas y en los Estados Unidos" [Discrimination in Chiapas and the United States]:

> *Es posible que durante los primeros meses asumiéramos una actitud de bene-volencia y aun de generosidad y acudiéramos con solicitud en ayuda de los menesterosos. Pero nos decepcionaría muy pronto comprobar que nuestros esfuerzos resultaban insuficientes no sólo como remedio de las necesidades que nos escandalizaban, sino también como causa de la gratitud de nuestros beneficiarios. (El uso de la palabra, 140)*

> It is possible that during the first months we assumed an attitude of benevolence and even of generosity, and we came to the aid of the needy with great solicitude. But we were soon disappointed to realize that our efforts turned out to be insufficient not only as remedies for the needs that shocked us, but also as cause of gratitude among their beneficiaries.

In the stories of *Ciudad Real* Castellanos contrasts the desires and demands of indigenous peoples themselves for land, education, and justice, with the various motivations of the Mestizo characters who speak or act "for" them. In "El don rechazado" [The Rejected Gift] an anthropologist working at the "Misión de Ayuda a los Indios" [Mission to Aid the Indians] (a thinly veiled version of the early INI) has the painful experience of trying to help a woman and her young daughter only to have his well-intentioned efforts met with incomprehension and even fear. In "La rueda del hambriento" [The Wheel of Hunger] a naïve young Ladina woman goes to work at a remote clinic run by the same mission. Her vague and romantic idealism is defeated by the hostility of the elements, the prejudice of the Ladinos and the misery of the Indians, and by the cynicism and corruption of her fellow missionary, Doctor Salazar, whose refusal to give out free supplies causes the death of a newborn child. The phrase "gente de buena voluntad" [people of goodwill] and missionary attitudes about charity and shared suffering are all shown to be meaningless in the face of the magnitude and complexity of the situation. The last and longest story, "Arthur Smith salva su alma" [Arthur Smith Saves His Soul], attacks the hypocrisy of the different "missions" to aid indigenous people through the story of a North American Protestant missionary who comes to Chiapas to translate the Bible into Tzeltal only to discover that his fellow missionaries are completely indifferent to the suffering around them and indeed serve as a front for U.S. covert activities. Smith sees his attempts to "save the Indians" as the way to save his own soul, but his growing revulsion with the situation leads to his expulsion from the mission; he renounces missionary salvation in favor of an idea of justice. While the story leaves the reader in doubt as to the possibilities of success for the individual, it does lead to the conclusion that, for the "missionaries" to save their own souls they must do more than share the suffering of those they are trying to help; they must work for social justice.[7]

An experience in Chiapas that had a great impact on Castellanos was her time as director of the traveling puppet show Teatro Petul. Her job was to write the puppet plays whose main character was the Maya puppet Petul and whose purpose was to teach a Maya audience to identify with the Mexican nation. Among other things, these didactic theater pieces promoted hygiene or explained about tourists and the flag. One piece called on the Maya to identify with the nation through the *vida ejemplar* [exemplary life] of Benito Juárez and explicitly promoted literacy and education as the means to better their lives.[8] In a 1965 article, Castellanos defined their task as follows:

Era preciso decirles todo: que eran personas humanas, que su patria era México, que el viento no estaba encerrado en una cueva, que los microbios existían y eran dañinos, que el hambre no constituía un estado natural sino era un mero accidente.

You had to tell them everything: that they were human beings, that their country was Mexico, that the wind was not shut up in a cave, that microbes existed and that they were harmful, that hunger was not a natural state but rather a mere accident.

Even allowing for the habitual Castellanos irony, the paternalism of the project is hair-raising. Although her intentions, and those of the people with whom she worked, were altruistic and even revolutionary, in these attempts to effect social transformation through theater, Castellanos was participating in the kind of crude colonialist *indigenista* action that presumed that the non-Indian intellectuals and bureaucrats from the city knew best what was needed and what should be done to solve the "Indian problem," and that the Maya themselves had no understanding of their own situation and no knowledge to contribute.

But these experiences disturbed certainties and began the process of questioning that would lead her to begin a critique of some of the underlying assumptions of *indigenismo*. A description of her work with Teatro Petul in a letter to a friend conveys some of the same paternalism in her relations to the Maya men with whom she worked, yet also describes the way in which comfortable hierarchies of competence and knowledge were being altered for her through the experience of reading together and talking about language:

> Estoy encargada del teatro guiñol y escribo las obras que se presentan así como acompaño a los del teatro en sus giras por la zona. Quiero familiarizarme con todo eso . . . Los que integramos el grupo somos siete. Tres muchachos tzeltales, tres tzotziles y yo. Los días que no salimos estudiamos juntos historia y geografía de México y leemos el Popol Vuh. Todavía el problema principal es el idioma. Aunque ellos concocen el español, lo conocen solo superficialmente. Hay que explicar el sentido hasta de las palabras más usuales. Pero hemos establecido, esos muchachos y yo, una relación muy buena. Amistad. Y yo me siento aquí muy protectora mientras les enseño cosas que ignoraban. Pero cuando vamos a caballo, los protectores son ellos. Y ese intercambio de carencias y debilidades nos iguala. (Calderón, 21–22)

I'm in charge of a puppet theater and I write the plays that are presented as well as accompanying the theater folks on their tours throughout the zone. I want to get to know all about this . . . There are three of us in the group: three Tzeltal guys, three Tzotzil guys, and I. The days that we don't go out we study Mexican history and geography together and we read the Popol Vuh. The main problem is still language. Although they know Spanish, they know it only superficially. I have to explain the meaning of even the most common words. But we have established, these guys and I, a very good relationship. Friendship. And I feel very protective here when I teach them things they don't know. But when we ride horseback, they are the protectors. And this exchange of lacks and weaknesses makes us equal.

The Maya men in the group translated the pieces she wrote into their languages, but she still had to communicate to them what she wanted expressed. Her descriptions of these interactions resonate with the image of Miranda as Caliban's language teacher, assuming that what she has to teach is what her pupils need to learn for their own good. But the scene she represents here has two crucial differences: this is not a scene of revolt but of collaboration, however unequal; Castellanos reads with the Maya one of the Maya's most important cultural legacies, the Popol Vuh, a book that is both vehicle and sign of the alternative cultural practices that *indigenista* action is seeking to change.

The impact of these efforts on her poetry of that period is clear: the poems in *El rescate del mundo* represent a clear departure from her earliest work as she abandons the highly abstract language of her earlier poetry in favor of more simple language, concrete images. However, the communication across cultures that she celebrates in her letter is represented elsewhere, in her fiction and essays, as an experience of frustration, misreading, and failure.

Her essay "Incidente en Yalantay" (recast in the story "El don rechazado") recounts an episode of failed communication that serves as an indictment of *indigenista* insufficiencies. Castellanos says that the Maya seemed to respond to Petul as if he were a person, one they could trust because he spoke their language and followed their customs, whereas Castellanos was an outsider, and the Indian men who formed the troupe wore Ladino clothes. This was all very well as long as it served the purposes of the INI; when a young girl asked Petul to help her get into the INI school, the INI group was elated. But when the director of the school returned with them to Yalantay to get her father's permission, the father refused, unless they were to pay him. The group was horrified by the idea that they would be buying the girl from her family and refused. The girl's tearful reproach to them was, "Why didn't you bring Petul?"

Some Maya did identify with the character Petul, but not in the symbolic way intended by the INI, as a form of interpellation into Mexican citizenship. The assumption of the *indigenista* promoters of Teatro Petul was that the Indians would take Petul literally, as if they were children or naïve readers who might be manipulated into taking on other cultural practices or identities through storytelling. The failure of the INI group to effect the kind of change it wanted (to bring the girl to school so she could have a better life) is a consequence of that underlying assumption, only now the failure is attributed to indigenous people's ignorance or superstition when the girl's father does not do what he is supposed to (understand the good intentions of the INI and do what he should do according to his role in the INI script). What can also be read in this story, both as it is told in the essay and as it is reelaborated in "El don rechazado," is the failure of the INI anthropologists to understand how their actions fit into a local hegemonic social narrative: when Ladinos express an interest in taking a young girl from her family to live in town, it is because they want to use her as a maid or a prostitute; their propositions have a different meaning from the one they intend in the context of social relations that take for granted the buying and selling of Indians by Ladinos. The failure of understanding on both sides is easily cast by Ladinos (including us as readers of the essay) into the available trope of "native superstition," or failure to read the codes of certain social transactions "properly," but that trope can also be understood by the reader of Castellanos' text as a defensive posture on the part of those who do not understand their own positioning within the hegemonic social narrative of colonial relations.

Her experiences in Chiapas with the INI brought Castellanos from simple good intentions to a wider critique of social structures that involved questioning her values and assumptions at every stage of her action and led her to focus on the paramount role of language and "reading" in interactions between people. In an essay in *El uso de la palabra* on the efforts to "defend" the Indians in San Cristóbal since Bartolomé de las Casas, Castellanos affirmed her faith in the power of language to effect change:

> *Si algún poder tiene la palabra, si alguna función tiene la teoría, si algún jugo ha de exprimirse del conocimiento, es éste de dar su nombre a las cosas. El nombre verdadero y exacto, aparte de producir un placer estético, mueve a la acción, a la conversión y a la corrección. Ya no es tan fácil continuar repitiendo el mismo gesto, la misma actitud, el mismo mecanismo cuando sabemos que ese gesto se llama despojo, ultraje; que esa actitud es rapaz y se aprovecha de ventajas ilícitas y choca de frente con todos los principios de la religión y de la moral, a los que se está adhiriendo; que ese mecanismo es un fósil que una mirada ajena contempla con curiosidad y con azoro, negándose a creer en su supervivencia en el siglo en que la tierra ha abierto sus puertos al universo.*
> ("El padre las Casas y la agonía del indio," El uso de la palabra, 146)

If the word has any power, if theory has any function, if there is any juice to be squeezed out of knowledge, it is that of giving things their names. The true and exact name, aside from producing aesthetic pleasure, moves us to action, to conversion, to correction. It is no longer so easy to keep on repeating the same gestures, the same attitudes, the same mechanisms when we know that this gesture is called despoiling, outrage, that this attitude is rapaciousness and profiting from illicit advantages and that it clashes with every religious and moral principle to which one adheres, that this mechanism is a fossil that the outsider's gaze contemplates with curiosity and surprise, unable to believe in its survival in a century when the earth has opened its gates to the universe.

In her Teatro Petul work in Chiapas, Castellanos was addressing an indigenous audience, and even after her return to Mexico City she continued to edit pedagogical material for the INI. Her novels, however, were aimed at a different public, the literate Spanish-speaking readership. The cultural gap between the readers of the novels and the people about whom she wrote, and its structuring of power relations, was an important thematic concern for Castellanos. In "El indigenismo y las literaturas heterogéneas: su doble estatuto socio-cultural" Antonio Cornejo Polar discusses how this gap structures such fiction by contrasting what he calls homogeneous literatures with heterogeneous literatures (7–8). In the first case, the production and reception of a text, the text itself, and its referent all circulate within the same sociocultural order, whereas in heterogeneous literatures one or more of these elements does not belong. In the case of *indigenista* writing, it is the referent, indigenous culture and history, that belongs to another order altogether, one that is not hegemonic with respect to the conventions, the production, distribution, and reception of the novel. Castellanos' novels can be read as examples of heterogeneous literature, but their reception reveals another order of heterogeneity, that of gender. When we look at the critical responses to the novels, we see that they generally fall into two categories: reading the novels as *indigenista*, and reading the novels as feminist, depending on which kind of "heterogeneity" the reader chooses as focus.

While in Chiapas Castellanos finished the novel she had begun in Mexico City. *Balún Canán,* published in 1957, won the Chiapas Literary Prize the next year and was immediately translated into English, French, and German. Critics praised the novel as a great work of *indigenista* writing for its portrayal of ethnic conflict and its denunciation of the exploitation of Indians. The book appeared two years after Rulfo's *Pedro Páramo* and one year before Fuentes' *La región más transparente,* and although from time to time someone recognizes it as part of this *nueva narrativa,* critics by and large continue to label the novel *indigenista.*[9] This classification, while valid, limits the way the novel is read, determining to a great extent what is seen and what we read for.

The work of Joseph Sommers addresses some of the ways in which the *indigenista* category functions to limit readings. First, as Sommers shows in his article on *Oficio de tinieblas* ("Forma e ideología"), the usual assimilation of Castellanos' novels into *indigenismo* hides the fact that this term names a discourse extending far beyond a literary practice, one that is implicated in wide-ranging social policies and concerted efforts to effect material changes in the lives of millions. As we saw in Chapter 3, *indigenismo* is not a completely unified discourse, but a set of parameters within which different interests vie for direction of social policy. Castellanos' novels are part of the critical mode of *indigenismo* in that, as she denounces the exploitation of indigenous people, she also criticizes the official mode of *indigenismo,* the government-sponsored policies and actions that she observed firsthand during her work for the INI. With its program of planned acculturation, in Sommers' words,

> Ya no se entendía el indigenismo como el fundamento potencial para una transformación radical y populista de las instituciones socio-económicas. De acuerdo a la nueva visión, el indigenismo serviría para adaptar el indio a las estructuras políticas y económicas establecidas. ("Forma e ideología," 77)

Indigenismo was no longer understood as the potential foundation for a
radical and populist transformation of socioeconomic institutions. According to the new vision, indigenismo would serve to adapt the Indian to the
established political and economic structures.

Thus, in some respects, Castellanos' literary work joins that current of *indigenista* debate that was in the minority at the 1940 Pátzcuaro Congress, where
socialists promoted radical changes in Mexican society itself while the majority promoted changing "Indians" instead. Written in the late fifties, *Balún
Canán* and *Oficio de tinieblas* anticipate in some respects the arguments of
the contestatory current that was to emerge vocally in the sixties, when radical social scientists branded *indigenismo* ethnocide. But if the novels anticipated this resurgence of a highly critical attitude, when they were published
the reigning assumptions about *indigenista* action were positive and, to some
extent, shared by Castellanos herself.

Joseph Sommers evaluates Castellanos' novels in terms of ideological re-
vision. In "Literatura e historia: Las contradicciones de la ficción indigenista,"
Sommers charts some of the ideological positions in Mexican *indigenista* writing by examining how three novelists, including Castellanos, construct and
mobilize the ideologeme *indio* in their novels. In his view, Heriberto Frías'
1893 novel *Tomochic* glorifies the indigenous past while it ignores the present,
promoting new class interests that ally modernization with the ideology of *mestizaje*. Here indigenous people as "Indians" are still outside the nationalist
program, as Barbarian threatening Civilization. Sommers cites the thirties'
novels *El indio* [The Indian] (1935) by Gregorio López y Fuentes and *El res-
plandor* [Sunburst] (1937) by Mauricio Magdaleno as examples of a populist
call for national mobilization through a paternalistic policy of assimilation
that was imposing itself on the national agenda at the time. He differentiates
Castellanos' work from this previous writing because he reads her disenchant-
ment with the assimilationist aspirations that perpetuate the existence of an
internal colonialism. Sommers praises her for this, but disapproves of what
he calls her "pessimism" ("Forma e ideología," 38). I would like to suggest
that there is another way to read her refusal to promote her own solution to
the "Indian problem."

If some critics do not always consider the specific political context of Mexican *indigenismo* when they speak about literary *indigenismo*, they do recognize that Castellanos' stance was not identical to that of earlier *indigenista*
writers. Sommers evaluates Castellanos' work in terms of ideology, but when
other critics include her in the literary category "new *indigenismo*," the political dimension of her work is treated primarily in aesthetic terms. The elements
cited approvingly as new include the more "rounded" or psychologically

complex characters, or the more sophisticated narrative devices.[10] The recognition that Castellanos does not put forth a Manichean vision of victim-victimizer is offered as an aesthetic judgment; her work is judged to be more literary and less overtly ideological, less propagandistic.

While Castellanos herself felt that aesthetic considerations were of primary importance for any writer and distanced herself from earlier *indigenista* efforts she judged as too clumsy, at the same time she stressed that literature did and should serve functions beyond the aesthetic. In several essays she repeated her view that Mexican literature has always had, and should continue to have, important social, moral, and didactic functions.[11]

An important claim made for the "new" *indigenistas* (such as Asturias and Arguedas) is that they present a more knowledgeable view of indigenous culture and experience, both through the inclusion of specifically "Indian" material and, formally, through certain poetic devices; their representation of indigenous characters is no longer a crude or exoticist caricature. Many critics focus on *indigenista* writing because they see it as the symbolic space for the utopian ideal of *mestizaje,* a discursive space in which social inequality would be resolved. We must ask ourselves how Castellanos' work is structured by this ideal, the Utopian desire to see resolved discursively what has not been resolved politically.

Martin Lienhard reminds us of some important factors, too often glossed over, to consider before the label "authentic" can be applied to any of the "new" *indigenista* writers. This claim is in fact based on conventions of reading and literary verisimilitude. For while it is true that Castellanos, Arguedas, Asturias, and others have more accurate knowledge of indigenous cultural traditions than some of their literary predecessors, they still present this material in a highly mediated form. The representations in *Balún Canán* of indigenous oral storytelling are not accurate representations of contemporary Tzeltal oral style. When we look at a Spanish translation of a Tzeltal story cited by Miguel León Portilla, we can see that the oral style of contemporary Tzeltal speakers is rather different.[12] The tales told by Maya characters in *Balún Canán* are an approximation in Spanish of the "Indian" literary style available to Castellanos and others through the contemporary translations of the Popol Vuh or the Libros de Chilam Balam. The average reader can hear echoes of the Spanish translations of the few ancient Maya texts he or she might have read, texts cited in the epigraphs before each of the novel's three parts. As Lienhard says, while the result is beautiful and often highly effective, it is not, strictly speaking, "authentic." Thus, our discussion of the "heterogeneity" of Castellanos' novels and of the presence of elements of indigenous culture in them must focus on the nature of this mediation.

Castellanos' representation of provincial Ladino society in Chiapas is *emic,* an inside view by one who was brought upwithin that culture, while her representations of Tzeltal or Tzotzil cultural practices may be highly informed but are necessarily an *etic* view, from outside that culture (Turner, 141–142). The novels Castellanos wrote represent discourse about Maya cultural practices, but are not themselves examples of Maya cultural practices. The novel must supply enough material for a person unfamiliar with Maya culture to reconstruct a context; one of the ways this works is by appealing to shared literary (non-Maya) conventions.

The first of the three parts of the novel, divided into twenty-four brief episodes, serves as dramatic exposition, creating for us a picture of the world of provincial society in the 1930s as seen through the eyes of the narrator, a seven-year-old girl who is never named in the novel except as *niña*, girl. Her first-person narrative provides the reader with a kind of doubled vision. The girl tells us about what she sees at her child's-eye level, and at the same time the reader is able to infer a great deal more about this world than the child is conscious of; the girl is the locus of a confluence of discourses. We see how the child constructs and derives meanings that, because of her lack of experience, are off the mark.

Her narrations frame the part of the novel that is not told by her, the second part, and they contain the voices of others; the reader filters meaning through the representation of her partial awareness of the significance of events. Because she is a child, she is also the object of the interaction of the discourses and value systems imparted by her family, the school, the church, and her Maya nurse, her *nana*. In the girl we see how an individual, in this case, a female child of a particular class, time, and place, is subject to conflicting interpellations, and how she acts in consequence. This process, banal at the beginning of the novel, will become the material of the third and last section of the novel, when the children's struggles to "read" events and symbols take on life-and-death consequences.

Two threads run through the first part: one is the series of signs of an imminent outbreak of violence that multiply as the conflict between Ladino landowners and the indigenous workers is exacerbated by the new laws of agrarian reform. The world of the Argüello family—the girl, her parents, César and Zoraida, and her younger brother, Mario—seems stable and ordered at first, but signs of conflict appear as landowners such as the girl's father resist what they see as an attack on their dominance in the region. Violence between Indian and Ladino is reported in the countryside; the girl's school, inadequate as it is, is closed by the government for violations of the anticlerical measures in force; one of the Indians loyal to César is wounded and dies upon his arrival at the family's home in Comitán. Despite the advice of their neighbors, who are selling their land and emigrating to Guatemala, the

Argüellos make their usual journey to their ranch, Chactajal; their arrival closes the first part and the open conflict predicted in Part One is narrated in Part Two.

The other narrative thread in the first part of the novel is the effort of the Maya *nana*, also nameless, to fight the girl's socialization into the prejudices of her class by giving her another vision of the world, an alternate set of values. This vision is conveyed through the device of tales the *nana* tells the girl. Framed by the first-person narrative, these are tales from the indigenous cultural world, spoken by a Maya woman's voice. The tale that opens the novel is that of the Conquest. The *nana* also tells the story of a magical creature, the *dzulúm* (in Chapter 4), and a creation story that is also a lesson on the proper relation between rich and poor (Chapter 9). At the end of Part One, the *nana*, who will not make the journey to the family ranch, says a prayer that is also a lesson for the girl, a summary of the values she is trying to instill in her. In an oral society the act of storytelling passes on the collective memory and instructs the young in the proper way to be in the community. The *nana*'s stories transmit indigenous cultural knowledge and memory as a means of cultural survival; they serve as well as the vehicle for the transmission of values, an education to counter the one the girl receives in school and from her parents.

In the second part of the novel, the narrative solidifies as the episodic premonitory quality of the first part gives way to a more sustained narration of overt conflict and action. There are fewer chapters and they are longer, more tightly linked through the chronology of growing tension between the family and the Maya. In place of the girl's first-person voice, the perspectives of the adult characters dominate. Each of them at one point has an internal monologue revealing his or her past, motivations, and delusions. Each of these characters is shown as struggling to reconcile a difficult personal situation with the conflicting ideological imperatives he or she confronts, imperatives that dictate contradictory loyalties. The crisis situation that has polarized the Maya and Ladino communities brings each character in some way into a conflict of allegiances.

César the patriarch, arrogant and described as "living by his own law," has received the benefits of education and travel available to a man of his class, but for which he has no use; his wife, Zoraida, was poor and fears being poor again, so she defends fiercely the position that is hers as wife and mother to Argüellos men; César's illegitimate nephew Ernesto, brought to Chactajal to give lip service to the law requiring a school for the indigenous community, longs to be part of the family from which he is excluded; César's timid cousin Matilde, who has fled her home because her older sister,

Francisca, seems to be going crazy, has almost no status except that of servant because she is an unmarried female relative.

Along with the adults of the Argüello family, two other important characters in this section are the Maya Felipe Carranza Pech, the only person in the Chactajal village who can read and write and leader of the opposition to César, and Felipe's wife, Juana. Felipe has traveled and seen President Cárdenas. He tries to tell his people what the new laws can do for them, and although his decisive actions win him a place of leadership, he now no longer fits in with his people because his experiences have changed him. His wife, Juana, is childless, a catastrophe for a woman in both the indigenous and the Ladino communities in Chiapas. Her husband could repudiate her according to the custom of her people, but instead he neglects her. She fears the changes she sees in him because they add to her isolation. Through her we see a process whereby Maya women are marginalized in their community and forced to work as servants to Ladinos—like the *nana* and her replacement, Vicenta, in Part Three, who are also alienated from their communities.

The last section of the novel narrates the final collapse of the family and the death of the boy, Mario, cursed by the *brujos,* the sorcerers, of Chactajal. The girl is again the narrator, and the action returns to the town Comitán. The terrain of struggle has shifted from the men's world to the women's and the children are the object of the conflict between belief systems. In this part of the novel, reading and interpretation of stories are represented as life-and-death matters for the characters, and as the girl tries to put into practice her lessons in reading and storytelling—lessons that are also lessons in power— she is inducted into those stories as actor with horrifying consequences.

The problems of reading that are dramatized in the novel are also apparent in the different kinds of reading that are brought to the novel by its critics. The use of the *indigenista* literary category generates critical discussion in a manner that privileges some aspects of the novels while silencing others. The most glaring suppression observable in many cases is that of the voices and experience of women. Those who come to Castellanos' novels from a reading of her other work, her poetry, essays, and theater pieces, immediately perceive the thematic continuity of her urgent attention to women's experience and the ways their lives are too often "forms of death." The feminist perspective that was to some extent still latent in her earlier poetry emerges clearly in the novels and would later be articulated more explicitly in her poetry and essays and in her play *El eterno femenino.*

The first phase of a critical rereading of Castellanos' novels that takes this perspective into account is the kind that Elaine Showalter has called "feminist criticism"; that is, it is primarily in a revisionist mode of interpretation, encompassing a wide range of practices that "offers feminist readings of texts which consider the images and stereotypes of women in literature, the omissions and misconceptions about women in criticism, and women-as-sign in semiotic systems" (12).

If we do not go beyond the binary oppositions strong/weak or oppressor/oppressed to discuss Castellanos' treatment of both ethnicity and gender, we run the risk of speaking as if these two categories are mutually exclusive while at the same time asserting an identical form of oppression.[13] The phrase "women and Indians" seems to oppose the two terms as if the only women were not Indians and the only Indians were not women.[14] Castellanos' fiction dramatizes a social reality of interlocking forms of oppression, but does not ask us to assume a common oppression and a common response to it on the part of Ladina women and Indians. It is precisely this parallel that the novels reveal to be painfully inadequate. Yes, Ladina women and Indians are exploited by Ladino men, but not in the same material ways. Ladina women also exploit Indians, treat them as objects, revile them. Indian men have control over Indian women, whose lives are defined in terms of their sexual and reproductive roles, as are those of Ladina women.

One Ladina in *Balún Canán* who owns land is Francisca, César Argüello's sister. Instead of relying mainly on arms and force, she manipulates Maya beliefs to retain her power. However, if she uses her knowledge and practice of Indian *brujería,* it is not because she shares completely the Maya worldview or sees herself as part of their community, but rather to hold her workers in fear and to continue the pattern of Ladino exploitation of the Maya. Moreover, because Ladina women in the novels are excluded from the rationalistic, legalistic systems of Ladino men (represented in the novel as the discourses of school, priest, and doctor), they do not therefore share a worldview with indigenous people. Zoraida and Matilde are both oppressed and excluded by the paternalistic sexual ideology of property and family, yet each in her way also conforms to it and defends it; their oppression as women never leads them to identify with the Maya community. If in the women's sphere of influence we see Ladino and indigenous cultural practices enter into contact in a way that allows a mixing or borrowing between them, this does not mean that Ladina women share either the indigenous worldview or the kinds of material oppression people suffer *as "Indians."* In fact, the *nana* tries to teach the girl to share certain values of her world, and while the girl is receptive to them because she is so firmly excluded from her own, in the end the novel refuses to hold the girl up as a solution: the ideal of *mestizaje* is shown to come up against the great obstacles of divided allegiances and complicity.

Since Mariátegui, it is recognized that the *indigenista* writer is a Mestizo writing from the dominant position in the social order about indigenous people who are in a position of relative dependence. But if that writer is a woman, even a woman of the most privileged class, her relation to that hegemonic pole is ambiguous at best. This would not, of course, endow her with a special insight into indigenous cultural reality, but it might lead to a questioning of some of the "generic" assumptions of hierarchy. More significant perhaps is the manner in which gender shapes the legibility of *indigenista* writing.

Nancy K. Miller quotes Gérard Genette on *"vraisemblance,"* or plausibility, as an effect of "reading through a grid of concordances" (36). We have seen some of the ways that *indigenismo* sets up its own grid of concordances for the thematics of ethnic conflict. But on a more fundamental level we can also seen how gender is another factor in shaping the reading process. The general assumption that the *(indigenista)* novel is a representation of a male speaker's utterance organizes the perceived hierarchy of discourses in these novels. A striking example of how this works can be seen in the way reviewers and, later, many critics dealt with a technical aspect of *Balún Canán* that they deemed less than successful.[15] A few seem to think that Castellanos must have changed narrators in the second part because she was not capable of presenting the entire narrative through the eyes of a child. This part contains events that the girl could not have communicated to us, so she had to put it in the third person. Indeed, one critic says she should not have used a child's perspective at all.[16]

There are several assumptions here that could bear closer scrutiny and that make one ask if what is being read and rejected as *"invraisemblable"* (implausible) is not perhaps something else altogether, some other aspect of the novel that troubles or does not fit. In the first place, this criticism distinguishes only two types of narrative voice; the first and third parts are narrated in the first person by the girl while the second part is always described as narrated in either a "third person" or by an "omniscient" narrator. But this description is incomplete. The girl's speaking voice, her "I," is the focal point for sections she narrates, but other voices are *represented* there, most notably that of the *nana,* her Maya nurse. Different belief systems or discourses are heard and enunciated through the dialogue she actually reports or reproduces, through the tales told to her by her *nana* and by Uncle David, and through the curious document she comes across and reads in her father's library, a document that we will examine in some detail later. Through this interplay of discourses and voices, the reader is able to infer a great deal that the girl herself could not consciously know or understand. Moreover, the quality of her own way of speaking should make it evident that this is not actually a seven-year-old speaking but the literary representation of one.

The terms "third person" and "omniscient" narrator imply a unified voice, a single speaker, one who is represented as producing the utterance. This concept is not adequate to account for the range of stylistic devices employed by Castellanos in the novel's middle section, which work to introduce many perspectives and voices: some chapters are internal monologues in the first person; one consists of a document written by Felipe's recounting his community's building of the school; in others, parenthetical inserts signify the eruption of a character's thoughts into the narration. In the chapter that tells of the fire that burns the ranch's sugar mill, Castellanos uses a rhetorical style similar to that of the oral tales we have seen represented in Part One, but here no speaker is identified. Castellanos avails herself freely of some of the resources of the novel's tradition as genre of heteroglossia.[17]

This brings up an important point: if the girl (whom the reader in some sense probably sees as the child persona of the author) is understood to be speaking the first and third parts, who is enunciating the second? In Part Two, the situation of enunciation is established by a sentence that appears between the epigraph and the chapter number: "Esto es lo que se recuerda de aquellos días" [This is what is remembered about those days] (75). "Se recuerda" is the impersonal reflexive, not the first person, and can be translated as "is remembered/one remembers/people remember/we remember"; there is no clearly identified source of the enunciation. This assimilates the narration into either a written account in which the recorder transcribes memories, not necessarily her own, or perhaps into an oral account of the kind the *nana* gives: a collective memory. In any case, this phrase focalizes Part Two as an enunciation, but the identity of its speaker cannot be determined. This device also has the ring of an oral formula used to begin a tale, thus echoing the oral style of two other written versions of (oral) collective memory presented in the novel in which a Maya man tells the story of Chactajal in order to preserve the community's history.

If the phrase "This is what is remembered . . ." situates the entire second part in the register of a narrated memory, then whose is it? That of the girl, years later after she's grown up? The community? If so, which one? Through the frames of a female voice and the conventions of oral discourse, experiences usually submerged can be read through the dominant register of the conventions of realist novelistic discourse used in Part Two.

The girl who tells us much of the story of Chactajal and of her family is not the "hermano mayor," the older brother of her community, but the "hermana mayor," older sister of Mario and custodian of his memory after he dies; the crucial difference is that, for the Maya community if not for the Ladino authorities, the "older brother" is entitled to speak; she is not. His authority is recognized whereas in no one's eyes is the girl is entitled to speak; reasoning with her mother, for example, has no effect, but Mario has only to whine wordlessly and he gets his way because he is the boy.

Sandra Messenger Cypess comments on the fact that critics have neglected the significance of the girl as narrator-protagonist (4). This neglect is linked to the way some critics have seen the girl as a vehicle through which the story passes. To dismiss the girl as merely a reporter of the action (or of what is significant and important to the adults—critics and readers) is to dismiss and silence crucial aspects of the novel's workings, the way it maps and analyzes the workings of discourse and dramatizes the consequences of taking one kind of discourse for another.

Cypess points out that there is something already subversive in making a child, especially a female, the speaker; it flouts the maxim "children should be seen but not heard." This is especially true because she is a female child.[18] The commonly accepted grid of concordances or rules of plausibility takes the passivity and complicity of women in their own oppression to be axiomatic as well. Cypess concludes that Castellanos' choice of speaker "disrupts the usual rules which govern who may speak and which topics are permissible" and sees in the narrative voice switch not a weakness but "a signifier of the restrictive social arrangements signified in the text," that is, as significant of the lack of communication that is a major theme in the novel (5–8).

Referring to the organization of her novel, Castellanos herself said:

> La estructura desconcierta a los lectores. Hay una ruptura en el estilo, en la manera de ver y pensar. Eso es, supongo, la falla principal del libro. Lo confieso, no pude estructurar la novela de otra manera. (Carballo, 419, emphasis added)

> The structure disconcerts the readers. There is a rupture in the style, in the manner of seeing and thinking. That is, I suppose, the main flaw in the book. I confess, I couldn't structure the novel any other way.

As we have seen in the discussion of Sobre cultura femenina, at times Castellanos may adopt a defensive posture, but irony is one of her favorite modes. What is disconcerting to the reader is not the rupture, the switch in narrative voice itself. After all, the works of Juan Rulfo, Carlos Fuentes, Manuel Puig, Mario Vargas Llosa, Gabriel García Márquez, and so on, are admired for precisely this kind of shift in narrative voice. Pedro Páramo is much more difficult to follow in terms of play with narrative voice, yet readers usually do not complain about the suitability of having the voices of dead people as vehicles for the narration. The disconcerting element is giving a voice to the socially silenced, to one who is "tangential," in Cypess' words, because of her age and sex if not her class.

The way the shift of narrative voices has been taken by some readers as a weakness or a flaw reveals a point of contradiction in the work's reception. It also points to a way of reading the novel itself as a palimpsest, a way of reading that reads *for* muted voices. (A palimpsest is a document that has been written upon several times, with traces of the older writing often still visible. By scraping or rubbing one can recover the older texts; many classical Greek and Latin literary works have been recovered in this fashion.) The novel illustrates this way of reading by staging a scene of "reading" a text as "double-voiced discourse," as a figurative palimpsest. This emblematic text is the document the girl finds in her father's library. Both a history of the indigenous presence in Chactajal and a history of the Argüello family's abuse, it presents a story told by a man who calls himself "el hermano mayor de la tribu," [the elder brother of our tribe/community] (57). A similar text is later written by the Maya leader Felipe to recount how his community built a school. Both of these documents are hybrids: written texts, they nonetheless use oral discourse's forms of address and narration and are written in Spanish, although speaker and audience speak Tzeltal. They can be seen as figurative "palimpsests."

These two texts, the document in the library and Felipe's account, do not literally show traces of another written discourse, but the voice that can be recovered through their heterogeneity is that of a community whose history has been suppressed, as indicated by the *nana*'s words in the opening lines of the novel:

y entonces, coléricos, nos desposeyeron, nos arrebataron lo que habíamos atesorado: la palabra que es el arca de la memoria. (9)

and then, full of rage, they dispossessed us, they robbed us of what we treasured: the word that is the ark of memory.

The tension between indigenous and Ladino uses of language is announced in the novel's title. Balún Canán is the Maya name for the place known in Spanish as Comitán, the setting of the story and Castellanos' childhood home. The Maya name asserts the continued Maya presence in the region, the persistence of a language and a history that have not been absorbed by those of the conqueror. The epigraphs Castellanos uses to frame each of the three parts of the novel stand for Maya culture and heritage as available through its surviving texts: the Libro de Consejo (the Popol Vuh), the Libro de Chilam Balam, and the Anales de los Xahil. These texts survived partly because they remained hidden from the Spaniards for many years. Each epigraph asserts the cultural survival of a Maya "we," a collective voice and history that filter through the text.

Even these citations from Maya texts recounting the region's history from a Maya perspective can be read and understood by the novel's reader only because they are translated into Spanish. Castellanos takes pains to acknowledge the authority of indigenous knowledge and experience, but they are always necessarily mediated through her voices, and through the language and conventions of nonindigenous culture. She foregrounds this as a problem of language and reading/interpretation in many ways, beginning with the most literal: communication is impossible when people do not speak each other's languages, and few Ladinos and Maya can do so. Ernesto's "teaching" of the boys of Chactajal is a mockery because they cannot understand what he says and he cannot understand them.

Understanding depends, on the most literal level, on the recognition by both speaker and listener of common conventions, starting with grammar. In Chiapas other linguistic conventions structure and signify social inequality.[19] The use of the other's language can itself constitute a kind of action, depending on the context of its use. When César speaks Tzeltal, it is as an instrument of domination: his orders are compared to *fuetazos* [whip blows] (65); he enacts rituals of fealty with his Tzeltal workers by speaking to them in their language while they respond "con monosílabos respetuosos y ríen brevemente cuando es necesario" [with respectful monosyllables and laughing briefly when necessary] (15). Use of Spanish by Indians is tolerated when it is used by women such as the *nana* to carry out their functions as servants to the family; the *nana* uses Spanish to speak to Zoraida and the children. But when Indian men dare to use Spanish to address Ladinos in any other relation besides service, this amounts to an act of revolt. Felipe astounds and frightens the Argüellos because he speaks Spanish and can thus call on them to comply with the new laws. The use of Spanish makes it possible for Felipe to challenge César, but it does not in itself give power. Ernesto knows this when he rages drunkenly to the uncomprehending schoolchildren

¿De qué nos serviría? No va a cambiar nuestra situación. Indio naciste. Indio te quedás. Igual yo. (160)

What good would it be to us? It won't change our situation. You were born Indian. You'll stay Indian. The same goes for me.

Ernesto uses "us" and "we," equating his situation to that of the "Indians" in that they all are excluded from power. But he does not feel any solidarity with them, and in fact, as the illegitimate Mestizo son of the patriarch, he does have alternatives in the new system that they do not have. To speak Spanish is not enough, nor is it enough to have the Argüello name, as Ernesto and Matilde know, because that use and possession are not recognized as legitimate.

In an early episode, the Indian man who uses Spanish to buy a ticket to ride the "rueda de la fortuna" [Ferris wheel] at the fair is called Antichrist by the crowd and punished for his temerity when the ride operator does not fasten his safety bar so that he almost falls to his death. The girl, who witnesses this violence, repeats the lesson she has learned:

Porque hay reglas. El español es privilegio nuestro. Y lo usamos hablando de usted a los superiores; de tú a los iguales; de vos a los indios. (39)

Because there are rules. Spanish is our privilege. And we address our superiors as *Usted,* our equals as *tú,* and Indians as *vos.*

In this elaboration of the three levels of hierarchy—superiors, equals, Indians—"indios" replaces inferiors on the scale, and in Chiapas the "indio" is opposed to "gente de razón" [rational people], and "indio igualado" [uppity Indian, Indian who takes himself as equal] is synonymous with "indio alzado" [rebellious Indian]. Castellanos presents the interaction of two communities whose worlds overlap, that have evolved a set of conventions for interaction, but that do not share and understand each other's conventions and values, even when they speak one another's languages.

Castellanos shows us how an individual is called on to recognize herself as a member of a community by showing how a child learns the rules, watches how others use them, break them, challenge and even refuse them. The girl's position with respect to the two communities is structured by the way she is addressed as audience in speech situations that can be called scenes of instruction. The novel opens with the *nana* in mid-speech, retelling the conquest of her people and establishing immediately the nexus of conflicting discourses in which the girl must try to situate herself. The girl interrupts; she has heard the story before and does not like it. When the *nana* teases her by excluding the girl from her audience—"Acaso se habla con un grano de anís" [Nobody talks to an anise seed] (9)—the girl takes her literally and responds to defend herself from this misidentification by telling her own story, such as she knows it: "Yo no soy un grano de anís" [I'm not an anise seed] (9).

The *nana*'s storytelling is not necessarily intended for the entertainment of the girl, but for her instruction. The first part of the instruction is that the indigenous community claims a "we," speaks from its own memory, its own representation of its history. The girl's community is identified in the process as "they," the despoilers, and in response the girl tries to extract the two of them from the speech situation of storytelling; she does not want to play by those rules anymore. This is because to "read" the *nana*'s story on its own terms would be threatening to the girl's own sense of her identity, not yet fully bound up with the "us" and "them" of Ladino and indigenous conflict, threatening also to the community of two she wants to maintain with her *nana*, the loving substitute for her mother.

When the girl tries to tell Mario what she has learned at school ("Columbus discovered America") we see the opposition between the two sets of lessons she has been given about her own past, the official lesson in school and the one she has just been given by her *nana*. But Mario's indifference to her teaching frustrates her attempts to imitate those speech acts that she has witnessed at school, speech acts whose purpose is to bring the children into a community through the representation of their "history." His refusal to take what she says in the way she means it is a refusal of her right to speak with any authority to him; because he is the male child he has already learned from others a sense of his importance, one that entitles him to refuse to be inducted into communities through (female) speech. And the girl's ethnic privilege in relation to the *nana* means that she does not have to listen to her either. To make the girl obey, the most effective threat the *nana* has, even more effective than divine punishment, is to tell her: "Te vas a volver india" [You'll turn into an Indian] (10). From the beginning, then, we see how the contradictions of the girl's relations to males of her own family and women of the dominated people are manifested in the dynamics of discourse.

Chapter 2 presents the extent and order of the girl's social world, the social hierarchy from the *señores* and ranchers down to the *indios* and the burros, as she sees it on her way to school. Everyone appears according to his or her station and role in this still-colonial world. Animals and objects are part of the child's social world: she is afraid that if the horse bites her it will laugh at her skinny arms, and that the balconies watch everyone pass. Her perception is of a magical order, and this mode of perceiving/interpreting is conveyed through the highly metaphorical language of certain passages in a narrative otherwise rather free of metaphor. The girl "reads" her world according to two codes; the social hierarchy, the place and order of classes, types, and stations, and also a secret magical life, an animating of things and animals that would have no proper place in that other order except as objects. Her magical way of seeing is reinforced by her contact with people who also believe in the magical qualities of reality, her *nana* and other Maya, and Uncle David.

At two moments on this walk through town the girl observes figures marginal to the social order. The Maya women weave and talk, then suddenly burst into sobs. She likens their language to a "ciervo perseguido" [hunted deer]. This deer image will recur when Ernesto kills a deer and angers the Maya for whom such an animal could be a *nahual,* somebody's spirit shadow, and it connects the Tzeltal language with the collective spirit of the people. The other marginalized figure associated with suffering is *la soltera,* the old maid. As is the case for most of the Ladina women in the novel, her identification with her role is not through her work but through her sexual relationship (or lack of it) with a man.

The reader's perspective is doubled, through simultaneous frames of interpretation, into the girl's and our knowledge of social conventions: the girl cannot be completely aware of what the label "old maid" means, and the horse she passes on the street looms large in her child's world. Another kind of doubling occurs in the two orders of explanations she gives for things: the rational and the magical. Finally, we see a doubled social order: these two scenes show two lines of cleavage, two axes of pain that run through this world: the Maya's suffering, presented as communal through the image of their language, and the Ladina woman's suffering presented as isolation and suffocation because of her sexual status.

This presentation of a doubled perception and a doubled interpretation is underscored in the scene of the family's automobile outing. The *nana* refuses to go along because she sees the car as demonic. The girl shares her magical way of seeing the car as alive. At the community gathering the boys fly kites for the men to bet on, while the women watch: "Nosotras miramos, apartadas de los varones, desde nuestro lugar" [We watch, separated from the men, from our place] (22). But while the girl is supposed to be watching her brother win the kite competition, she is instead making a discovery of her own—the wind. Like the car, to her it is an "animal" and she recognizes its voice as one she has always heard but never before recognized, and this place as "la casa de su albedrío" [the house of its will] (23). Her parents scold her because she does not see what she is supposed to see, her brother's victory, but she has been doing what her *nana* taught her to do: she lowers her eyes to show respect. The family has no idea what she has seen, but the *nana,* later on, understands and approves the girl's announcement that she has "met the wind." The girl is being taught codes of behavior, two sets of values through which to act. The Ladino community instructs her in her proper female place and role while her *nana* teaches her to respect the proper relations between natural and supernatural orders. That these two orders will conflict and demand different actions of her is already shown in this minor incident. It is her place as female, her duty, to witness and validate the male competition. What she admires instead, according to another set of values, is not the use of the wind but the wind itself, its freedom and beauty and its place in the various seasons of her life. The second kind of seeing is more real to her, and she receives approval for it from her *nana* whereas she is scolded by her family. For now, these two codes or sets of conventions are parallel for her, and only she and the *nana* are aware that both exist. The *nana*'s values are opposed to Ladino values and identified with the indigenous world; we might have been tempted to identify them as female values but we see how the girl's mother, Zoraida, fiercely upholds the values of the Ladino patriarchy. Social hierarchy cuts across gender lines and prevents solidarity between women.

The *nana* tells the girl that "el viento es uno de los nueve guardianes de tu pueblo" [the wind is one of the nine guardians of your people] (23). As the reader learns in the next chapter, Balún Canán means Nine Guardians. But what does the *nana* mean by "tu pueblo"—the place called Balún Canán? Or "your people?" The pueblo, the people who live in this place, have different names for it, names that come from the double heritage of colonizer and colonized. The Maya recognize the nine guardians, but the Ladinos do not. The *nana*, by teaching the girl to recognize them as well, is trying to make it possible for the girl to *mean* both communities when she will say "mi pueblo."

This dream of unity, of community, is sharply undercut in the very next chapter with the visit of Uncle David, a strange and scruffy old man who used to hunt *quetzales*, the bird sacred to the Maya. His song about the end of the "*baldillito*," the institution of unpaid Indian labor, is a prophecy of change and a warning, one of the many given in Part One. As he explains to the children, the ranchers will now have to pay the Maya for their work, and all will be "igual de pobres" [equally poor] (25).[20]

Uncle David also tries to teach the children something. He used to hunt *quetzales* but in doing so he transgressed, violated a place sacred to the nine guardians. He refers only obliquely to this action, but the reader connects his present state of dissolution with the consequences for this transgression. His story links this kind of offense against Maya cultural beliefs with the political change to come, when the ranchers will have to pay in both senses of the word. He is an example of a Ladino who does acknowledge Maya beliefs; his recognition inverts the hierarchy recognized by most Ladinos. When he first enters, he calls the children "gente menuda," young folks or little people, and refers to the adults as "personas de respeto," people of respect, the elders (24). When he uses these terms later he shifts them from the hierarchy of age to an ethnic hierarchy:

Los mayores lo saben y por eso dan a esta región el nombre de Balún-Canán. La llaman así cuando conversan entre ellos. Pero nosotros, la gente menuda, más vale que nos callemos. (26).

The elders know this and that is why they give this place the name Balún-Canán. That's what they call it when they talk among themselves. But we, the younger folks, would do better to keep silent.

He acknowledges the Maya as elders, whose knowledge gives them the right to name in their language while the Ladinos, like children, should show respect.

When the *nana* said "your pueblo" she was trying to include the girl in her community through their shared recognition of the nine guardians, but Uncle David's "we, the younger folks" reverses the hierarchy the girl recognized in the incident at the Ferris wheel while acknowledging the division rooted in Ladino transgression against the Maya, thus echoing the novel's opening.

The girl is shown as interlocutor in many different discourse situations. When her *nana* tells her tales from Maya oral tradition such as the tale of the Conquest or the tale of the creation of human beings and of the relations of rich and poor (the story of "el hombre de oro," the man of gold), the girl is addressed as part of a collective audience. As part of this audience she is instructed in the values and norms of the Maya community embodied in these tales. At the Ladino school, she is the audience for another kind of moral education, if only a fragmentary and incoherent version. In an important scene the girl is also shown as a reader. When the school is closed and her *nana* is too busy to talk to her, the girl goes to her father's library where she finds a curious document, handwritten with drawings, "figuras como las que Mario dibuja a veces" [figures like the ones Mario draws sometimes] (56).[21] The opening words, "I am the elder brother of my tribe. Its memory" (57) are a reply to the *nana*'s words that opened the novel; this document will attempt to reclaim the word for the indigenous community, their memory and history. The story the elder brother tells is the story of Chactajal and the two peoples who came to live there. The relations of the two are figured through language: "el cashlán . . . amurallado en su idioma como nosotros en el silencio, reinando" [The Spaniard . . . walled up in his language as we were in silence, ruling] (58). The Maya name for the place is Chactajal, but another name is substituted for it, that of the Argüello family. What is narrated now is the history of indigenous labor and Argüello abuse, ending with

> *y es aquí, hermanos míos menores, donde nos volvemos a congregar. En estas palabras volvemos a estar juntos, como en el principio, como en el tronco de la ceiba sus muchas ramas. (60)*

and it is here, my younger brothers and sisters, where we are gathered once more. In these words we are together once again, as in the beginning, as in the trunk of the ceiba tree with its many branches.

The community is called up and reconstituted through the anonymous Maya writer's discursive act.

The girl, reading this document, is reading the history of her family and its relations to the land and to the Maya, but she is not part of the audience directly addressed ("hermanos míos menores"). When her *nana* told a different version of the same story, the girl could resist her identification with the oppressor by interrupting and demanding a different story, asserting her own identity as she saw it. But as a reader, this kind of interaction is not possible. As a reader, the girl must make sense of the conflictual relations between these two stories, between the oral mode of discourse used by the speaker and its written form. To make sense of these stories, the girl would have to realize how they position her and what her place is in the scheme of relations whose history the story presents. But she is prevented from concluding by her mother, who takes the book away from her saying: "Son la herencia de Mario. Del varón" [These are the inheritance of Mario. The male] (60). Her mother instructs her that as a female she is not a proper reader.

The reader, in turn, looking over her shoulder as it were, knows more than the girl, is aware of the hybrid discourse of this text. This is especially clear when we learn, through the mouth of César, that this story was ordered written by César's father to serve as documentation of the family's property rights. The document, because it is written, has authority and legal status; it upholds power when the reader suppresses (or cannot recognize as valid) the oral tradition it represents, the voice that recounts oppression and a silenced history.

When in Part Two Felipe writes a similar document telling how the Maya community of Chactajal built a school, he too calls himself the older brother. Like the first document, his tale uses the forms of oral tradition to relate the same events that are presented in Part Two. But whereas most of the second part of the novel presents Ladino perspectives through stories of fear and defeat, Felipe's tale is one of optimism and affirmation. We can read the first "hermano mayor" document as a palimpsest because it contains two versions of the history of Chactajal. We can also read Felipe's story as palimpsest, not because it superimposes two stories, but because it is the countermemory to the Argüello story in which it is embedded.

These hybrid texts, palimpsests of domination and resistance, are also sites of discursive struggle over meaning between Maya and Ladino constitutions of community through memory. The girl, who is the site of struggle between two sets of lessons in cultural literacy, finds that her reading of one of these texts is mediated by her positioning as female. Gender also inflects the telling of ethnic conflict in the second part of the novel, a conflict that is laid out as both struggle over colonial forms of oppression and male domination.

One level of struggle is the overt conflict between men over land and power, fought with rhetoric, whips, machetes, guns, fire, laws, and the force of "el mando"—command. At first César has no intention of complying with the new laws issuing from the capital, but Felipe organizes his community to build a new school and demands compliance. César has them build the school and gives them his illegitimate nephew Ernesto as a teacher although he does not speak Tzeltal and the children do not speak Spanish. Catalyzed by Ernesto's drunken abuse of the children, the Maya community's resistance turns violent: the Maya set fire to the harvest and sugar mill, kill Ernesto as he rides for help, and force the family to flee back to Comitán.

César enunciates the colonial patriarchal values to which he adheres. He scorns the education he received abroad and rules his ranch, his family, and his Maya workers as he wills. In this attitude, he is not radically individual but simply conforms to the idea of what it is to be a rancher. He inherited the people with the land, and, in his eyes, their labor and the women are as much his property as the land itself. Of his illegitimate children he says, "lo legal es lo único que cuenta" [legality is the only thing that counts] (81). The law he means is the legal fiction that designates one male child of his blood the heir while the others are abandoned in squalor. But other laws coming in from outside—the laws ordering distribution of some lands to the indigenous people from whom it was stolen—challenge this patriarchal law by which name and land are passed on.

The Chactajal community is divided over what to do. Some men who have remained loyal to César continue to bring tribute (euphemistically called "supplies") to Comitán, but they also bring the corpse of one of their number murdered for that loyalty. The *brujos*, the sorcerers, punish loyalty to the family, says the *nana;* she shows the girl a wound she says is the result of the sorcerers' curse and the girl is brought face to face with the pain and suffering brought on by loyalty to her father.

Castellanos does not present the Maya community as homogeneous; she takes care to show that they recognize their oppression, but are divided in their responses to it. One response is the ritual in the chapel at Chactajal, where they pour out their frustration to the saints. Another is presented in the discussion among the men of the community wherein some express resignation, or pragmatism in the face of Felipe's exhortations to resist or demand compliance with the reform laws: "Pero el guardián de la ley está lejos. Y el patrón aquí vigilándonos" [But the guardian of the law is far away. And the boss is here, watching over us] (103). They name his weapons: the whip, the dogs, the gun (103). They are limited by their lack of knowledge of the world outside Chactajal and Comitán—what or who is the president? Where is Mexico? Why should they believe Felipe based on these phantoms when the *patrón* is over there in the house? Felipe Carranza Pech combines old beliefs and new experience to become their leader. He sees himself as the "hermano mayor," the guide such as their ancestors had. He is able to assume this role because he has traveled far and returned with knowledge of the state; he met Cárdenas and shook his hand; he heard the speeches about equality and justice, the new laws—the rhetoric of the Revolution that has just arrived in Chiapas. But what separates him from others who also have traveled or speak Spanish is that he knows how to read and write. These are the tools of the Ladino. He is able to invoke their power when he demands that César open the school: "Lo manda la ley" [The law commands it] (99). In the Ladino system, the written word ratifies power. Ownership of the land is proven by documents, notice of the new laws comes in the newspapers, in letters.

As great a threat to their power as the new minimum wage is the idea of education for the indigenous people. César drags his feet by providing a docile, incompetent teacher and making the Maya build the school themselves, but he does not refuse to comply with the law; he complies with the letter but not the spirit. Felipe is able to win the support of the other men at first because he claims to have implicated them all to César. He does not trust their resolve because for them the law, the force of the written word, is intangible while the weapons of the landowner, the whipping post and the pistol, are not.

César fails to understand the magnitude of events. In addition to the Maya, other enemies he and his class have made turn to the new laws. His Mestizo godson, Gonzalo Trujillo, is now working for the government and is openly hostile to César. The relation of godfather entails great responsibilities in both Ladino and indigenous communities, responsibilities that César has ignored and neglected. As government representative and because he too speaks Tzeltal, Gonzalo is able to tell the people of Chactajal that they no longer must obey César. Ernesto shares Argüello blood, but is not "legal." Both of these "sons" aspire to be included in the patriarchal ruling order by being recognized by the father. Their exclusion makes them turn to an alternative power structure, the state emerging from the Revolution.

The other conflict narrated in this part, along with the political struggles among the Ladino and Maya men, is based on a sexual encounter. Matilde, César's cousin, has arrived at the ranch in a state of hysteria, telling how her sister, Francisca, claims to be a *bruja,* a witch, sleeps in her coffin, and rules her Maya workers through fear and the whip. Both Matilde and Ernesto are of the Argüello family but are defined as marginal to it by the crushing patriarchal sexual ideology in force: Ernesto is male, but a bastard; Matilde is legitimate, but a female and unmarried. The two react to their precarious situations by exaggerating the behavior expected of them in these sexual roles, Ernesto with machismo and Matilde through stereotyped fantasies of seduction. Ironically, each is shown to behave quite differently when circumstances change. Matilde, who has never worked in her life and never expected to, takes over running the household in order to ensure that the family will not tire of her and want her to leave. Ernesto, who wants to be as tough as his uncle, is squeamish, in fact, sickened by the cruder aspects of life on the ranch. Ernesto and Matilde sleep together once, but the possibility of communication and tenderness implied by their encounter is frustrated by their confused loyalties to the sexual ideology that they share and that punishes both of them. Matilde finds out she is pregnant and secretly has an abortion; when the family learns this, she is expelled to wander into the wilderness to die. Once again, solidarity between the victimized is prevented by their confused allegiances to the forces of their own victimization.

The story of Ernesto and Matilde as it illustrates the workings of sexual ideology and the ideology of the family is intertwined with that of the Maya resistance to the rule of the Ladino family. Together they illustrate the dynamics of gender and ethnic relations that maintain the institution of family on which Ladino ideology and power are predicated.

If Part Two narrates conflict between men, in Part Three, when Jaime and César leave the room after their last conversation, they also leave the realm of effective action in the novel. César will be absent, stalled in his petitions for aid from government cronies in Tuxtla; the doctor does not act to save Mario; the priest is too late and too harsh; the neighbor, Jaime Rovelo, gives up because his son in Mexico City has turned against his father's class. The violence that erupted in Part Two, violence between oppressor and oppressed, is now played out in the sphere of the Ladina women.

The Ladina women do not "define" patriarchal ideology; they are not its subjects. They may benefit from it, or give their allegiance to its hegemonic values, but it also relegates them to a place of dependency. Their choices within it are extremely limited. They repeat its maxims and defend its privileges, but pay a high price, and it does not grant them the same alternatives as the men have. Ernesto, Gonzalo, Jaime Rovelo's son, all can turn away from the landowners' colonial system by giving their allegiance to the state as it challenges the local oligarchy's power. They have choices of action in the public realm of laws and even through the use of force. The Ladina women, whose lives are circumscribed into the private domain of the family, find their choices determined largely by their sexual roles. Alternatives exist, but for the women of the ruling class in the world shown in *Balún Canán* (and *Oficio de tinieblas*), these alternatives are usually expulsion, madness, or death.

Zoraida is defined and defines herself almost completely in relation to the men in her family: she is the wife of César and the mother of the heir to the Argüello name. For a woman of her poverty-stricken origins, she has risen as high as she can in her world. It was possible for her to be attached to this class through her honor, her clean sexual reputation before marriage, and her desirability to César. But this identification is precarious; when Matilde, César's cousin, arrives at the ranch, Zoraida says: "Tienes más derecho a estar aquí que yo" [You have more right to be here than I] (117). Part Two, Chapter 2 is her internal monologue: her poverty, her escape through marriage "como gallina comprada" [like a bought hen] (91), the lack of love and understanding between her and her husband. If it were not for the children he would have left her and they are all she has. She defends even more fiercely than César the ideological underpinnings of patriarchy—machismo, fear and contempt for "Indians"—because they symbolize the power and position that she enjoys only through the men. By *speaking* thus she tries to cement a position for herself, but as a woman she is not entitled within the values of that system to dispose of her own life.

Zoraida's access to the world outside her home is extremely limited. Her public functions include social visits: to the poor, to a friend, to clean the church closed by the government. Her position is measured by what she can buy. By contrast, there are two women who do move freely in the outside world. When Doña Pastora, the traveling merchant, appears, she has the right to use the familiar form of address, *tú*, to Zoraida, who then addresses her more formally as *Usted*. Zoraida's respectful mode of address signifies the power this woman has because her mobility gives her knowledge. Doña Pastora's gossip connects the families, her knowledge is her power. Like the *curandera* (a female shaman or healer), another woman of special knowledge, she has a freedom of movement that comes from her lower-class origins and from controlling her own economic situation, something that is impossible for women of Zoraida's class, whose class affiliation is derived from economic dependence on a man. Zoraida's role in the family is to oversee indigenous labor and to reproduce the values of the patriarchal family, as we saw in the episode where she takes the "hermano mayor" story away from the girl. According to these values, the family is the male line, the inheritance.[22]

Two other Ladina women represent alternatives that women like Zoraida fear. Ernesto's mother, Doña Nati, is from the same social level that Zoraida escaped, but she was "dishonored" by another Argüello, then abandoned to raise her child in poverty. She has achieved some marginal respectability because she has sacrificed herself completely to raise Ernesto. If Doña Nati represents what Zoraida's legal marital status saves her from, Zoraida's friend Amalia the spinster represents another frightening alternative. Amalia names the only three socially acceptable possibilities for a respectable Ladina woman when she says "No, no me casé, no tuve hijos, no pude ser monja" [No, I didn't marry, I didn't have children, I couldn't become a nun] (251). As an old maid she is "un estorbo, como una piedra contra la que tropiezan los que caminan" [an obstacle, like a rock tripped over by those who walk] (251). The only way her empty, confined life takes on any meaning is if she upholds the legitimacy of the powers that condemned her to it; she serves by hiding priests from the government and passing on the church's values to the children; when she teaches them the catechism, she announces: "Entonces es necesario que sepan lo más importante: hay infierno" [So you have to know the most important thing: hell exists] (254).

Three women bear the Argüello name: César's cousins, who live on their ranch, Palo María. Matilde and Romelia are also identified by their marital status, that is, the way their sexual relationship with a man (or the absence of it) defines their legal status in society: Matilde is "soltera" and Romelia is "la separada." Francisca, the oldest, is not identified this way when she first appears in the novel; she is simply named. It soon becomes clear that this is because she is the one in charge; not only does she have the name but she also owns the property. This makes it possible for her to assume the role of a man and not be defined exclusively by her sexual role. Like César she adheres passionately to the Ladino ethic of ownership and exploitation, but she shows even greater ruthlessness than César, using the whipping post to punish defiance. But in order to maintain control she also must use Maya cultural beliefs in magic, a weapon available to her because she is a woman. The price is complete isolation and maybe madness. Zoraida and Romelia argue over whether or not she is crazy, faking it or really a witch, but both secretly believe that Francisca has supernatural powers. When the family flees Chactajal, it is apparent that Francisca has power because she already knows what has happened to Matilde and even who has killed Ernesto. But is she in control or a prisoner? She is barricaded in the house, a prisoner of her need to master.

The Ladino landowners in the novel are fighting to preserve title to the land. Jaime Rovelo's son has rejected his father's ideology and is working in Mexico City for land reform; Rovelo disowns him and, when Mario dies, says that he too has lost his son. César wants to turn Mario into a rancher like him, yet the true heir to the family values is Francisca. Because she is a woman, she succeeds through ideological manipulations, to the point where it is unclear whether she is inside or outside: to retain her position as landowner she adopts Maya power practices, loses Matilde, and cannot be seen to offer hospitality to her own family; she is virtually a prisoner on her own ranch. She retains power, but no longer has a proper place in her family or in the Ladino order of things.

Another hybrid version of Chactajal history that combines a Maya perspective with the story of the Argüello family is the story of the *dzulúm* the *nana* tells the girl in the first part of the novel. The two palimpsest documents, the deed found in the library and Felipe's story, are written and told by men who explicitly claim the right to speak as the elder brother of their people, thereby defining an individual speaking voice within their narratives. The *nana*'s tale does not set itself up as a record, as a history. Its style is not as formal as that of the other two either, although it does share the poeticized tone that signifies indigenous oral narrative in the novel. Told by a woman to other women in a traditional women's place, the kitchen, it is about a woman of the Argüello family. The narratives of the two men give voices to an otherwise silenced history, that of the Maya community of Chactajal, and are the alternatives to the Ladino versions of history or events. The *dzulúm* story stands in relation to these histories of Chactajal as that "wild zone" of women's tales about women's lives (Showalter).

The *dzulúm* story prefigures what happens to Matilde later in the novel. The *dzulúm* is a supernatural being, perhaps an animal, never seen, but whose passage is marked by terror and fascination on the part of both animals and people in the surrounding area. "No se mueve por hambre sino por voluntad de mando" [It does not move because of hunger but because of the will to command] (20). Its power is such that "hasta las personas de razón le pagan tributo" [even the rational people (Ladinos) pay it tribute] (20). The tribute the Argüellos pay seems to be the lives of women of the family. Angélica, the woman in the tale, and Matilde are both orphans and, for different reasons, neither of them is eager for marriage. Both suffer great anxiety, are visited by a *curandera*, later wander in the wild and return with torn dresses. Angélica disappears, and the explanation given is that she was carried off by the *dzulúm*, which is portrayed as a kind of demon lover, "bello y poderoso, con su nombre que significa ansia de morir" [beautiful and powerful, with its name signifying a longing for death] (21). In the style of an oral tale, Angélica is young and beautiful, and supernatural explanations account for all the elements in the story; the tale is presented as an account of a real event, but it follows the conventions of an oral folktale.

In contrast, the narration in Part Two of the novel of what happens to Matilde follows the conventions of novelistic realism. Matilde was raised by her sister, Francisca, but because her society defines family through the male and there is no man in her life, she is pitied and made to feel that she owes her place to grudging charity. She flees to Chactajal when it seems that Francisca has gone mad, after she claims to have made a pact with the *dzulúm*. At Chactajal, Matilde is as terrified as Zoraida of not belonging: "estaba en casa ajena y tenía que agradar" [she was in another's house and had to please]

(119). She makes herself into a housekeeper despite the fact that she has never worked before, but even so, the only way she finds to feel at ease is to have César, the man of the house, perform the ritual of "el soplo" (taking a mouthful of alcohol and blowing it on her). She is thus symbolically assured of a place, but it is one that is entirely dependent on his approval.

Matilde fantasizes about a man, a Prince Charming who will solve all her problems, but her naïve sexual daydreams are destroyed by her encounter with Ernesto. Despite a moment of tenderness that comes when they confess to each other the fears that torment them, they retreat into hostility and incomprehension, with disastrous results. Ernesto is tormented by his illegitimacy while Matilde suffers because she is an aging spinster. Neither recognizes the injustice of their suffering; each identifies with a degrading image and with the sexual ideology that degrades the other.

In her own "longing for death" Matilde attempts suicide three times. The first time, she tries to follow the example of Angélica, walking off into the wilderness to die. But her vivid imagination of the crude realities of thirst, heat and exhaustion, wild animals, all frighten and discourage her. She not only uses the story of Angélica as a model, she also asks herself questions about what the story leaves out: "Y Angélica ¿estaría desesperada como ella? ¿O se perdió sin querer?" [And Angélica, was she desperate too? Or did she get lost without meaning to?] (140–141). Matilde is grateful when she finds the little girl crying because she can take the girl home and not die. The second time she tries to kill herself she does not hesitate but tries to drown herself in the river only to be saved by a Maya boy. Finally, when she sees Ernesto's body, she fully expects to die when she confesses hysterically that she has aborted Ernesto's child. Her confession does turn out to be suicidal after all for it is answered by a murderous gesture: César tells her to leave, and he and Zoraida turn away. All of them know what is supposed to happen next in the story, and once again Matilde walks off into the wilderness like Angélica, this time not to return. Francisca performs the interpretive act that turns the event back into story when she says: "Ya lo sé. El *dzulúm* se la llevó" [I already know. The *dzulúm* carried her away] (218).

Francisca seems to take the *dzulúm* literally. But we can see many other ways of reading the *dzulúm* tale. The telling of the *dzulúm* story shows how events in the history of the Argüello family are incorporated into Maya tales, given magical explanations. Literally, a magical being carries off a Ladina. According to another way of reading, the Maya could be said to be telling in symbolic form the price the Ladinos must pay for the power they exercise; the telling of the story then becomes a kind of symbolic revenge (of the kind that is activated in the last part with the curse of the *brujos*). In the interpretive economy of the realist narrative, the reader can see that Matilde was cast out of the family for sexual behavior that transgressed patriarchal sexual norms. Under these norms, the sexuality of servants or lower-class women is at the disposal of males such as César or Ernesto, but the sexuality of women in the family is subject to their rigid control for the protection of the legal fiction of patriarchy that underwrites possession of land and wealth. The *dzulúm* story functions as a warning and a prophecy to Ladina women of what will happen to them if they give in to sexual desire, a desire that is figured in the *dzulúm* and located outside, in the wilderness. It is a sinister version of the wind that the girl recognized as freedom and free will.

Another way we are invited to read the *dzulúm* as symbol is through its identification with "el mando," or command, the characteristic used over and over to identify César and that is identified, through the *nana*'s tales, with Ladino oppression of the Maya. The *dzulúm* is a demonized representation of the landowner, an incarnation of the ideology of possession to which he pays tribute. The *dzulúm* story thus also links symbolically the punishment and regulation of women's sexuality with the "voluntad de mando," the will to command, that oppresses the indigenous community, especially in the figure of Francisca.

The reader has available these interlocking ways of making sense of the *dzulúm* story, but it can also be read as an illustration of how the oral narrative-acts that are represented in the text are a mode of expression for Maya women and how they circulate in and between the Maya and the Ladino worlds. They express, subversively, a curse on the family, one of the many warnings in the novel. First the *nana*'s storytelling act is narrated, then we see how Matilde and other Ladinos use it as a model for action. Matilde will join Angélica in the *dzulúm* story the next time it is told. But we also see how the subversive element in the story, the Maya's condemnation of Ladino exercise of power, is recuperated by the Ladinos as a punishment for transgressive Ladina behavior.

When Francisca pronounces that Matilde has been carried off by the *dzulúm*, César objects to this literal acceptance of a magical explanation for events. This exchange opens the third part of the novel and figures the opposition that will be played out until the end, between the belief systems maintained by Ladino men and those held by the Ladina women that incorporate Maya beliefs. The *dzulúm* story functioned smoothly as a model for action and explanation of events, but the last part of the novel tells the breakdown of this mechanism and the children's attempt to mediate the breakdown and survive.

The action of the third part is precipitated when the *nana* tells Zoraida that the sorcerers of Chactajal have cursed the family and that the boy will die. In response to Zoraida's threatening stance, the *nana* says:

No me toques, señora. No tienes derecho sobre mí. Tú no me trajiste con tu dote.
Yo no pertenezco a los Argüellos. Yo soy de Chactajal. (231)

Don't touch me, señora. You have no rights over me. You didn't bring me
with your dowry. I don't belong to the Argüellos. I am of Chactajal.

Although the *nana* had herself been cursed by the sorcerers for her loyalty to
the family, she finally is forced to take sides and identifies herself with Chactajal
and not the Argüellos. Zoraida responds by beating her and casting her out.

The battle between the Maya and the landowners is now being fought as
a battle of beliefs. Zoraida professes not to believe in the Maya discourse of
magic, but secretly she is afraid and so seeks to marshal defenses in the other
belief systems around her. When she turns to the official representative of
the church, the priest (in hiding from government persecution), he commands her to submit to God's will. Her response is to try to turn the force of
the curse away from her son: "Si Dios quiere cebarse en mis hijos . . . ¡Pero
no el varón!" [If God wants to feed on my children . . . But not the male!]
(250). In effect, she has pronounced a curse against her daughter.

The stakes are the cornerstone of the landowning oligarchy's ideology, the
male heir. The son bears the name that *is* the family. Jaime Rovelo's son is
cast out when he gives his allegiance to the revolutionary discourse of social
justice; more powerful than flesh and blood is the discourse that defines family through ownership of the land. The stakes for the girl are her life; to choose
allegiance to the male, to the family, means her death.

The children have heard many stories. But they take them all on the same
level: the games they play with Maya servants, Amalia's terrifying stories of
the torments of hell suffered by lying children under the eye of an all-seeing
God, the murder of the Maya man who looks like the bloody statue of Christ's
death, the new servant Vicenta's stories of the devil, and their mother's outburst. All of these speech acts seem to have the same reality for them, the
same force. The children themselves try desperately to mediate conflicting symbolic realms. Trying to make sense of these powerful stories, the children
construct a narrative in which they are all combined. The reader must decide
what causes the boy's death—appendicitis, the curse of the sorcerers, or the
fact that the girl hid the key to the chapel, thus preventing Mario from taking
first Communion so that he might be protected while the curse fell on her.

In an interview Castellanos said that she wanted there to be various possible interpretations of Mario's death:

Quería que ésta tuviera varias interpretaciones: en primer lugar, que pudiera ser
la consecuencia de una serie de elementos mágicos que operaban, no sólo sobre

los enemigos de los indígenas que eran los patrones, los fuertes, sino también
sobre sus hijos, los inermes. En segundo lugar, esa muerte debería también ser
explicada como un hecho natural debido a la incompetencia del médico y al
estado general de atraso en que estaba ese pueblo. Y por último, quería que esa
muerte pudiera ser atribuida a la protagonista y narradora como una culpa. Es
decir, ella podía haber escogido entre la muerte de su hermano y la suya—y
decidió sacrificar a su hermano. (Dybvig, 32–33)

I wanted it [his death] to have various interpretations: in the first place,
it could have been the result of a series of magical elements that were
operating, not only on the enemies of the indigenous people—the bosses,
the strong—but also on their children, the defenseless. In the second place,
that death also had to be explainable as a natural occurrence due to the
doctor's incompetence and the general backward state of the town. And
finally, I wanted that death to be attributable to the protagonist-narrator as
her fault. That is to say, she could have chosen between the death of her
brother and her own—and she decided to sacrifice her brother.

The process of interpretation that is the crux of the action in the third part of
the novel involves the reader in a reading that is more complex and ambiguous than the clear doubling of perspective so easily negotiated in the first
and second parts. The ending is constructed in such a way that the reader
cannot clearly reject the girl's interpretation of events as simply erroneous or
childish. By this time, the novel has created a context in which enough force
is associated with indigenous values and shared beliefs and the beliefs and
values of the dominant Ladino systems have been so discredited as blind and
oppressive that a new process of evaluation and interpretation must be used,
one that reads the text as palimpsest.

The end of the novel constitutes a deliberate rejection of a powerful trope
of self-fashioning in Latin American literature: by reclaiming a relation to the
land and to indigenous status through an indigenous mother figure, the Mestizo son (Caliban) can assert himself as legitimate national protagonist: "This
island's mine by Sycorax my mother." *Balún Canán* deliberately stages the
relationship of the *nana* and the girl as an alternative fostering of the Europeanized child by the indigenous mother, along the lines of this Utopian dream
of union. But this ideal resolution is clearly rejected by the novel's end. The
nana had tried to form the girl as protector of her people and as the custodian or guardian of her brother, the heir. When they pray together before the
trip to Chactajal, the *nana* tells how she has tried to teach the girl humility,
gratitude, and love instead of contempt, vengeance, and pride. She wants the
girl to recognize that she owes what she has to those who serve her. The girl

represents an ideal possibility of culture that would make possible a different kind of relation between them. The dream of another relation between Ladino and indigenous people passes through a dream of another relation between daughter and mother. But if there is space to dream this fusion, it is still within the order that values the male and leaves her powerless. And at the very end of the novel, when the girl thinks she sees the *nana* on the street, she says: "además, todos los indios tienen la misma cara" [besides, all Indians look the same] (291).

After her brother's death, the girl feels tremendous guilt and writes his name everywhere; this burden of guilt inscribes her into the patriarchal order and separates her from her *nana*. As the boy was lying wounded, like one of Uncle David's quetzal birds, the girl refused to go with Uncle David to Balún Canán to see the nine guardians, see their faces and learn their names, as she had with the wind. She refuses the symbolic discourse of the Maya because, she says, she has to return the key to the chapel, the key that in her mind represents her defense against her mother's curse. But she has no intention of doing so. The story of danger and survival in which she is enmeshed prevents her from choosing the dream in which she is reunited with her *nana*, in the kite field with the wind where Mario's kite flies the highest and the circus arrives after all. This dream is a kind of wish fulfillment, a mythical order without history. In the end, two forces prevent a resolution of cultural conflict through the ideal of cultural syncretism: the continuing material conflicts over land and justice, and the mother's curse, motivated by oppressive patriarchal constructions of womanhood. The girl starts to write out of a sense of guilt, but what she writes over and over is her brother's name. His story subsumes her own story.

We have seen the figure of palimpsests inside the novel, the double histories of Maya and Ladino, of Chactajal and the Argüellos. But in a sense, the novel itself is a palimpsest. The "I" of the girl narrates the memory and the history of women and her experience of Maya culture even as her story encloses and transmits the "official" story of conflict between the law of the patriarch and the new laws of reform, represented by Mario's name. The struggle between Maya and Ladino occupies the heart of Part Two but it is entwined with Matilde's story. A reading that recognizes only the *indigenista* story without recognizing the women's stories reproduces the kind of reading César gave of the palimpsestic text in his library.

Castellanos shows clearly how the oligarchy's subordination of indigenous people is connected to the ambiguous situation of its women, linked by the "will to command." She also shows that reforms promoted by the national government help bring down the colonial oligarchy's power but that the gap between the law and justice for the Maya continues to be enormous. The anticlerical law closes the girl's school with the result that girls have no classes and the teacher gives private lessons to the children of the new elite, the rich bourgeoisie. Power and schooling have passed to another group of Ladinos while the people of Chactajal get nothing.

In her essay on women and education, Castellanos recognized that education, although vital, was not in itself enough to change the situation of women as long as the situation of the family did not change and there was no consciousness that the family as an institution was oppressive.[23] Felipe is conscious of the oppression of his people, but not of that of his own wife at his hands. The girl has the possibility of this consciousness, but it has not yet grown in her. Castellanos' critique does not go so far as to represent a new consciousness, but, rather, gestures toward its necessity through the claims made on the reader as reader. It is in the reader that this consciousness must grow if we are to decipher the other voices of the palimpsest. In this novel we see the beginning of Castellanos' own consciousness of how she could write *Sobre cultura femenina* and "forget" what she grew up with; through the story of the girl's education we are presented with competing versions of history and competing claims on allegiances. Castellanos' next two works of fiction broaden her scope to take on the constitution of community through the relation of story and action.

꧁ 5 ꧂

Ciudad Real: *The Pitfalls of* Indigenista *Consciousness*

It so happens that the unpreparedness of the educated classes, the lack of practical links between them and the mass of the people, their laziness, and, let it be said, their cowardice at the decisive moment of the struggle will give rise to tragic mishaps.

Frantz Fanon, *The Wretched of the Earth* (148)

While still in Chiapas working for the Instituto Nacional Indigenista in the mid-fifties, Castellanos began to write the short stories of *Ciudad Real* (1960) and her second novel, *Oficio de tinieblas* (1962). Both texts extend her critique of racism and economic exploitation in Chiapas and, by extension, in Mexican society. Her narratives present social dramas of struggle and survival played out by Indians and non-Indians at the critical historical conjuncture of state efforts at national integration. In *Ciudad Real,* and in a somewhat different form in *Oficio de tinieblas,* Castellanos centers her analysis around the problems of an intellectual's actions, consciousness, and allegiance.

The range of Castellanos' writing and cultural work during this period is astonishing. Between the publication of *Balún Canán* in 1957 and of *Oficio de tinieblas* in 1962, she published *Al pie de la letra* [Literally] (1959), *Salomé* and *Judith* (1959), *Ciudad Real* (1960), and *Lívida luz* [Livid Light] (1960). She wrote literary criticism and essays for major newspapers such as *Excélsior,* edited school texts for the INI (1958–1961), taught classes at the National Autonomous University of Mexico, and was director of UNAM's Department of Information and the Press. During this time she also married, had two miscarriages, and finally gave birth to a son in 1961, challenging her own contentions in *Sobre cultura femenina* that women must choose between motherhood and writing. The reader of her fiction can trace an intellectual trajectory shaped both by her early poetry's idealism and by the shocks and disillusionments of her experiences.

Like *Balún Canán, Ciudad Real* and *Oficio de tinieblas* focus on the heterogeneity and conflict out of which Mexicans were attempting to "forge a nation," in Manuel Gamio's phrase. Until this point in her prose, Castellanos' critical consciousness has been manifested as a double voicedness in her writing. In *Sobre cultura femenina,* a feminist critique emerged from the doubled voice, but also wavered between consciousness and unconsciousness, between ironic and conformist talk. In discussing *Balún Canán,* I have used the palimpsest as a metaphor for the way the text figures the dynamic of two discourses in tension; it is a figure for our reading of competing versions of history and counterhistory in terms of cultural conflict. The palimpsest figure also raises the problem of positioning for the female intellectual and her consciousness: we are able to read the novel's lessons in cultural literacy, and we see how the girl tries to negotiate them for herself, but at the end she is still guiltily writing Mario's name yet nameless herself. This novel contrasts men's and women's spheres of action, but the locus that organizes our response to the lessons is a girl, not a woman. Castellanos' next two works of fiction raise the particular problem of the woman intellectual's relation to the conflicts they narrate. Jean Franco's reading of *Oficio de tinieblas* in *Plotting Women* lays out very clearly the ways that the plots and conventions of the novel as Mexican national allegory provided little space for imagining effective forms of action for women or other marginalized people (129–146). If Miranda speaks, writes, or emits a critique of Prospero's order with its Manichean opposition of Civilization and Barbarism, where do her new allegiances lie? Where does she stand? What forms of action does her consciousness entail?

These questions are most directly presented in *Ciudad Real,* a collection of ten stories, written from Castellanos' experiences while she worked at the Centro Coordinador in Chiapas for the Instituto Nacional Indigenista. The book is dedicated to the INI: "Al Instituto Nacional Indigenista, que trabaja para que cambien las condiciones de vida de mi pueblo" [To the National Indigenist Institute, which works to change the living conditions of my people]. As was the case in *Balún Canán,* the word *pueblo* is here a site of contested meaning: it means both a place and a people, but who is included in "mi pueblo"—the indigenous *pueblo,* the Ladino *pueblo,* the Mexican *pueblo?* Castellanos' dedication announces her allegiance to the project of national reform and inclusion just as her work in Chiapas with the traveling Teatro Petul puppet troupe translated those intentions into direct attempts to interpellate the Tzeltal and Tzotzil Maya as Mexican citizens.

Yet *Ciudad Real* and *Oficio de tinieblas* are unflinching in their analysis of the failures of the integrationist projects of the INI. In these two books Castellanos sets out to work out for herself some answers to the questions of justice and responsibility facing people like her, the Mexican "educated classes," as Frantz Fanon would call them: writers of ethnography or fiction, anthropologists, government officials, teachers, journalists, witnesses, and agitators. This is the group that Fanon scrutinizes with such severity in "The Pitfalls of

National Consciousness," where he warns that political independence and nationalism do not necessarily eliminate colonial relations. Using the example of Latin American nations, he points out how the national bourgeoisie becomes the intermediary for new articulations of neocolonialism, often promoting ethnic conflict as a means to consolidate its power. In place of this division, Fanon lays out a vision in which the educated classes and the masses would work together consciously. Fanon's analysis is extremely useful for understanding the promises and the pitfalls of Mexican *indigenismo*, and Castellanos' compassionate but devastating portrait of it.

Ciudad Real affirms the commitment to social change that motivates *indigenista* discourse even as it offers a critique of some of its assumptions. The violent and oppressive nature of relations between Ladino and Indian are delineated through the social geography of city and the highlands, along with the failure of those who come from outside the region to comprehend adequately the situation they propose to change.

The predicament of these outsiders (from both the United States and Mexico) is the subject of Cynthia Hewitt de Alcántara's *Anthropological Perspectives on Rural Mexico*, a project she says is a history of anthropologists' attempts to answer two questions: "Who are these people still organizing their livelihood in ways outside our immediate experience?" and "What is their relation to us?" (1). She places the efforts of Mexican *indigenistas* as policymakers in the context of debates over the production and use of knowledge among *indigenistas* as anthropologists. She reminds us that in the late fifties and early sixties "the area around San Cristóbal became . . . a laboratory for the study of interethnic relations by functionalist anthropologists" (63). Many Mexican *indigenista* anthropologists were questioning the ahistorical approach of the structural-functionalist school of anthropology, although they were indebted to its work of "cultural mapping." In the period from 1955 to 1962, while Castellanos was writing *Balún Canán, Ciudad Real,* and *Oficio de tinieblas,* she was very much a part of the ferment of anthropological debate and activity in her home state, both as a participant and as an observer. Among her colleagues were Gonzalo Aguirre Beltrán, physician, ethnographer, and director of the INI since 1948, who formulated the idea of the regional *indigenista* approach to social change, and Alfonso Caso, who initiated the pilot project of the Centro Coordinador in the Chiapas highlands in the early fifties. Along with other *indigenista* anthropologists they insisted that contemporary conditions in Chiapas could be understood only as patterns of domination rooted in the colonial period. In this view, indigenous culture should not be seen as a holdover from the times before the Conquest, as some anthropologists had assumed. Maya villages in Chiapas were not static, self-contained communities, nor could a city like San Cristóbal de las

Casas be understood as a modern urban center. What these anthropologists called for instead was an understanding of the regional dynamics of social relations in which the Ladino "ciudad señorial" [the seigneurial/feudal city] dominated the indigenous rural population both through force and through the continued manipulation of ethnic identity (50–52). Hewitt summarizes the working idea about the ethnic category "Indian" that emerged at this stage of Mexican *indigenismo* as follows:

> an inhabitant of a relatively remote rural region, exploited for the benefit of urban counterparts in an anachronistic (colonial) way, not as part of a modern class structure, but rather as a member of a culturally defined caste to whom all possibility for advancement within the larger society had for centuries been absolutely denied. (52)

This paradigm of interethnic relations in Chiapas owes much to the work of Julio de la Fuente, a radical organizer who went on to become an anthropologist in the forties and who collaborated with Bronislaw Malinowski on a groundbreaking study of Oaxaca. One of de la Fuente's important contributions was to assert that the Indian/non-Indian dichotomy, so central to the organization of Mexican provincial society, was a social construction manipulated by the dominant group to justify the inferior status of the dominated, a division used as an instrument of domination in a "dual society." De la Fuente and Malinowski's work was presented at the 1940 Pátzcuaro conference, which resulted in the founding of the INI, and was the first anthropological study in Mexico to examine indigenous culture in terms of economic relations. Hewitt points out that de la Fuente made the crucial observation that Mestizos (who are called Ladinos in Chiapas) in the provinces "based their own livelihood on control of Indians rather than upon participation in a modern capitalist society" (48). This premise emerges particularly clearly in the stories of *Ciudad Real*.

In an article called "Relaciones étnicas en los altos de Chiapas" de la Fuente presents an ethnographer's summary of ethnic relations in the highlands of Chiapas that details the ways that status is recognized by the inhabitants of the region. The physical characteristics of racial typing are not what determine or mark social location; rather, social distinctions are easily made on the basis of clothing, housing, forms of transport, language use, food, and customs. Castellanos, who had lived these relations from the inside, as she documents so compellingly and painfully in *Balún Canán*, had returned as an adult to join the efforts of *indigenista* intellectuals such as Aguirre Beltrán, Caso, and de la Fuente to transform this society. We can read *Ciudad Real* and *Oficio de tinieblas* as works of fiction that are also part of the ethnographic writing that includes *indigenista* scholarly publications and Ricardo Pozas' fictionalized ethnography *Juan Pérez Jolote* (1952).

Ciudad Real maps the social geography of Chiapas, encompassing the Maya villages in the orbit of the Ladino city. The title is the colonial name for the city now known as San Cristóbal de las Casas and emphasizes the idea that resistance to change is the heart of an anachronistic, self-contained backwater province undergoing the transformations brought about by the Revolution, modernization, and the imposition of national priorities no longer represented by the local elite.

The collection is structured as a kind of display of "interethnic relations" and their history in the region, with the progression of stories unified around a critical gaze that moves deliberately from periphery to center of power: from Maya village to Ladino city, and from a historical overview with a Maya perspective through stories that might have occurred before the Revolution, and ending with those that narrate very specifically the contemporary regional crisis. This spatial and historical movement is a map of forms of violence as well, articulated as a series of portraits or situations of characters ascending the social hierarchy, always marking the relative power and privilege of men and women, from the poorest and most exploited indigenous village dwellers to the most privileged of Ladinos. The stories are important as acts of naming and representing these situations, of registering experiences so completely erased from the political agenda of *indigenismo* that the programs for social change elaborated by the *indigenista* intelligentsia are inadequate to respond to the suffering they hope to diminish.

The careful structure of the collection as a whole is reinforced by figurative parallels and connections that weave the stories together. The first three stories anchor contemporary Maya dependence and exploitation in the history of conquest and colonization. The four middle stories of the collection lay out the fixed rules of the social game in Chiapas and the violence that reinforces them. The broader national and international context of change appears in the last three stories, which have outsiders from Mexico City and from the United States as protagonists. These educated outsiders have all come to this place, like Castellanos and other *indigenistas,* to change the conditions described so powerfully in the first seven stories. Yet they are largely unaware of the dimensions of their own positions in the ascending hierarchy of privilege, and their efforts will not necessarily bring the kinds of change that will challenge injustice. Castellanos vividly conveys the wrenching shock to values and self-image experienced by those intellectuals or professionals who are brought face to face with the forms of everyday violence in Chiapas and reveals the inadequacy of their understanding and action in these circumstances. The book as a whole forces the reader to grapple with a question it does not itself answer directly: What form must their (our) solidarity take in order for it to be effective?

Three themes that recur in the collection as a whole are introduced in the opening story, "La muerte del tigre" [The Death of the Tiger]. First, the society of Ciudad Real is presented as a decadent colonial holdover whose panoply of rigid roles is enforced by those who cling to fixity in the face of change, and whose social and economic privilege derive from "the fix" of a racist hierarchy. Second, Castellanos foregrounds the use of "language as an instrument of domination"; in a key essay by that title, she uses the metaphor of the word as coin whose exchange has been corrupted. Finally, this story presents Maya beliefs and cultural practices as ways of understanding and negotiating collective experiences of violent and oppressive social structures. Castellanos seems to indicate that any meaningful form of change will have to spring from indigenous forms of knowledge and action.

Castellanos uses the same decentering strategy that she analyzed in *Sobre cultura femenina* and performed in *Balún Canán:* Maya history rather than the hegemonic perspective becomes the point of departure for the reader's guided tour through the world of Ciudad Real. This deliberate alignment with the perspective of the oppressed expresses an initial gesture of solidarity. "La muerte del tigre" begins with an account of the Bolom clan's lineage from their earliest migrations and era of prosperity through their conquest and struggles for survival, both placing their experience at the center of the region's history and evoking the continuity of their present economic situation with the colonial period. The reduction of a proud and audacious people to a scattered group of fearful and exhausted village dwellers has only been accelerated by their further dispossession after Independence. As they are forced onto the poorest land, the men must leave to work in the lowlands, entering the system of debt peonage that is a modern form of slavery.

The privileging of the Maya perspective is also suggested by the way the third-person omniscient narrative voice employs rhetorical echoes of Mesoamerican indigenous storytelling language, such as repetitions of pairs of terms like "del hombre blanco, del ladino" [of the white man, the Ladino] (16), and the anaphora of "allí . . . allí . . ." [There . . . there . . .] (15). Maya beliefs are foregrounded as source of metaphor and explanation: a key element in the story is the Maya belief in the relations of humans to animal protector spirits (like the deer *nahual* in *Balún Canán*). The Bolom *waigel,* or animal protector spirit, is the jaguar; this idea is extended in the metaphor of the *caxlán* (the Maya word for "castellano," meaning non-Indian, Spaniard) as iron with the gaze of a vulture. The use of indigenous cultural referents and rhetorical devices to signal or signify an indigenous perspective to non-Indian readers is, as was the case in *Balún Canán,* still an outsider's construction; it should not be taken for an indigenous perspective. Yet clearly its intention, and to some extent its effect, is to deliberately "de-authorize" the hegemonic values and perspective that deny Maya history, Maya values, Maya voices.

The panorama of increasing suffering culminates in the specific events recounted in the story when the men of the village, forced by starvation, go to the city to sell themselves to the *enganchador,* the recruiter who will broker their labor to the plantation owners in the lowlands. As the story moves to the city of Ciudad Real itself, the narrative voice begins to incorporate Ladino views of the world (18–19) in a portrait of a community in decline. Brief sketches of social types such as the townswomen or the lawman illustrate, in a line or an image or two, the hierarchy of ethnic and gender relations. The two labor recruiters, Don Juvencio and his associate, are more fully drawn types whose elaborate forms of address, legalistic rationalizations of exploitation, and manipulation of language suggest the ideas in Castellanos' essay "Language as an Instrument of Domination" (translated in Ahern, *Rosario Castellanos Reader,* 250–253). Don Juvencio speaks the language of the Bolom men and knows enough about their beliefs to manipulate them into giving him their true name Bolom (jaguar) because they think he has magical power over them. Most of them will die on the coast from hunger and illness; this death is the death of their name, their history—the death of the tiger.

In this story, as in most of the others in this collection, Castellanos raises the issue of specific cultural practices involving magic and belief. One way of reading this is to say that the Indians are easily manipulated because of superstition, as if their beliefs were the cause of their suffering. This view, a variation on the Prospero thesis, holds that if they would only abandon these "primitive" beliefs, they would be less easily exploited and might be assimilated into modern society. Yet at the same time, this story (and others) also offers an alternative way of interpreting the villagers' actions, an interpretation that takes into account material causes and the history of oppression just narrated. Whether or not the Bolom men believe that Don Juvencio has *magical* power over them, they have in fact almost no choice when they sign on with him; they are being forced to work on the plantations not by magic or superstition but by uses of power that have created starvation.

These two ways of reading and understanding indigenous people's actions, in terms of a cultural symbolic repertoire, or in terms of a more materialist view, are juxtaposed in the second story, "La tregua" [The Truce], as well. The title suggests that the war of Conquest and resistance has not ended, but has only taken on new and degraded forms. The story has three parts: an encounter between a young Maya woman fetching water in a mountain village and a Ladino stranger who does not speak her language; the explanation, through flashback, of the context of this encounter; the death of the outsider at the hands of the villagers. Rominka Pérez Taquihequet is described as "mujer como las otras de su tribu, piedra sin edad" [a woman like the others of her tribe, an ageless stone], an image that suggests at once the survival and continuity of her people over time and the inability of the narrator-outsider to see her as a fully individual human being.

The stranger is lost, hungry, and sick, but the man and the woman cannot communicate with each other. Rominka is sure he is an evil spirit, a *pukuj*. Since those who see the *pukuj* go mad, she is terrified and falls to her knees, weeping and confessing her life to him. Not only do her words go uncomprehended, the man's response is to push her, and she flees. This scene suggests a "first encounter" between indigenous and European people, and also between anthropologist and "native." Two people in their human condition of need and want face each other across a gulf of radical cultural incomprehension, and the response of the stranger is an act of violence. But this particular encounter is not a first encounter; it has a context, a long history of almost ritual violence. The narrator attributes the woman's reaction to a magical belief, but the next part of the story, in the form of a kind of flashback, gives another explanation of her fear and expectation of violence. News of her encounter is brought to the men of the village, who are off making illegal alcohol, thus defying the Ladino monopoly on a substance necessary to the Maya's ritual life. In the past, this defiance had been met by savage repression on the part of the *secretario municipal,* who burned people alive in their huts as punishment for their defiance of Ladino control. The Maya village's economic dependence is enforced by extreme violence. An encounter with a stranger in this context and his violent gesture are clearly read by the villagers as the kind of threat whose consequences are only too well known.

In the last scene of the story the villagers discharge their hate and fury on the stranger, killing him in a ritual scapegoating that is said by the narrator to conjure away, for a while, their bad luck. His death is a response to the violence of the authorities, another act in the centuries-old war between the two peoples. Indigenous beliefs are said here to provide a paradigm for their actions—destroying an evil spirit—even as their action is also clearly presented as a political response to tremendous social pressures. Yet the language of the narrator, through its presentation of the killing in terms of a frenzy of orgiastic violence, brings us back to the tension between the historical and materialist analysis present in these stories, and to the readily available trope of native ignorance as the factor frustrating the most well intentioned efforts of civilizing outsiders to understand and narrate such events, latent in the assimilationist premises of Castellanos' own participation in *indigenista* action. The fact that those premises are themselves the object of her critique in these stories does not mean that Castellanos has succeeded in moving completely away from them. This ambivalence also raises problems for us as readers: while the stories suggest that we understand "magical" interpretations as a cultural form of political understanding, it is still too easy for us to read according to the "plots and plausibilities" (Nancy K. Miller's phrase) of our own colonialist reading traditions—the inevitability of native victimization due to their superstition—and to ignore the political consciousness that is also presented here.

The third story, "Aceite guapo," is about another kind of scapegoating. The title, literally, "Handsome Oil," might perhaps also be translated as "Fire Water" because it is the name of the cheap alcohol sold by Ladinos to Indians, one of the commodities of colonization. In the previous story, the stranger, the outsider, is made responsible for the suffering of the village and killed. Ironically, although this individual is weak and helpless, he stands for the perpetrators of social violence (his response is to shove Rominka) on a much larger scale (the burned village, the economic exploitation that results in their hunger). In "Aceite guapo" the setting is once again the Maya village, but now the story shows how external oppression is reproduced internally. Daniel Castellanos Lampoy is growing old, his wife is dead, and his children neglect him; he is a marginalized person in his own community. Looking for security in his old age, he fixes on the idea of holding the office of *martoma,* or caretaker of a saint, one of the communal positions that combines religious and civil duties in Maya villages. Because he has not participated in the *cargo* system before, he does not have the necessary status to claim that office, so he decides to get the post through bribery. The Ladino landowner he has worked for in the past will not give him a loan, so he in effect sells his two sons to the labor recruiter and then uses the advance money to bribe the village council into giving him the post.

Daniel talks to the statue of the saint as if she were real; he tells her gossip, confesses his suffering to her, much as Rominka confessed hers to the *pukuj.* As in the previous story, this verbal outpouring is not real communication. The sacristan, Xaw Ramírez Paciencia (a character who reappears in *Oficio de tinieblas*), tells him that since the saints are Ladinos he should not expect them to understand Tzotzil. Xaw is mocking Daniel, but he is also commenting indirectly on the Catholic Church's perpetuation of ethnic hierarchy and its unresponsiveness to indigenous suffering. When Daniel follows Xaw's mocking advice to buy *aceite guapo,* the other community officials disapprove of his drunkenness because it is a solitary act and not part of their ritual communal practices. They throw him out of the church, and it is implied at the end of the story that he dies as a result. Daniel's participation in his community's institutions is corrupt and ineffective, and his attempts to survive are all mediated through Ladino institutions—the debts owed to the boss, the sale of his sons' labor to the recruiter, the unresponsive church, the accustomed humiliations of buying the *aceite guapo*—but these institutions can only provide for his further degradation.

"La suerte de Teodoro Méndez Acúbal" [The Luck/Fortune of Teodoro Méndez Acúbal] along with the two stories that follow, "Modesta Gómez" and "El advenimiento del águila" [The Coming of the Eagle] move from the outlying indigenous villages to Ciudad Real itself. They provide variations on the theme of fortune and the ways that people's lot in life is fixed in Ciudad Real. "La suerte de Teodoro Méndez Acúbal" also has an indigenous protagonist and is also about the distortion of ordinary human commerce—verbal and monetary—by a crushing history. As in the first two stories, all commerce between Maya and Ladinos is shown to be rigged. The coin that Teodoro finds will be the "proof" at the end of the story that he is a thief.

The reader's perspective is situated once again in alignment with Maya village life in relation to the Ladino city they call Jobel. Teodoro finds a coin because he's walking with his eyes cast down in the proper attitude of humility. His point of view is contrasted with the gaze of the city-dwelling Ladinos, who walk with their heads held high as a sign of their pride. In the second half of the story, the focus of the narration shifts to a Ladino shopkeeper, Don Agustín. We are given access to the inner turmoil of both characters as they act out in miniature the dynamics of indigenous self-assertion and Ladino rage and ever-present fear of an Indian revolt. Teodoro's luck is to have access to the cash economy without having to take the usual path of selling himself or his sons into debt peonage. Yet he does not tell his family; he feels shame. The find leaves Teodoro "disturbed," even "another man," because now "Era tan rico como . . . como un caxlán" [He was as rich as . . . as a *caxlán* (54). Teodoro's modest aspiration, to be able to buy something in a store, and the seemingly insignificant changes of behavior that result, will be perceived by Ladino eyes as of a piece with the threat of a caste war.

Don Agustín notices Teodoro because he walks on the sidewalk (to look in the store windows), customarily reserved for Ladinos. Don Agustín's jewelry store bears the name of his conquistador ancestor, and he prides himself on not selling to Indians. Yet his own sense of personal failure (he's a "niño viejo," an old bachelor; 59) is entwined with his class fear. "La seguridad de su vida era tan frágil que habría bastado la cara de un chamula vista a través de un cristal, para hacerla añicos" [The security of his life was so fragile that it would take only the face of a Chamula seen through the glass to shatter it] (57). To maintain the sense of self predicated on a superior class status always under siege, he resorts to inciting communal violence that is a mirror image of the last scene of "La tregua." The face-to-face encounter between Teodoro and Agustín, like that between Rominka and the stranger, measures the abyss between Indian and non-Indian. Teodoro does not speak Spanish and is so afraid to enter the store that he must get drunk even to venture inside. Don Agustín experiences Teodoro's gaze as a judgment, and his response to Teodoro's presence produces a judgment: "¡raza de ladrones!" [race of thieves!] (59). It is not necessary for any words to be exchanged. An Indian steps out of his place, has a desire, has access to the means of satisfying it, in short, lays claim to the kind of personhood supposedly conferred by a liberal economy of monetary exchange between two subjects, and he thereby threatens the foundations of ruling-class identity. The power of the Ladino's word is such that he can name a man a thief because he has dared to leave his place.

"Modesta Gómez" tells the story of a woman who becomes an *atajadora,* one of a group of poor Ladina women who survive by routinely attacking and robbing the Maya women who come to the city to sell their goods in the market, throwing them a few coins in the pretense that their acts are not theft. This peculiar way of earning a living is a product of the elaborate, rigid gender and racial codes of Ciudad Real. A similar scene, but told from a Maya point of view, has an important place at the beginning of *Oficio de tinieblas.* Here, it is the life of Modesta Gómez that is told as the narrative moves back and forth between the account of Modesta's first day as an *atajadora* and flashbacks that show how she has come to this state.

Monique Sarfati-Arnaud reads this as a story of the stages of Modesta's degradation told in three acts illustrating the venues of commercial exploitation in this society. The first "market" is the Ladino household to which Modesta herself is traded as a child. She becomes a *cargadora* (a poor child who is part baby-sitter, part plaything for the children of the wealthy) for Jorge, the family heir. Her first lessons are about her place, in the kitchen, but she dreams of ways to better her lot. Of the two options of escape she imagines, marriage or the brothel, the second seems just as attractive as the first. She is raped by Jorge, the boy she grew up with and cared for as a child, then thrown out by the family after being publicly humiliated. Left a widow with three children by a drunken husband who beat her, she finds work in a butcher shop, where she reproduces the brutal ethnic and class hierarchy in her treatment of the customers. The last forum for exchange in the story is the scene of her first day as an *atajadora.* She chases and beats the girl she has chosen to rob, drawing blood: "Se miró las uñas ensangrentadas. No sabía porqué, pero estaba contenta" [She looked at her bloody fingernails. She didn't know why, but she was happy] (74). Even the most abused and degraded Ladina woman can maintain a sense of social self through institutionalized violence against Indians.

116

The socially enforced forms of degradation and violence in everyday life in Ciudad Real confer power in radically unequal exchanges across the divides of race, class, and gender. Every form of commerce is rigged, every form of communication is vitiated in this world. Teodoro and Modesta's luck or fate is fixed before they can act to realize their modest dreams. But there is a niche for Modesta; Ciudad Real condones institutionalized robbery as long its victims are Indian, while Teodoro's mere presence in a store condemns him as a thief. And the next story shows how fortune is rigged differently when the poor Ladino is a man. In "El advenimiento del águila" a Ladino man who is almost as poor as Modesta is able to improve his lot because, as a man, he has access to more lucrative forms of institutionalized robbery.

The eagle of the title is the protagonist Héctor, described as macho and compared physically to a bird of prey, although the description sneeringly makes him sound more like a vulture than an eagle. Héctor, a widow's son from a family with an old title, fails as an altar boy, fails as a student, and finally is fit for nothing but hanging around, although this behavior is considered absolutely appropriate for a man with his family name: "Para ser un señor, a Héctor no le faltaba más que la fortuna" [To be a gentleman, all that Hector lacked was a fortune] (78). This is the story of how he acquires that fortune by following in the path of his conquistador ancestors, but with a modern twist. The first socially acceptable means to a fortune for a man of his class is living off of women. He runs through his mother's money first, then that of the woman he marries precisely for that purpose: "A oscuras todas las hembras son iguales" [In the dark, all females are the same] (79). Penniless again, Héctor has no option but to leave Ciudad Real, when a friend gets him an appointment as *secretario municipal* in the village of Tenejapa. He sees this job as a loss of status, complaining, "los indios no son personas. No entienden el cristiano" [Indians aren't people. They don't understand the Christian language] (82). The common substitution of "Christian" to mean Spanish underscores the colonial nature of categories still at work. As when the Spaniards first arrived, Héctor's sense of superiority is based on the possession of a language and a religion as signs of civilization, and on the exclusion of "Indians" from personhood. When the official government seal wears out, Héctor refuses to do his job. The village elders, the narrator says, see the seal's eagle as flying with news to the capital and petition him for a new one. He tells them a new seal will cost a thousand pesos because it is "el nahual del Gobierno" [the protector spirit of the government] (84). When Héctor realizes that the elders are seriously considering paying this outrageous bribe he raises the price of the ten-peso seal to five thousand pesos. With the money from this extortion, he opens a store; now he monopolizes both government and commerce in the village. The last sentences of the story—"y los rasgos del águila eran casi irreconocibles. Ya parecía un borrón" [And the features of the eagle were almost unrecognizable. Already they seemed almost a blur] (87)—let us know that he will pull the scam again. The irony of the oligarchy's pride in a glorious past as compared to its actual behavior is also a moral judgment on this new form of institutionalized theft; the colonial extortion of Héctor's ancestors is reproduced in a modern form under the new national government. Like the word *eagle*, the word *señor* is stripped of nobility, and the power structure remains intact behind its screen of empty values.

Like Modesta, Héctor runs through the gamut of gender-prescribed options for survival and escape from poverty. But if the situation is rigged against Modesta from the start because she is female and poor, Héctor fails in spite of all his advantages and a far greater range of possibilities at school, in the church, at a trade. It is precisely the values of his class that make him a useless parasite. Incapable of following one of the professional paths acceptable to his social status, and once he has used up the available women, he turns to the third traditional option available to the gentleman, institutional exploitation of the Indians. Despite the fact that he can barely read or write, he succeeds in gaining power and wealth because he can manipulate the power of institutions. Do the village elders really literally believe that the eagle seal is a magical thing that flies off to the capital? Or does it matter? They recognize that, in effect, Héctor's control of their access to legal documents is a means of power over them, and they are forced to pay the bribes he demands.

Héctor is without a fortune at first but finds a new way to exploit in the name of a distant and empty nation. The seventh story, "Cuarta vigilia" [The Fourth Vigil], is also a story of the former ruling class in ruins yet clinging to its power after the Revolution. The *niña* Nides is an old woman (the title *niña*, or girl, is the familiar form of address used by those of her class and by servants) who maintains a grotesque fiction of class status by murdering an Indian man. In this act she follows family precedent. Her grandmother was a rich and stingy woman who promised the unmarried Nides the security of a share in her fortune. When the Revolution came, the grandmother buried their chests of money with the body of a Chamula man murdered to keep the location secret. Carranza's men find the chests and steal her money anyway, and they lose the land. But Nides is able to live on the charity of those of her class, because she tells herself and everyone else that she still has that money. This crazy, frightened old woman still has nightmares about Carranza's soldiers during the Revolution. She orders a passing Indian man to come in and dig a hole in her garden, kills him, and buries him with a chest that contains her "fortune." In fact, the chest contains worthless junk, "*bilimbiques*" substituted for her money by soldiers during the Revolution when they robbed her. After she has repeated her grandmother's deed, for a moment she's afraid of "un espanto," a ghost, but then is reassured at the thought that this is only an Indian, not "una gente de razón" [a rational person] (99). Where Héctor is able to make a real fortune out in the world with real money and goods, albeit by institutionalized theft, Nides enacts the pathology of her class. The means of exchange do not even have to be real; their value is not conferred by their use, but rather by the kind of paranoid and murderous fictional economy that we saw in "La suerte de Teodoro Méndez Acúbal." The chest is empty but the death of the Chamula man is still real.

The last three stories break open these closed circuits of oppression by introducing protagonists who are outsiders, people who are in Chiapas in order try to change the conditions of life that involve such suffering and violence. Each continues to illustrate a progression up the scale of privilege, and the last story sets the situation of Chiapas in an international context. In "La rueda del hambriento" the protagonist Alicia is a woman from Mexico City, whose naïve and romantic illusions about her new job as a nurse in a clinic for the Misión de Ayuda a los Indios [The Mission to Aid the Indians] are destroyed by the sexism, hardship, injustice, and hostility toward change that she meets. In "El don rechazado" [The Rejected Gift] the male narrator is a person of greater professional prestige and assurance, an anthropologist with fewer illusions about the possibilities of change, who works for a government agency with more resources, but who still feels guilt and confusion about the failure of his efforts to help a woman and her children. And the last, and longest, story, "Arthur Smith salva su alma" [Arthur Smith Saves His Soul], presents a person at the pinnacle of social hierarchy—a white, male, Protestant linguist-missionary from the United States, as naïve and romantic in his way as Alicia—who meets his own disillusionment. He comes to Chiapas to work for the Organization, an agency (modeled on the Summer Institute of Linguistics) with huge resources supposedly dedicated to helping the poor but which, as Arthur learns, is in fact a front for U.S. covert activities.[1]

The first seven stories present a world that cries out for change and the struggles of individuals to survive within it; these last three are complex examinations of the motives and consciousness of agents of change from the educated classes. Questions about what kinds of changes are necessary, what means might make a difference, and about the nature of good intentions torment these characters. By the time we read these stories, we have been provided with an education about the social conditions of Chiapas that allows us to measure the actions of both the individuals and the agencies that are trying to intervene. While Castellanos shows compassion for their dilemmas, which one supposes to be closely based on her own experiences, she is ruthless in her judgment of their/her blindness and insufficiencies.

The title "La rueda del hambriento" again plays on the idea of the wheel of fortune, of a cycle, but also on the idea of the wheel as instrument of torture, and the suffering of hunger. The story's epigraph is taken from the poem by César Vallejo whose title Castellanos has given her story: "pero dadme / en español / algo, en fin, de beber, de comer, de vivir, de reposarse, / y después me iré" [but give me / in Spanish / something, finally, to drink, to eat, to live with, to rest on / and then I will leave]. For the first time in this collection of stories, those who suffer address directly those who might come to their aid (the intellectual, the *indigenista,* the reader). All of the forms of suffering, of blind resistance and survival that have been described previously, are now re-presented as a call that demands a response from the interlocutor.

The story recounts Alicia Mendoza's time in Chiapas as a journey toward insight, or a process of disillusionment in three parts: she arrives by bus in Ciudad Real; she then goes by horse to the village of Oxchuc; and finally she leaves Oxchuc altogether. The first stage is the bus trip itself, the transition from her old life into the new, between her memories and her dreams for the future. When she first arrives she thinks she's going to find jungles and "bungalows," images from the movies, but the reality is much different. In an ironic deflation of the fairy-tale attitude she takes toward life ("No hay mal que por bien no venga," the equivalent of "Every cloud has a silver lining"; 107), her *madrina* [godmother] has died of cancer, and now Alicia must seek her fortune. This is her first job, her chance at independence since the other two options open to women of her class are closed: "para monja no tenía vocación, y para casada faltaba el novio" [I didn't have the vocation to be a nun, or the husband to be a wife] (106). Yet she's still captive of the romantic feminine dream; when she learns that the doctor at the remote clinic where she'll be working is unmarried, she plunges into fantasies of adventure and romance. Although in education and opportunity she is far more privileged than Modesta Gómez, Alicia's dreams of a future reflect the limited ideals available to a woman whose unmarried status is a source of vulnerability and fear.[2]

Her arrival in Ciudad Real itself is structured by three encounters that signal the obstacles she (and the mission, or at least its stated objectives) must overcome, but whose significance she does not understand. First, her friendly neighbor on the bus ride cuts her off when she learns Alicia will be working for the mission. Next, the small boy who guides her to the hotel strikes an Indian man in passing, for no apparent reason. When she asks why, he says "pues . . . porque sí" [well, just because] (109). This dirty beggar boy states his absolute certainty of social superiority to an adult Indian man in the baldest of terms: "¿Acaso yo soy indio para que me igualen?" [Do they think they're as good as me? I'm no Indian!] (109). Random violence is his ethnic right. Finally, when the hotel owner learns from Alicia that she has come to work in the mission, she raises her prices, saying:

Ustedes . . . vienen a Ciudad Real a encarecer la vida. Cuando los indios se
alzan ya no quieren trabajar de balde en las fincas, ya no quieren vender su
mercancía al precio de antes. Los que padecemos somos nosotros. Es justo que
ustedes paguen también por el perjuicio que nos causan. (110)

You . . . come to Ciudad Real to raise the cost of living. When the Indians
get uppity they don't want to work for free on the *fincas* anymore, they don't
want to sell their goods at the old prices. We're the ones who suffer. It's only
fair that you should pay too for the wrong/damage you do to us.

This version of what is fair, of who is the victim, explains local Ladino hostility to any change. Alicia's education has begun, but she is not yet able to
understand the lessons she is receiving. The director of the mission tells her
she is being initiated into the local reality, explaining what we as readers have
seen illustrated in the preceding stories: "Aquí no se trata de razones sino de
intereses" [Here it's not a question of reasons but of interests] (111). Alicia
has to choose sides, and she chooses the mission over the interests of the
local Ladinos. But this choice of commitment is no guarantee of understanding; while waiting for the rains to end so she can go to her post in Oxchuc,
she finds that she cannot make contact with either the Indians or the Ladino
employees at the center.

The next stage of her journey is the excruciating ride by horseback through
the rain into the isolated village of Oxchuc, scandalizing the local Ladinos as
"una mujer que monta como hombre" [a woman who rides like a man] (114).
It seems to her that "estaban condenados a errar siempre en las tinieblas"
[they were condemned to wander forever in darkness], a phrase that resonates with *Oficio de tinieblas*. When she arrives, her colleague, Doctor Salazar,
no romantic hero, rages about the lack of supplies and the farcical nature of
their mission sponsored by people interested in the image of doing good
rather than the reality. Yet although Alicia wants to work in the clinic, she
ends up serving as the maid-housekeeper for Salazar, a role she does not challenge, clinging to the shreds of her romantic illusions with the phrase "él es
hombre" [he's a man] (121). Salazar's absolutely humiliating treatment of
Alicia is of a piece with his moral failure as a doctor.

Even when the clinic receives some medicine at last, they are unable to
administer it; they are called Protestants and Communists by the Ladinos,
and the Indians are suspicious and afraid. Their good intentions are not
enough, and their responses to frustration veer wildly, as Salazar admits,
between idealism and cynicism. It all seems useless. Salazar looks back on
his days as a working-class student who had always felt excluded and oppressed by the rich, but who now finds himself in a village where he is one of

the Ladinos, a person of the most privilege, wealth, and power. His response, also, has positioned him with the local Ladinos; his anger and resentment are now directed at the poor: "En cambio, los pobres piden, piden sin descanso. Quieren pan, dinero, atención, sacrificios. Se nos ponen enfrente con su miseria y nos convierten en culpables a nosotros" [On the other hand, the poor ask, ask endlessly. They want bread, money, attention, sacrifices. They put themselves in front of us with their poverty and transform us into the guilty ones] (122). What is being requested, echoing Vallejo's poem, is dignity as well as food, but Salazar flees from that imperative when he withholds food and medicine from a child, allowing it to die. When a sick woman gives birth to an infant whom she cannot nurse, Alicia is horrified that Salazar refuses to give the family milk unless they pay; he even refuses to let Alicia pay for it herself, and the child dies. Nor can Alicia comprehend the apparent passivity of the villagers or their magical explanation of their misfortune: "el pukuj está comiendo a mi hijo" [the *pukuj* is eating my child] (132).

We have learned in "La tregua" to read the association of *pukuj* with *caxlán* in the context of the social violence that Salazar perpetuates and rationalizes as he raves about how the root of the problem is educating the ignorant, ungrateful Indians. In all of these stories Castellanos has also been consistent in undermining a reading that would see traditional beliefs as the cause of suffering; rather, the appeal to magical explanations is shown always as a response to extreme and desperate conditions. As in the story of the *enganchador* or of the eagle seal, indigenous people who find themselves in extreme situations of need, injustice, and oppression both call on their traditional beliefs to explain their plight and take the actions that they might have taken in the absence of those beliefs: the men sign on to work because they have no choice; the village pays the bribe because it has no choice; the family accepts the death of their child because it has no choice. The possible choice of active resistance on their part is represented as almost unthinkable given the violence with which hierarchy is enforced and with which transgression is punished, as when the *secretario municipal* burns people alive in their huts for daring to make their own alcohol. Castellanos will explore the history of active resistance by indigenous people in *Oficio de tinieblas*. Meanwhile, in these last three stories she focuses on educated people like herself who came with good intentions to break the cycle. The kind of reading that takes a magical explanation at face value and sees it as the cause of poverty and suffering is presented as a form of ignorance that leads to moral failure.

Alicia packs and leaves. The last phrase, "afuera llovía" [outside, it was raining], signifies dreary failure, but Alicia leaves a different person. She may have started out ignorant and naïve, but by the end she has learned some of the lessons of this place and made a choice; she has no answers or solutions either to the oppression she witnesses or the discrimination she experiences as a woman, but she will not allow herself to be corrupted, as has Salazar.

The story is a devastating portrait of the missionary version of *indigenismo* as charity, failing not only from lack of resources and local hostility amid the enormity of the "cycle of hunger," but also from cultural ignorance of its agents. This story, along with the one that follows, explores the situation Castellanos describes in her essay "Incidente en Yalentay" in which a young girl approaches the Teatro Petul troupe and announces that she wants to attend the INI school. The attempts of the troupe and the director to help her are frustrated by the girl's father, who refuses to give permission unless they give him money (see Chapter 4). As the teller of the story in the essay, Castellanos lays out her own experience of frustration, guilt, and incomprehension.

"El don rechazado" returns to this theme but with a protagonist who is now a professional, has better resources, more support, and clearer and, to some extent, more objective perceptions of the social realities of Chiapas than does Alicia Mendoza. It is also the only story in the collection narrated in the first person, by José Antonio Romero, an anthropologist working in Ciudad Real. In his self-presentation in the first paragraph he immediately digresses into issues of the professionalization of this work. No longer are the social workers of *indigenismo* recruited from the urban poor, like Alicia and Salazar, who might cling to their posts as their only chance in life for a decent salary. The mission is now in the hands of the government; it has technicians and programs, Romero has a Jeep for his travels to the villages instead of a horse. And now those in need approach the outsider for help rather than hiding in suspicion. A young girl throws herself on the Jeep as Romero is inching his way through the foot traffic of the city. This encounter, an inversion of Roinka and the stranger, is framed by the narrator's self-conscious disclaimers distinguishing his values from the reigning social values of Ciudad Real. First, he says: "aquella vez solté tantas groserías como cualquier ladino de Ciudad Real [that time I let out as many obscenities as any Ladino from Ciudad Real] (138); second, he shows his awareness of the local assumption that any Ladino man who goes off with an Indian girl must be going for sex when he claims: "mis gustos son un poco más exigentes" [my tastes are a little more demanding] (138). With the last phrase he sets himself above the Ladinos but without necessarily differentiating himself from their contempt for Indians. In fact, the girl is seeking help for her mother, Manuela, dying from a postchildbirth infection; Alicia and Salazar failed to save a woman in a similar situation. But Romero can take this woman to a clinic, buy her medicine with his own money, save her life and that of her child, and conceive the idea of putting the daughter in the mission school or acting as godfather to the newborn as ways of helping the family out of their desperate situation.

Yet his efforts to help are met with incomprehension and resistance. First of all, nobody at the Center speaks Tzeltal except the linguist and the maids (104), but more to the point, the mother, Manuela, does not believe that his motives could be different from those of other Ladinos. She proposes a price for her daughter as his mistress and prefers to have her abusive boss, Doña Prájeda, be godmother of her child. Romero recognizes that he has failed, but tells his readers not to blame Manuela for thinking that all *caxlanes* are the same; he understands that because his actions do not fit any known local pattern of interaction, they must seem to be a trap. He knows all this, and yet he feels guilt and remorse. "Debe de haber algo. Algo que yo no les supe dar" [There must have been something. Something I didn't know how to give them] (146). He is like the mission director, who tries to explain the situation to Alicia: he seems to know better than she does and has not degraded himself like Salazar, yet he has no answers either, and is tormented by his own insufficiency and limits. His confession to the reader challenges us to imagine what needs to be done differently.

Ciudad Real as a whole traces the survival and adaptation of colonial structures in Chiapas after the Revolution and places the region in the broader national context by illustrating the ambiguities and failures of *indigenista* efforts to intervene. The last story, "Arthur Smith salva su alma," ties the history of struggles between indigenous peoples and the heirs of European cultures to an international context of U.S. influence and covert activity. At nearly forty pages, it is the longest, almost one-fourth of the book. It is also the third story about outsiders who come to Chiapas as part of organized projects for social change, but who end up themselves challenged and changed by their experiences. Arthur Smith is a North American technician, a "foreign expert" who represents the pinnacle of privilege and material power in this provincial society. The organization that sponsors his missionary work has vast material resources in comparison with the Mexican agencies; its sponsorship of translations of the Bible into indigenous languages is modeled on the Summer Institute of Linguistics, which has been banned from some regions in Latin America because it is seen as a front for U.S. government intelligence-gathering and intervention.

Like the earliest Spanish missionaries, Arthur learns Tzeltal in order to translate the Bible and to evangelize. The story is as much a commentary on early Spanish evangelization as means of colonization as it is an early documentation of the Protestant missionary activity whose success in Maya communities in Mexico and Guatemala in recent years Castellanos did not live to witness.[3]

Arthur's story begins very much like "La rueda del hambriento," with the young outsider's journey to Chiapas, where he is going to make a new life. It is punctuated by flashbacks that reveal the dreams and illusions rising out of his past. Like Alicia Mendoza, Arthur has been left alone when his mother dies of cancer. Unlike her, however, he is able to travel in comfort, by helicopter, and he seems absolutely certain of the superiority of his origins and of the rightness of his mission, of having a place in the world—or at least he is able to clothe any uncertainties he may have in the language of absolutes. His approach is defined through a series of plays on the idea of seeing and certainty. His helicopter provides him with a God-like view, from which the world appears to him "bien hecho" [well made], at least in its external aspect. "La confusión viene de una mirada desatenta y rápida. En cuanto el ojo se detiene puede discernir, puede calificar con exactidud" [Confusion comes from an inattentive and rapid gaze. Whenever the eye stops, it can discern and qualify exactly] (151). Arthur Smith, like the other U.S. citizens he will meet in the settlement, is absolutely certain about what he sees and knows, about his power to read and interpret parables for the ignorant *pueblo*. The material wealth of the organization he has joined—the airstrip, the helicopter, the technicians—is in painful contrast to the pitiful resources of the mission or even the INI center. He is given complete material support for the completion of his project of bringing the message to the "indios salvajes" [wild Indians] (159), but like Alicia and the anthropologist Romero, Arthur will be confronted with situations that challenge his way of understanding the world and call on him to take sides and to act in opposition to the interests of his class.

The epigraph, "un hombre, / en el mejor sentido de la palabra, bueno" [a man, / in the best sense of the word, good], poses the question of moral and ethical action as the heart of the story. From the beginning of the story, the narrative voice presents Arthur's self-satisfaction with a sly irony that ridicules his values and pretensions. In Chiapas, his privilege reinforces his belief that he is on the right side, that he comes from a superior culture (156–157). If the narrative voice in "La rueda del hambriento" also reveals the gap between Alicia's naïve illusions and the realities that awaited her, it is with a considerable amount of compassion; as a poor, single woman, Alicia is not one of the most privileged, and if her illusions are pathetic it is because they are so impoverished. Arthur, on the other hand, sets out to save his soul by doing good deeds (154) in part because, like Héctor, he has not done very well in the more traditional avenues to success available to a man in his society: bureaucracy, business, war. Like Salazar, he found it difficult to imitate the example of Christ at home because of his repugnance for poverty: "ser bueno era entonces fácil. Tan fácil como caminar sobre las aguas" [Then, it was easy to be good. As easy as walking on water] (154). The people he has come to evangelize are to be the instruments of his salvation. But "nadie se salva sólo" [nobody is saved alone/nobody saves himself] (a phrase of Sartre's that Castellanos cites often in her essays) becomes one of the refrains of Arthur's story.

What Arthur finds at the U.S. settlement is the same kind of hierarchy, privilege, and injustice characteristic of local Chiapas society, but with a more modern veneer. The attitudes of his compatriots differ little from those of the Ladinos; the wives complain about Indian maids, most of the Indians work without pay, as they do on the Ladino *fincas,* and when Smith proposes distributing pamphlets of his translations, he discovers that most of the Indians are illiterate and nobody is interested in starting a school.

Arthur's assistant in translation, and later in preaching, is the Maya Mariano Sántiz Nich. Arthur does not realize just how different his versions of texts are from Mariano's:

> A Mariano se le bañaba la cara y el cuello de sudor y cuando Arthur le pedía la correspondencia precisa de un vocablo, respondía con el primero que se le venía a la mente. Y si el texto decía Espíritu Santo, Mariano interpretaba Sol y principio viril que fecunda y azada que remueve la tierra y dedos que modelan el barro. Y si decía demonio, no pensaba en el mal, no temía ni rechazaba, sino que se inclinaba con sumisión, porque después de todo el demonio era sólo la espalda de la otra potencia y había que rendirle actos propiciatorios y concertar alianzas convenientes. Lo que echaba de menos, porque no se mencionaba jamás, era la gran vagina paridora que opera en las tinieblas y que no descansa nunca. (165)

Mariano's face and collar became bathed in sweat when Arthur asked him for the precise equivalent of a word, and he replied with the first thing that came to mind. If the text said the Holy Spirit, Mariano interpreted that as the Sun and the virile principle that fecundates, the hoe that turns the earth, the fingers that mold the clay. And if it said "devil," he didn't think of evil, he didn't fear or reject it; rather, he bowed in submission because, after all, the devil was only the other face of the other power and one had to render him propitiatory acts and make appropriate alliances. What he missed, because it was never mentioned, was the great vagina that gives birth, at work in the shadows, never resting.

In their first collaborative sermon, Arthur chooses the theme of "libre iniciativo" [free enterprise], that most important of American values, and uses his own case as an example. Ironically, he preaches to the mixed congregation of U.S. citizens and Maya using the Sartrean formula "nadie se salva sólo. Si quieres salvarte tú, tienes que salvar a otro" [nobody can save himself by himself. If you want to be saved, you must save another] (166). His compatriots do not like his message, and the version the Maya receive through

Mariano's translation is that the gringos cannot go to heaven without an Indian as a kind of passport (This cross-cultural misunderstanding of the value
of reciprocity is illustrated in *Balún Canán* as well; see Chapter 4). Mariano
translates this as a commentary on the relation of the Maya to the North
Americans: "Así pues, eran verdaderamente hermanos de los otros y, aunque
menores, indispensables" [So that means that they really were brothers of the
others, and, although younger ones, still indispensable] (167). The irony is
that Mariano's phrasing does indeed sum up a paternalistic relation that
maintains Maya inferiority but that might seem a preferable alternative to
their position in relation to the Ladinos, but Arthur is completely unaware of
how his message about free enterprise has been subverted, or even of how
his own words reflect ironically on his conduct.

The presence of the Organization and its Protestant evangelizing in Oxchuc provoke a hostile reaction from three sectors: the neighboring indigenous communities are threatened by the departure from traditional practices, including the ritual use of alcohol, which is tolerated by the Catholic
Church but prohibited by the Protestants; the Catholic clergy, including the
bishop, wage a campaign from the pulpit against their rivals using rhetoric
that ranges from the anti-Lutheran to the invocation of Maya demons; the
indigenista center at the mission is threatened because its activities are oriented around nationalist efforts to cultivate Mexican citizenship and *castella-
nización*, teaching the Maya Spanish. When violence breaks out between indigenous communities, Pastor Williams is eventually able to broker a truce
with the Ladino authorities based on a cynical recognition of separate spheres
of influence for the two churches and what Arthur recognizes as "una solidaridad de raza" [racial solidarity] (188–189), the agreement that bloodletting
between Indians is a kind of safety valve that keeps them from rising up
against the whites. The INI/mission as representative of Mexican government
to the indigenous population is not even a player in this political arena.

The incident that provokes a crisis in Arthur's certainties and leads him to
a horrified recognition of moral bankruptcy is the same as the one that confronted Alicia: a child's death that could have easily been prevented with the
medicines and knowledge available to the outsiders, the rationalization of
neglect by those with the means to act but who choose not to, and the resignation of victims whose fatalism is understandable or appropriate when nothing can be done but seems appalling to those who know that the death was
not inevitable. When Mariano's child dies, Arthur cannot understand his
apparent resignation. As we have already seen, Arthur is absolutely unaware
of how much he does not understand of Mariano's culture or values, even
when he thinks they are saying the same thing in different languages. But
when Arthur starts to ask questions of those whose language and values he

does share—the pastor, the doctor—he learns that the Organization has the money and supplies to help these people but is not interested, that the technicians who are there are not working to improve the people's conditions at all. Rather, their obsession seems to be danger from savage Indians, Catholics, and Communists, even to the point that when violence erupts one technician proposes bombing Oxchuc. Arthur protests that this would be a moral crime, but the proposal is ultimately rejected only because of qualms about "international law" and not because it is outrageous or repugnant.

When Mariano himself is murdered, Arthur has a moment of lucidity and solidarity that takes the form of a recognition of Mariano's humanity (187), that Mariano was the one who could have "saved" him. During this self-questioning, Arthur tries to escape his guilt with sleeping pills: "al que le temo no es a mi enemigo, sino a mi guardián" [the one I fear is not my enemy but my guardian] (182). Arthur's former certainties dissolve into doubts, and he is finally expelled from his community as a traitor when he speaks out because, as he says, "Yo estaba pidiendo lo que debe ser el pan nuestro de cada día: la justicia" [I was asking for what should have been our daily bread: justice] (191). These words are the response to Salazar's demand that the cause of all this suffering be addressed (although he blames the victims), and the answer as well to José Antonio Romero's anguished recognition that "there must be something." "Justicia" is the word that obsesses Pedro in *Oficio de tinieblas* and that replaces the idea of charity. Arthur's new consciousness is presented as a crisis of representation, a failure of the old story:

> *Porque ahora todo lo que antes era nítido y ostentaba un rótulo indicador, se había vuelto confuso, incomprensible. Entre el lado bueno y el lado malo no había fronteras definidas y el villano y el héroe ya no eran dos adversarios que se enfrentaban sino un solo rostro con dos máscaras. La victoria ya no era recompensa para el mejor, sino botín del astuto, del fuerte. (190)*

Because now everything that before was clear and displayed a name tag had become confused, incomprehensible. Between the good side and the bad side there were no defined boundaries and the villain and the hero were no longer two adversaries confronting each other but a single face with two masks. Victory was not the reward for the best, but, rather, the booty of the cleverest, the strongest.

The story ends when Arthur leaves behind his Bible, his religion, his country, and his certainties, but feels free, relieved, and sets off to find the hut of a Maya. The last sentence in the story is "Será cuestión de ponerse de acuerdo.

Por lo menos estos hombres y yo hablamos el mismo idioma" [It will mean coming to an agreement. At least these men and I speak the same language] (194).

How should we read this ending, as straight or ironic? The images of *tinieblas* [shadows] and *amanecer* [dawn], of speaking the same language suggest hope and change. Shall we read the story as the straight portrayal of the good man? Arthur does go from being the arrogant, naïve gringo to becoming a more enlightened human being; he does move from seeing only the surface of things through a Manichean lens of racism and intolerance to a recognition of the hypocrisy of those values and a clearer moral vision. A. K. Stoll characterizes this trajectory as that of the "mythic hero" in the terms of Joseph Campbell. But this hopeful reading is contradicted by the paragraph cited above that sums up Arthur's new consciousness in terms of an explicit rejection of the paradigm of heroes; the image of "a single face with two masks" has more in common with the system of values we saw sketched by Mariano's translations, where good and evil, male and female, are not represented as antagonists in combat but as complementary forces.

That Arthur wants to think for himself and is willing to make great sacrifices in the name of new values is celebrated in this story, but his confident assertion that he and the Indians speak the same language has already been revealed as another illusion, a false certainty. Like Alicia and Romero, Arthur struggles for recognition of what it means to do the right thing. But that struggle, so vital for the integrity of the individual, will not itself do anything for the poor and the oppressed. At the end of this story Arthur is not an enlightened savior figure; his new consciousness is a step in saving his own soul perhaps, and that's all. Yet without that first step he will never be able to go the rest of the way toward an encounter with the Maya in their world, on their terms.

The dedication that begins *Ciudad Real* places it under the sign of change, Castellanos' aspiration to change the conditions of life for her people. As *indigenista* fiction, these stories denounce injustice and oppression and describe what needs to be changed. The kinds of change, or, rather, the forms of action undertaken by these characters, are understood and even treated with compassion, but are shown to be almost entirely inadequate, whether they take the form of individual reactions or communal violence, survival through accommodation or the perpetuation of the oppression of others, even well-intentioned but ignorant institutional efforts. Castellanos does not in the end prescribe another form of action for the characters most like her. Instead, she limits herself to an exploration of her dilemma. Perhaps this is because in this collection she hovers on the threshold of the recognition that she will explore more directly in *Oficio de tinieblas,* the recognition that change, when it comes, will have to be collective and will probably involve some measure of upheaval and violence. It will not be the result of the work of intellectuals; it will not take the form of accommodation. In the meantime, the most important change those intellectuals can make—maybe the only one—is in themselves.

6

Versions of History in Oficio de tinieblas

Mas he aquí que toco una llaga: es mi memoria.
Duele, luego es verdad. Sangra con sangre.
Y si la llamo mía traiciono a todos.

Rosario Castellanos, "Memorial de Tlatelolco," *Poesía no eres tú* (288)

But here I touch an open wound: my memory.
It hurts, therefore it is true. It bleeds real blood.
Yet if I call it mine I betray them all.

Trans. Maureen Ahern, *A Rosario Castellanos Reader.*

Oficio de tinieblas was awarded the Sor Juana Inés de la Cruz Prize when it appeared in 1962. Although translated into French, Russian, Hebrew, Polish, and German, this powerful work has yet to be published in English.[1] Ethnic and discursive heterogeneity again provide the dynamic of the text, but the second novel presents a wider scope of national issues than *Balún Canán*. Ethnic conflict is represented through both Maya and Ladino versions of history. These versions are not only alternative accounts of events, they are also ways of knowing the world, and hence of acting on it.

In *Oficio de tinieblas,* Castellanos also returns to the problems of women's creativity and agency in new ways through the figures of the Maya woman Catalina, leader of a cultural revitalization movement, and Idolina, the adolescent daughter of landowners, who uses writing as a means for individual, isolated resistance. These two figures represent a step beyond the negation with which *Balún Canán* ends, but there is still no resolution imagined in this novel for the violence of ethnic conflict or women's oppression.

The title of the novel lends itself to several readings. Among the meanings of the Spanish word *oficio,* from the Latin *officium,* are a craft or trade, a function or office, an official written communication, and church services. The word *tinieblas* means shadows, obscurity, or darkness and is used figuratively to mean ignorance, uncertainty, or idolatry. As a proper name, Oficio de Tinieblas means the Office of Tenebrae, the Catholic Mass celebrated on Good Friday. This refers to the climax of the novel when a Maya boy, Domingo, is crucified on Good Friday as the Maya of San Juan Chamula resignify the Christian cultural paradigm of the Passion of Christ as part of their struggle against Ladino oppression. Read more figuratively, the phrase could be taken to suggest a Dark Service in the sense of idolatry; from the perspective of the Ladino townspeople, the Maya's appropriation of Catholic rituals to their own purposes would thus be seen as superstition or ignorance. Another meaning of *oficio*, that of ministry or function, has to do with the religious and social role the Maya woman Catalina Díaz Puiljá assumes; as *ilol*, a person versed in magical powers, she occupies a "dark calling," but one traditional in her society. And given the resonance of the word *oficio* with Castellanos' essay writing (see Chapter 8), where she frequently uses the term to insist on the writer's task and vocation as social critic, the phrase *oficio de tinieblas* calls to mind the difficult calling of the writer in the struggle over signification in the arena of national culture. These different meanings converge in the novel's subject, the Maya community's attempt to constitute authority and power over its own fate by appropriating the rituals of the church but reading them through its own alternative cultural tradition. In the process of telling this story, Castellanos struggles with her own positionings as female Mexican intellectual, as Ladina from Chiapas, as *indigenista,* as she tries to imagine grounds for solidarity.

Other meanings suggested by the title link the dimension of cultural conflict to the roles of women. Because Catalina is frustrated in her desire to carry out the usual office assigned to women in her community, that of motherhood, she attempts to define another place for herself in a new role as mediator between the past and future action. Stacey Schlau points out how the title has meaning for the other female characters in the novel as well: "Its title suggests the physical, intellectual, and emotional enclosure to which all female characters are subjected in the novel's rural setting" (45). The constraints of prescribed gender roles on women in both communities, figured as enclosure or *tinieblas,* channel and shape women's actions and their intervention in the redistribution of power that results from the revolt. Idolina, the daughter of the Ladino patriarch, is a Miranda figure in this novel, the daughter of a powerful landowning family who strikes out blindly against her confining circumstances. The other female characters whose roles as female cultural agents make them central here are two Maya women: Idolina's Maya *nana,* Teresa, and Catalina Díaz Puiljá, one of the leaders of the Maya uprising. It is their actions that make possible Joseph Sommers' observation of a key dimension of the title's meaning:

El título sugestivo de la novela, evocando la pasión de Cristo, contiene una
implicación, aunque no muy definida, que en la capacidad indígena de absorber
una historia de opresión y sobrevivir en tinieblas, se nutre la chispa mágica de
una posible resurrección. ("El ciclo de Chiapas," 259)

The suggestive title of the novel, evoking Christ's Passion, contains an
implication, although not a well-defined one, that in the indigenous capacity
for absorbing a history of oppression and surviving in the shadows is
nourished the magical spark of a possible resurrection.

Although Castellanos is not able to imagine a successful revolt in this novel,
or what such a resurrection might look like, she is able to offer an analysis
that anticipates subsequent powerful critiques of the assumptions of *indige-*
nista policies and writing by challenging from within some of the most important premises of Mexican nationalism.

Oficio de tinieblas gives a literary version of a real event that was one of a
series of violent confrontations between Maya and non-Indians starting with
the European invasions. Castellanos said she based her fiction on an actual
revolt that occurred in Chiapas between 1867 and 1870 ("Una tentativa de
autocrítica," *Juicios sumarios*, 433); the Ladinos of Chiapas call it the Caste
War of 1867 or Cuscat's War, while the Maya themselves call it the War of
Saint Rose of Chamula (Bricker, 119). The kind of conflict Castellanos narrates in *Oficio de tinieblas* still persists in Chiapas as it does on a national scale
in Guatemala and elsewhere in the Americas; the uprising of January 1, 1994,
brought the situation in Chiapas to the attention of the world. The initial
phase of the Spanish conquest of the Maya took over twenty years; their last
stand in the Yucatán against the Spaniards was in 1546–1547, and some
peoples were not brought under Spanish rule for another 150 years. The Maya
views of the Conquest were recorded in the Books of Chilam Balam, books
of prophecy written in Maya languages but using the Latin alphabet, which
also contained accounts of historical events. The oldest are the Chilam Balam
de Tizimin and the Chilam Balam de Chumayel, which Castellanos quotes in
her novels' epigraphs. The *chilams*, or priests, acted as intermediaries between
the natural and the supernatural. Such intermediaries have played crucial
roles in many indigenous rebellions, such as the ones in Chiapas in 1712 and
in 1870, as well as the Caste War of the Yucatán in the nineteenth century.[2]
In *Oficio de tinieblas*, the Tzotzil woman Catalina is such an intermediary;
through her office as *ilol* and later as voice of the supernatural, Catalina channels her own individual spiritual energies and also gives form to the collective desires and needs of her community.

Many Maya revolts over the centuries have taken the particular form that

anthropologists call a "revitalization movement." Anthony Wallace has defined such a movement as "a deliberate, organized, conscious effort by members of society to construct a more satisfying culture" (265). Wallace stresses
the idea that this kind of movement, while taking the form of religious renewal, represents a conscious attempt on the part of the community to effect
social change. In her study of Maya revitalization movements, anthropologist Victoria Bricker expands this definition and also refers to the events that
inspired Castellanos' novel:

> (1) an attempt to reinterpret (i.e., "revitalize") the symbols of the Catholic
> cult forced on them by their Spanish conquerors, in order to make it more
> relevant to the Indian experience, or (2) an attempt to throw off what they
> considered to be the yoke of "foreign" domination and establish their own
> government, based on the Spanish model. In two of the movements under
> consideration here, the reinterpretation took the form of "Indianizing" the
> concept of the Passion of Christ. In highland Chiapas, in 1868, the Indians
> of Chamula crucified an Indian boy and proclaimed him to be the Indian
> Christ. (5)

While religious practices are the locus of conflict in these movements, Bricker
insists that the main issue is power: "Religious revitalization movements . . .
did not reject Catholicism per se. What they did reject was Spanish monopo-
lization of the ecclesiastical hierarchy" (20). The underlying causes of the
rebellions of 1712 and 1867–1870 (and of other ethnic confrontations in the
Yucatán and in Guatemala) were and are economic misery and exploitation,
aggravated by the greed and extortionate practices of the clergy and civil
officials and their mistreatment of indigenous leaders.[3]

In the novel, the Ladinos of Ciudad Real (present-day San Cristóbal de las
Casas) fearfully recall the Maya rebellion of 1712, and use it to justify their
brutal repression of Maya communities. During the years 1708–1713, four
religious movements culminated in an organized armed political rebellion in
the Chiapas highlands. In the Tzotzil towns of Zinacantan, Santa Marta, and
Chenalhó, the Virgin and other saints appeared and promised to help the
Maya. The communities came to make offerings at the new chapels and
crosses they erected, but in each case Spanish authorities destroyed the chapels, claiming that the rites were idolatrous, although, according to testimony,
the rites were the same as those held for other saints. At issue was Spanish
control over doctrine, and over indigenous people's lives and tribute.

In 1712, while the trials for those involved in the Santa Marta cult were
taking place, the Virgin appeared to a young woman, María de la Candelaria,
in the Tzeltal community of Cancuc. The first cross erected in her honor was

removed by the priest, but the Tzeltales built another chapel and asked the bishop to recognize it. When, instead, arrests were made, a man from Chenalhó named Sebastián Gómez organized the surrounding thirty-two towns, including Tzeltal, Tzotzil, and Chol Maya communities, proclaiming a Maya republic and a native church. Literate men were chosen as vicars to serve the saints and a Maya bishop was ordained. Mary, not God, now ruled heaven and María de la Candelaria was her intermediary. An army was organized on the Spanish model, but although the Maya outnumbered the Spaniards, they had no guns, and troops from Guatemala eventually defeated them. During the battle, Ladinos brought out the image of the Virgen de la Caridad, and Ladino oral tradition still claims this as the reason for their victory.[4]

The uprising that Castellanos uses as her source was not against the Spaniards; it occurred after Mexican Independence, a period during which conditions actually grew worse for indigenous people. This rebellion, called Cuscat's War by Ladinos, actually began as a revitalization movement in 1867 and became violent only after Ladino suppression. Castellanos follows the general outline of events that she found in written Ladino accounts by Molina and Pineda.[5] According to these sources, a Chamula woman, Agustina Gomes Checheb, found three stones in Tzajalhemel that she said fell from the sky. A Chamula official, Pedro Díaz Cuscat, began a cult around the stones, claiming they could speak, and organized their worship.[6] The priests and Ladino officials tried to suppress the cult by arresting its leaders, but failed. A Mestizo teacher named Ignacio Fernández de Galindo took up the organizing while Cuscat was in jail. When he exchanged himself for the release of the Maya leaders, he was executed. The rebellion was crushed and the rebels were massacred, again with the help of troops from Guatemala in an alliance between regional elites that disregarded national boundaries. These events provide the bare outline of the story told in *Oficio de tinieblas*.

Wasserstrom points out the economic roots of these rebellions, and also the extent to which Maya cultural practices adapted for survival:

> As native communities in general began to recover and grow after 1720, so also did the notion of communal solidarity, often in the form of collective ritual, acquire new significance and urgency. By means of such ritual, indigenous people kept alive that spirit of resistance, that insistence on their collective distinctiveness and dignity, that mitigated the daily outrages of colonial life. For it must be remembered that colonial society brought Spaniards and Indians together not simply as distinct ethnic groups but as members of antagonistic social classes—that ethnic relations quickly became a pretense for perpetuating inequities and injustices of a much more familiar sort. Then too, the options of emigration and transculturation, of *mestizaje*,

which many chose to pursue, remained open to Indians in most parts of
Mexico and Central America. But in Chiapas, at least, a significant number
of these men and women chose instead to modify their beliefs and customs
and traditions in every way possible so as to avoid the one fate they
evidently feared most: the loss of their right to be *naturales*. (119)

Wasserstrom reminds us that the two ethnic communities are not two separate worlds; their relations must be understood in terms of economic relations of class. He also points out the extent to which remaining Indian signified a choice, a strategy for survival.[7] Castellanos develops these two premises
in her fiction at a moment, in the late fifties, when these views were a subject
of great contention among anthropologists, *indigenista* policymakers, and
those intellectuals concerned with setting national priorities concerning Mexico's heterogeneous society. This way of understanding the situation of the
Maya challenges the assumptions of the more assimilationist version of *indigenista* social policy as well as the utopian premise of *mestizaje* as Mexican
national identity. It is also something to keep in mind while reading *Oficio de
tinieblas,* for it informs Castellanos' organization of her narrative. On the one
hand, Castellanos stresses the failure of outsiders' attempts to realize the
promises of the Revolution, or to effect any kind of significant positive change
in Chiapas. She also stresses the adaptive capacity of indigenous people, their
aspirations for change. Yet she too seems to draw back from asserting full
agency as a possibility for them.

As in *Balún Canán,* Castellanos situates the action of *Oficio de tinieblas* in
the thirties, during Cárdenas' land reform. By situating her stories after the
Revolution, she is able to insist on the persistence of fundamental social inequalities between landowners and indigenous peasants and to distance herself from the fifties' rhetoric of triumphant reform and progress (Sommers,
"Forma e ideología," 73). In her second novel she expands her scope to the
entire highlands region of Chiapas; her goal is to convey the complexity of
social relations between Ladinos and Maya, accounting for class, gender, and
social institutions such as the church, the schools, and the national government. The novel presents the circumstances leading to the uprising and its
failure through the portraits of two communities, indigenous and Ladino. A
key element in her analysis is her portrayal of a social world polarized between two interdependent communities, two cultures, two modes of historical consciousness. She focuses on the cultural differences that mediate
people's relations to institutions and their discourses and that structure community identity and action.

The action moves back and forth between two places: San Cristóbal de las
Casas, the center of Ladino society, and San Juan Chamula, the Maya village

where the revolt is centered. The novel as a whole is framed by the telling of two tales in a mythic mode, but most of the narrative is told chronologically by an impersonal voice of limited omniscience with the help of interior monologues, explanations of psychological motives, and flashbacks to provide background.

The Ladino world we are shown has its seat of power in the former colonial capital, whose regional dominance has been challenged by the transfer of the provincial government to Tuxtla Gutiérrez and by the reform directives issuing from Mexico City. As in *Balún Canán,* a wealthy landowning family serves as focus for the action, but other Ladino characters and institutions play important roles as well as they vie for power and status and struggle for survival. The Tzotzil Maya world is also shown in terms of many characters and social institutions. One Maya institution is the *cargo* system, which evolved during the colonial period, wherein Maya couples are chosen by the community to occupy posts of civil and religious authority for a year. During this time they must leave their fields and live in the main town, spending their own money on the drink and ceremonies necessary to carry out their duties; in return, they achieve status in the community. Pedro González Winiktón occupies the *cargo* of judge and embodies the masculine virtues of his community. His wife, Catalina Díaz Puiljá, has no children and suffers both because she wants a child and because a childless wife is considered a failure (at least as the novel represents indigenous values). When she turns to supernatural forces for a remedy, she comes to be respected for her power as *ilol,* one who uses magic. Both Catalina and Pedro are to be important leaders of the Maya uprising: Pedro becomes a political leader because he has heard the Revolution's promises of justice and represents them to his people, aided by Ladino land reform agent Fernando Ulloa, while Catalina is the leader of a religious revitalization movement that gives form to the Maya's attempts to survive, resist oppression, and redefine the circumstances of their existence. These two movements for change come up against a power struggle between Ladinos, the local oligarchy on the one hand and those who see their future with the new government in Mexico City on the other. Because local Ladino power depends on control of indigenous labor by landowners and the church, the Ladino community of Ciudad Real must deal with any threat to that control whether it comes from the revolutionary government or from indigenous people themselves.

About half of the novel's chapters are narrated from the perspective of the Maya, while the other half are narrated from the perspective of the Ladinos. Shift in perspective is established, first of all, by alternating between the two geographical spaces of the two communities. But along with shifts in setting and social milieu, shift in perspective is effected by alternating between the different sets of cultural values through which the reader must understand characters' actions and motivations. *Oficio de tinieblas* differs markedly from her first novel in that, at times, Castellanos does not hesitate to use direct commentary by the narrator to tell the reader what these values are, a technique she does not use at all in *Balún Canán*. Another means she uses to mark the difference between Maya and Ladino worldview is through shifts in the kind of language she uses; many of the sections associated with San Juan Chamula, especially those concerning Catalina, are told with a more varied, poetic language that sometimes echoes both the Bible and Spanish translations of Maya texts such as the Popol Vuh (see Chapter 4).

The representation of two ethnic communities in conflict whose antagonism is figured as an opposition between two modes of historical consciousness is a key to questions of form and ideology in the book. Some have been tempted to characterize this difference as an opposition between "myth" and "history." An example of an approach that assumes an absolute difference between these two constructs is illustrated by the following paragraph from "Women in the Work of Rosario Castellanos":

> The vision of time in the work of Rosario Castellanos also contributes to the creation of a universe of "magic realism." She does not conceive of time as historical but employs a time which follows a circular development and which seems to be immobilized throughout eternity. It is the time of the perpetual cycle of sowing, harvests, seasons, subdued rebellions, which hold man in mysterious submission. The last image of *Oficio de tinieblas* (as in *Balún Canán*) completes the cycle that began with the novel's opening image, thus closing the circle of time and projecting us into the process of the eternal return. Everything reverts back to a state of normalcy, which is ruled by the indomitable cycle of the earth and the will of the gods; rebellions are put down and forgotten, another cycle begins. Events, penetrated by history, are tainted with fetishism and ancient mythological beliefs, which make the burden of tradition hanging over mankind all the heavier. (Tron de Bouchony, 69)

This view equates myth with circularity, and, by pointing to a structural circularity in the narrative, equates circularity with the impossibility of change, superstition, and acceptance of oppression as "normalcy." It also casts indigenous people as doomed, by their "fetishism" and its "mysterious submission," to helpless barbarism.

A more subtle, and more convincing, view is the one proposed by Joseph Sommers, who sees the contrast as a problem of "history" in the narrative. Because Sommers' work is so important in situating *Oficio de tinieblas* as social critique in terms of the moment when it was published, the social reality it describes, and the literary traditions on which it draws, it is useful to see how he reads the novel through this question of history.

Sommers wrote about *Oficio de tinieblas* several times. "Forma e ideología en *Oficio de tinieblas* de Rosario Castellanos" provides a systematic reading of the novel fifteen years after its publication; he explains some of the neglect it suffered because of discomfort with its strong social criticism. In particular he points to how the novel demystifies the idea that the situation in Chiapas was different from that of national society because Chiapas was "feudal." Part of this demystification involves showing that, while indigenous people and Ladinos may have profound cultural differences that serve to prolong conflict, they do not inhabit separate social worlds but, rather, live in intimate interdependence.

Sommers praises the novel's achievements, but is critical of what he calls two points of ideological contradiction. Specifically, he states that Castellanos' representation of the two cultural systems is structured by an opposition between "history" and "myth," with these terms indicating two kinds of consciousness: "history" is aligned with the Ladino worldview while "myth" refers to that of the Indians. One way he sees the formal presence of this opposition manifested in the novel is in the opening and closing tales or "myths" that show how indigenous culture narrates its history in a mythic mode. Sommers sees the tone of these two scenes (which he compares to Miguel Angel Asturias' "realismo mágico") as inconsistent with the psychological realist mode of the rest of the novel (86). The second limitation, stemming from the first, is what he calls Castellanos' "cultural pessimism" (91). He claims that the representation of the Maya's consciousness as mythic shows them as incapable of the historical consciousness necessary for social change, and that Castellanos fails to suggest alternatives to the failed revolt. The formal element that he identifies with this ideological contradiction is the transposition of the real historical events to the Cárdenas era.

Sommers' criticism is based on his opposition of myth to history, with the assumption that a mythic worldview is unhistorical and that the representation of the Maya as having a mythic cultural system is therefore regressive. Castellanos clearly represents the two communities as having different ways of understanding the past and of narrating their experiences, and thus of constituting their identities as groups, that is, as having different ways of knowing and telling their histories. However, I do not think that she therefore claims that the Maya lack any kind of historical consciousness or the capacity to enact change. Rather, she represents an "insurrection of subjugated knowledges" and its possible alliance with the radical potential of the discourse of social equality legitimized by the Mexican Revolution. In her representation of conflict, the Maya do indeed initiate action, although their action fails; they understand their past and its relation to their present quite clearly—more clearly indeed than the sympathetic Ladino agent Fernando Ulloa, who has a historical theory about the situation but who consistently misreads and misinterprets the social systems of Chiapas despite his sincere desire for change and justice. How then to talk about the real differences between the cultural modes of experiencing and knowing history that Castellanos represents in her novel? And how to account for the novel's failure to imagine a revolutionary consciousness? What issues of "plausibility," in Miller's terms, are at stake here as they were in the readings of *Balún Canán*?[8]

When we consider the question of the novel's relation to history we must distinguish between the events themselves, what Castellanos called the "indispensable facts" (see below), and the textual and oral records of them that historians or anthropologists take as their objects of study. The other sense in which the term "history" has been used in discussions of the book, such as those of Sommers and Julio Rodríguez-Luis, is as a code for designating one of the cultural poles in the situation of conflictive heterogeneity described by Antonio Cornejo Polar. The fact that the novel refers to two cultural systems in close and antagonistic relation and makes the nature of those relations its theme is posed as a problem of "history" taken to mean the historical consciousness of indigenous and nonindigenous communities. This reading of the novel is structured around an opposition between Maya's and the Ladinos' collective relations to the past, their differing modes of experiencing time and events, and their differing modes of narrating that experience—what I have been calling modes of historical consciousness. The issue at stake in these readings seems to be whether or not Castellanos was capable of imagining Indians as historical agents; because she tells the story of a rebellion that fails, does that mean she considers indigenous people culturally incapable of constituting themselves as historical subjects? Perhaps a better way of asking the question is to look at the extent to which her representation of Maya self-constitution and political mobilization is still grounded in colonialist forms of *indigenista* thinking.

One place to begin an examination of questions of myth and history raised by a novel about cultural conflict is with the relation of Castellanos' narrative act to these three levels of "history." First, there is the series of events in Chiapas known as the Caste War of 1867–1870, the events to which Castellanos' novel refers. Second, there is the set of narrative acts, the accounts of these events both written and oral, through which Castellanos and others (including ourselves) have knowledge of or access to these events. In addition to sources she mentions, Castellanos could have heard Ladino oral accounts of these events, either when she was growing up or when she was working for the Instituto Nacional Indigenista in Chiapas while she wrote the novel. Unknown to Castellanos for linguistic reasons is the Maya oral history of ethnic conflict. Both oral traditions, Ladino and Maya, have been recorded and translated by Bricker.[9]

Castellanos used written and oral sources for the "facts" about the events, their chronology, and the story of the Maya's crucifixion of a child in the belief that this would give them power against their foes. This last incident plays a central part in the novel, but, as it turns out, probably never happened. Jan Rus quite convincingly demonstrates that this story is apocryphal, a Ladino calumny that was, in fact, not part of contemporary Ladino accounts of the uprising, but was added some twenty years later in order to justify one side of a political struggle (157).[10] In the 1888 account by Pineda from which Castellanos got this distorted information she could also read Ladino justifications and explanations of causality. Her comments on the events in a letter show that she assumes Pineda's characterization to be accurate:

> No son más que datos indispensables para formarse una idea de los acontecimientos, pero la impresión que queda es que las rebeliones podían reducirse a un arrebato dionisiaco, una orgia de sangre, una embriaguez colectiva de violencia que no quería ir más allá, que no tenía ningún plan posterior, y que desaparecido el primer ímpetu no se aprovechaba de las ventajas logradas.[11]

> There are only the indispensable facts for getting an idea about the events, but the impression that remains is that the rebellions were nothing more than a Dionysiac convulsion, an orgy of blood, a collective intoxication with violence that didn't intend to go any farther, that had no subsequent plan, and that, once the first impulse had disappeared, did not take advantage of the gains it had realized.

The attitude toward the Maya in Pineda's text that Castellanos summarizes here, that the Indians were bloodthirsty savages, has left its traces on the novel. Although the novel clearly presents the indigenous revolt as a response to extreme forms of oppression and is careful to present such motives as cultural survival and the desire for land and justice as forces that shape the revolt, the language that is used to describe Maya actions during the armed struggle itself is shaped by Pineda's presentation of the Ladino victory over the Maya as the result of Maya cultural failure or moral inferiority, enabling the reading of "mysterious submission" cited above. And at least one major "fact" about the uprising that takes on central importance in the interpretive economy of the novel, the crucifixion, appears to have been invented by the victors to justify their brutality toward the vanquished.

In *The Indian Christ, the Indian King* Victoria Bricker examines the common opposition of "myth" and "history" in order to debunk the assumption that myth is not also a way of dealing with time and the past, and that "history" as it is defined in the West does not also propose myths—paradigmatic explanations of events—or search for patterns of repetition. So-called mythic cultures do indeed understand chronology and deal with events in sequence, but the teleology of this understanding is different. Myth chooses to ignore an overwhelmingly linear temporality in favor of a more paradigmatic model. In Bricker's view, mythmakers have a different theory of history (3–9).

The opposition of myth and history is more usefully seen as depending on the idea of two narrative modes, two symbolic repertoires used by groups to represent their existence in time.[12] Bricker concludes that the modern Maya emphasize structure at the expense of personality in their folklore of ethnic conflict, that the individuality of the hero is not important in their tradition and ritual. The hero of one cycle or century or millennium is the hero of all time. He may be referred to by the names of all heroes or the name of any one of them. The villain who opposes him can be called by the name of any villain from any time period. The passion of Christ is conflated with the Spanish Conquest of the Maya and with the many colonial uprisings as well as the most recent conflict with landowners and soldiers. What is important is the structural message: ethnic conflict is characterized by warfare, death, rape, soldiers, weapons, and the division of people into two groups, the conquerors and the conquered (8). This in no way implies that the Maya are fatalistic; indeed, such stories keep alive a spirit of resistance. In *Living Maya,* a compelling account of Maya survival and cultural renewal that places women at the center, Walter Morris underscores the continuity of this process and provides yet another link in the series of events Castellanos narrates:

> The Maya blend history and myth. They place events not in the order of
> their occurrence but in order of their importance. The leader of land reform
> in 1938, Erasto Urbina, appears in Chamula stories about "the beginning of
> the world." Some storytellers are old enough to remember the actions that
> Erasto undertook to restore Chamula land and basic rights, yet Erasto is an
> actor in ancient myth because he changed the world of Chamula and caused
> its renewal. (33)

In our Western division of academic disciplines, the oral self-representations of communities are studied as myth or folklore, and not as history. In *Oficio de tinieblas* Castellanos represents the ways the two ethnic communities narrate their histories as different, but she does not cast this difference as an opposition between those who somehow understand history and those who do not. Rather, she shows the workings of two kinds of historical discourse, competing versions of history that in fact are not completely separate but that share some modalities and one important paradigm: the central mythic paradigm of Christianity, the crucifixion. In *Oficio de tinieblas* what is as important as what happens is how events are told and why they are told that way: how each community constitutes itself as such through its acts of narrating.

We might be tempted to recast the question in terms of orality and literacy, and, indeed, this difference is an important aspect of the differentiation between the two cultural communities. However, the pair orality/literacy, like the pair myth/history, characterizes the ways people mediate their experiences, but these two modes are not in and of themselves the source of conflict, which is economic exploitation and an ideology of ethnic superiority. Rather than seeking to maintain an opposition, we can look at how Castellanos seeks to represent the painful, conflictive heterogeneity of her society.

The tale that opens the novel points toward the syncretic religious practices of the Tzotziles; it is a founding myth that blends Christian elements with indigenous religious beliefs and is told from an indigenous perspective. This tale acts as a seed narrative in the novel in that it gives us an initial version of the tale of conflict that the various characters will try to "rewrite" through their actions in the course of the novel. The story that closes *Oficio de tinieblas* recasts in a similar oral/mythic mode the events just narrated in the novel. Both tales are narratives that try to account for the continued oppression of indigenous people by Ladinos.

As in *Balún Canán,* the narrative is preceded by an epigraph taken from a Maya text—the Popol Vuh, or Libro de Consejo—that prophesies an end to the dominance of those who have ruled. And, as in *Balún Canán,* the reader's entry into the narrative passes through a tale marked as indigenous. The novel opens with the story of the founding of the Tzotzil town San Juan Chamula, which, like a myth, includes the origin of the world and a supernatural causality. The culture from which such a story emerges, however, is one whose beliefs have been shaped by the Conquest, for we see elements of Christianity blended with Maya beliefs.

San Juan Fiador wants a temple, so he turns the sheep in the valley into stones as a sign to the pre-Christian Tzotziles (whose name means *murciélagos,* or bats) that they should build one. But they do not understand that this is "the sign of a will" (9) and thus the arrival of the Spaniards, the "others" (9), is explained as necessary to the fulfillment of this design. However, the new arrivals do not really understand the sign either. They do build the church, so they have "understood" the purpose of the sign by using the stones. But, unlike the Tzotziles, they do not know that the stones are "ovejas petrificadas" [petrified sheep] (9). In this tale, two interpretive systems confront each other, two codes that are at odds without the divine intervention of San Juan Fiador, who must step in when the walls of the church keep falling down. The temple that is finally built is the site of two kinds of expression, *caxlán* (the Maya name for the Spaniards) and *indio*, prayers and laments (10). The languages themselves are signs of difference from the Tzotzil perspective; their language is for dreams while "*castilla*" (a deformation of *castellano*, or Castilian; *castilla* means castle) is for orders, sentences, threats, and rewards: "ferreo instrumento de señorío, arma de conquista, punta del látigo de la ley" [iron instrument of lordship, arm of conquest, the tip of the lash of the law] (9).

This doubleness of expression and of interpretive systems is figured as a syncretic coexistence structured by unequal relations of power and mutual incomprehension. The church is the site of a partial integration of the two belief systems, a transculturation whose heterogeneity is both represented and embodied in this opening parable. The indigenous view of the saints is syncretic: "San Jerónimo . . . protector secreto de los brujos" [San Jerónimo . . . secret protector of the sorcerers] (10). The form Castellanos gives to her representation of the syncretic cultural practices of the Maya signifies this heterogeneity through her novelistic incorporation of conventions of oral discourse:

> Así como se cuentan sucedieron las cosas desde sus orígenes. No es mentira. Hay testimonios. Se leen en los tres arcos de la puerta de entrada del templo, desde donde se despide el sol. (10)

> Just as we tell them these things happened from their beginning. It is not a lie. There is testimony. It can be read in the three arches of the door at the entrance of the temple, from where the sun takes its leave.

The cultural survival of Maya beliefs and practices represented by the tale itself is inscribed in the church building; the "testimony" that can be read in the figures carved over the main door of the temple evokes a common sight in Mexico: indigenous symbols among the Christian symbols, placed there by the indigenous artists who built the churches. But the workings of this syncretic process are shown as founded on misreadings by both communities and on mutual incomprehension. This tale implies that Ladino understanding of the foundation of this society is as partial as that of the Maya. In other words, it is not the "mythic" discourse of the Maya that prevents them from understanding their history; rather, what is understood by each group is different. The parable can be read as a story about the dilemma facing

Mexicans as a nation: the history of the Conquest can be read in the institutions built under colonialism, but where is the reader who, like San Juan Fiador, can keep the walls of the nation from falling down?

After this "mythic" entry into the novel there is a change in narrative mode. In *Balún Canán*, shifts in narrative voice corresponded to place and are clearly marked by first-person and third-person narrative conventions. Here, shifts occur as well, but they are of a different nature: from an unidentified speaker who seems to be using the indigenous oral conventions and who gives a supernatural explanation of causality for the arrival of the Spanish conquerors, the voice shifts to a standard impersonal omniscient voice; from a perspective that accepts the Maya's beliefs as the norm we move to one that must explain for us the social structures of the Chamula world, of which San Juan Chamula is the center. It is here that Maya men live when they are chosen to carry out *cargos*. This section approaches a kind of ethnographic discourse; it assumes readers unfamiliar with these cultural practices who are outsiders to this world. Here, too, the syncretic nature of Chamula beliefs is evident. *Cargo* holders work within the church when they organize saints' festivals, but as part of their responsibility for the sacred, they must also respect "su padre, el sol" [their father, the sun] (11).

The first kind of narrative, the tale, approximates the Tzotzil mode of remembering and explaining their history while the second gives us an external view of their social structures. The third level of entry into the narrative is marked by the phrase "Amanece tarde en Chamula" [It dawns late in Chamula] (11). This temporal verb marks an opening, the beginning of the novelistic narrative in the mode of critical realism, just as the oral formulas marked the preceding story; it moves the narrative from the general into the particular, chronological flow of events that will be told in the novel. This line will also be echoed in the last line of the novel: "Faltaba mucho tiempo para que amaneciera" [It would be a long time before the dawn] (368).

Pedro González Winiktón is "hermano mayor," or Elder Brother, to his people (the role so important in *Balún Canán*). He is a man respected for his character who this year occupies the *cargo* of judge. Despite his good fortune, he has no children; his wife, Catalina Díaz Puiljá, has even turned to the power of magic to become pregnant, but to no avail. She herself is now so knowledgeable about magic that she is recognized as a practitioner, "una 'ilol' cuyo regazo es arcón de los conjuros" [an *ilol* whose lap is the repository of spells] (13). But she is bitter and afraid that Pedro will repudiate her for being barren, as is his right. This is, of course, the same situation that exists for Juana in *Balún Canán*, but Catalina is a central character in this novel, one whose resolve to control her situation motivates much of the action.[13] She and Pedro will represent different courses of resistance against Ladino oppression: Pedro acting as mediator of an outside, nationalist discourse and Catalina as mediator of an indigenous past.

The opening of the novel thus situates the reader in the social world of the Tzotziles. What happens next gives a picture of the Ladino world from that perspective and suggests metaphors for ethnic relations. The Chamula women journey to market in the city they call Jobel and that the Ladinos call by its colonial name, Ciudad Real. The official name, San Cristóbal de las Casas, is a reminder of Fray Bartolomé de las Casas, the bishop of Chiapas, who became known as the defender of the Indians. The linguistic and historical tension between the two communities signified by these different names emerges starkly in the first episodes narrated, which figure their relations in two ways: as routine and violent robbery, and as rape. As they enter the city, the Maya women are attacked by *atajadoras,* the poorest of the Ladina women, who fall upon them and take part of their merchandise, throwing a few coins at them in supposed recompense.[14] The Maya community is preyed upon by the Ladinos, and Maya women are preyed upon by other women who themselves are desperately poor; in the story "Modesta Gómez" in *Ciudad Real,* Castellanos shows us how one of these women fallen on hard times is glad to be an *atajadora* when the alternatives for feeding her children are starvation or prostitution. These women despise their victims and are in turn despised by "decent women." Maya are exploited by Ladinos because they are kept in economic dependence, but this is part of the entire Ladino social system, shown as one of brutal exploitation of the weaker by the stronger.

One of the Maya women, a girl named Marcela Oso, is separated from the others and lured into a house by a Ladina woman, Doña Mercedes, where she is brutally raped by the wealthy landowner Leonardo Cifuentes. The fact that Doña Mercedes speaks Tzotzil makes it possible for her to procure Maya women for her *patrón,* Cifuentes. Marcela's rape reenacts the common historical metaphor for the Conquest, but Castellanos does not use rape merely as a figure, as does Octavio Paz in *The Labyrinth of Solitude,* where rape is a central metaphor of Mexican identity, but shows rape as a fact of everyday reality for Maya women.

These opening scenes show two common forms of *caxlán* abuse of Maya, by both women and men. The women act out of their own economic desperation, while the man systematically sexually abuses women with the help of another woman, Doña Mercedes; both illustrate the "(ambiguously) non-hegemonic" situation of Ladina women. Doña Mercedes herself was Cifuentes' first prostitute and now serves as his pimp because the only other possibilities for her are "atajadora, custitalera or placera" [robber of market women, traveling peddler, or food vendor in the plaza] (21). As with the *atajadoras,* economic necessity and the extremely limited economic possibilities for Ladina

146

women structure her participation in exploitation of Maya women. Doña Mercedes owes her livelihood to her sexual services for the *patrón* and works to perpetuate sexual exploitation. Paradoxically, of all the Ladina women in the novel she has the most mobility, but she is cut off almost completely from the society of other women; she talks endlessly to herself, justifying her situation. Doña Mercedes can give a form to her experience through language, but she has no audience.

Language and naming can be instruments of exploitation but also of consciousness, as can be seen in the ways that Marcela's rape is named, understood, and acted upon. At first Marcela has no name for what has happened to her, and she is lost, literally and figuratively. She wanders dazed through the streets, and is tormented by Ladino children. Language fails her. The bishop and the young priest Manuel Mandujano notice but do not help her, with the excuse that they do not speak her language. When she rejoins the other women, her mother abuses her, discharging her own suffering on her daughter, until Catalina rescues her. Only Catalina realizes what has happened; Marcela herself is immensely relieved when she hears Catalina tell Pedro: "un caxlán abusó de ella" [a *caxlán* abused her] (29) for she hears her suffering named. Just as Marcela's rape is a figure for the historical exploitation of indigenous people by Ladinos, so Catalina's naming of it prefigures the role she will play later on, of channeling the community's experience of suffering into a form, an expression they can recognize.

Catalina sees in Marcela the opportunity to remedy one of her problems, how to care for her brother Lorenzo, who is retarded and unable to care for himself. In the scene where Catalina and Pedro work together to negotiate the marriage of Marcela to Lorenzo, Castellanos skillfully conveys the interplay between custom and emotion, between the form of the ritual and the personal motivations of each party as they read each other's reactions and negotiate the names for Marcela's experience. Although Lorenzo is known to be impotent and thus not a fit husband, Marcela's rape means her parents receive almost nothing for the customary bride price. Pedro feels that their union is another form of injustice, but Catalina is satisfied for she has the answer to her prayers: Marcela is pregnant. In revulsion Marcela tries to get rid of the child, but Catalina wants it for herself.

Marcela's pain awakens a different response in Pedro because it reminds him of the horrible rape of his own sister. Then, he was overcome with sorrow and the desire for justice, and now as a judge he recognizes the situation of his people as one of injustice. He feels the need to act, but cannot see how. Pedro sees Marcela's pregnancy as a sign of judgment against his lack of action: "la injusticia engendró delante de ti" [injustice was engendered before you] (48). Catalina names the boy Domingo and sees him as the answer to her desires, but the community calls him "el que nació cuando el eclipse" [the one born during the eclipse] (49). The child is read as a sign differently by each person, but at a crucial moment these meanings will converge.

Pedro finds a possible response to the injustice Domingo signifies to him when he learns a new language. After Pedro's year of service as judge, the family endures great hardship back on their land in Tzajalhemel. To pay the rent they owe the Ladino landlord Pedro is forced to join a plantation work gang.[15] On the ranch of a German, whose Maya wife is treated as a servant, the whip is still used, but the German sees himself as enlightened because he provides a toilet and a school. The other Ladinos fear that education and Indian knowledge of Spanish will produce the "indio alzado" [rebellious Indian], but he sees this as a way to make them better workers—the logic of modernization. Of course, the school is largely a failure since the workers must attend after their grueling day's work, but Pedro sets himself to learn. Because of his aptitude he is favored by the *patrón*, has more contact with the Ladino world, and learns to speak Spanish. When President Cárdenas tours the region and asks to see a plantation, he is shown the school. In his speech, Pedro hears the word *justice* linked with possession of the land, and when he shakes Cárdenas' hand, for him it signifies a promise, "el sello de un pacto" [the seal on a pact] (61). Pedro takes literally the promise of the Revolution that the government will come to the aid of indigenous peoples in their struggle against exploitation and for self-determination.

Pedro thus finds himself positioned differently in the world through the education that gives him access to the language of the Ladino and to literacy. This new interpellation is validated in his eyes by his encounters with Ladina prostitutes; through possession of the women of his oppressor, he feels himself equal to the men. Equality is predicated on a model of masculinity defined by possession. Once he has been with the prostitutes he loses some of his awe for Ladinos because he sees their women as just women: "Hembras sí, hembras, barro que la mano del varón moldea a su antojo" [Females, yes, females, clay that the hand of the male molds to his whim] (61). Once again, Castellanos conjugates the sexual and the social as relations between Maya and Ladino are mediated by gender roles. The image of women as clay to be molded will be redefined when Catalina herself molds clay into images of the old gods, asserting female creativity and action as a means to mobilize her people.

The word *justice* pronounced by the president is a promise for Pedro, but the men in the community know that to take this speech act seriously also means promises of violence and another kind of suffering. To say the word means to take action; Pedro is trying to make the word into something real, to redefine it through action. On his return Pedro abandons outward signs of rebellion, but retains his lessons from the school and begins to talk to others of justice. They are wary:

> Decir justicia en Chamula era matar al patrón, arrasar la hacienda, venadear a los fiscales, resistir los abusos de los comerciantes, denunciar los manejos del enganchador, vengarse del que maltrata a los niños y viola a las mujeres. Decir justicia en Chamula era velar, día y noche, sostenido por la promesa de un hombre remoto cuya buena fe ninguno había probado aún. Era preferible callar. (62–63)

To say justice in Chamula meant to kill the boss, to raze the hacienda, to hunt down the tax collectors, resist the abuses of the merchants, denounce the manipulations of the plantation recruiters, take revenge on those who mistreat the children and rape the women. To say justice in Chamula was to keep watch, day and night, sustained by the promise of a remote man whose goodwill no one had yet tested. It was better to keep silent.

They imagine forms of resistance but fear the consequences. They hesitate as well because, if they believe Pedro, it means that their suffering has been in vain.

Pedro's empowerment comes through a non-Indian discourse of justice and equality, but one that resonates with his experience, a discourse that appears to have the power to enforce its claims. Catalina's empowerment, on the other hand, comes through her community's traditional beliefs and practices and their recognition by the community. Catalina's sterility and her yearning for transcendence can find no *form* in her community, but whereas Juana's choice was to leave, to find a place elsewhere, as the *nana* did, Catalina is shown as a strong, active woman who searches for a solution on terms recognized within her own community, first through magic and then in an attempt to reconstruct her community's past and heritage through the old gods. Castellanos portrays this motivation as at once the response to an individual and profoundly personal dilemma, and as the way an individual realizes herself through the forms and paradigms available in her culture. Catalina's "dangerous memory," grounded in her experience of suffering as female and in her community's subjugated knowledge, represents a powerful force for collective mobilization.

Although Castellanos shows the religious revival that Catalina inspires as an extraordinary event, through the subsequent work of anthropologists and historians we now can see that the use of "talking cross" or talking saint cults as catalyzers of rebellion was not an isolated incident but has a long history in the Maya region. Wallace's definition of a revitalization movement as the attempt to create a more satisfying culture in response to stresses that have become intolerable finds an echo in cultural anthropologist Victor Turner's ideas about "social dramas," those times when an event polarizes elements in a society to the point where the society must resolve its tensions or split apart. Like Wallace, Turner looks at the process through which the group attempts resolution, but he is interested in the paradigms a culture uses to understand and to act out the social drama as kinds of narrative. When the Tzotziles try to reshape the metaphors with which they must live, they turn to other paradigms. Catalina attempts to enact maternity while Pedro attempts to make concrete the promise of Cárdenas, and both will use the story Bricker calls "The Indian Christ, the Indian King."

The metaphors for ethnic relations—of plunder, rape, the birth of the *mestizo*—and the attempts to establish new paradigms using both traditional and revolutionary models are all gender inflected. Rape casts ethnic relations in terms of sexual violence and reproduces a false alignment of the indigenous with female and Ladino with male. The attack of the *atajadoras* on the Maya women shows another way that gender constructs a metaphor, for if ethnicity itself is not symbolically aligned with gender in this figure, gender still determines the social positions of these two groups of women both within their respective communities and in relation to each other.

The first part of the novel privileges the perspective of the Tzotzil community and foregrounds female characters. We have already seen women's complicity in violence against other women and the barriers to solidarity between women who are objects of that violence. The possibility of alliance and solidarity between poor women and privileged women, Indian and Ladina, or among Ladinas is rendered practically unthinkable by the interaction of racism and class division with gendered identity. In following scenes, the portrait of Ladino society that emerges through the lives of Ladina women is one in which the lives of women of privilege are shown as structured through their relations to Ladino men. Their allegiances are dictated within a system that defines their place through their sexual roles, which are in turn mediated by forms of racial solidarity. Three principal characters are identified—and identify themselves—through their sexual relations to the patriarch Leonardo Cifuentes: the legitimate wife, Isabel Zebadúa; the mistress, Julia Azevedo; the prostitute/spy, Doña Mercedes.

Cifuentes' wife, Isabel, occupies the highest position on the Ladino social scale for women. She witnesses Marcela's flight after the rape, but does nothing to prevent it or to help Marcela; rather, she feels humiliated and angry for the insult to her status. She clings to the superiority of her name and her place as legitimate wife, but is unable to shame Leonardo by the example of her virtue because of her complicity in his murder of his foster brother,

Isidoro, her first husband. She is completely dependent on Leonardo, who enjoys humiliating her. Her allegiance to a code of ethnic and racial superiority precludes identifying with other victims of her husband, and her own treatment of her daughter's *nana*, Teresa, is a horrifying story. Like Zoraida, Isabel is a cruel and tormented figure, Miranda's mother, whose allegiance to her own oppression within patriarchy and complicity in the oppression of others is both understood and condemned.

Her chief rival is the newcomer, Julia Acevedo, who is known as the wife of the government reform agent, Fernando Ulloa, but who, in reality, is not married to him. Julia is a beautiful redhead who walks freely through the town, earning herself the nickname "la Alazana" (the red mare). Her unconfined sexuality is dangerous to the social hierarchy, yet her own internalization of gender norms contains that threat more effectively than any of the townspeople's attempts to police her. Although she was reared by her mother to take care of herself, came into contact with radical ideals at school, and is now living with a man who is a sexual freethinker, Julia yearns to be accepted in the most traditional terms by the town's elite.

> *Era una de esas mujeres para quienes el mundo, su propio destino, y hasta su personalidad, no se revelan, no adquieren un contorno definido más que al través del contacto amoroso con el hombre. (127)*

> She was one of those women for whom the world, her own destiny, and even her personality are only revealed, only take on a definite outline through a love relation with a man.

A relation with Leonardo would give her an entry, but, however hard she tries, she is not accepted by the upper-class women, who are threatened by her overt sexuality, a situation illustrated elsewhere by Castellanos in the short story "'Vals capricho.'"

Doña Mercedes, acting as go-between, advises Julia to play Cifuentes for his money in case Ulloa leaves her, thus underscoring the fear of economic insecurity that motivates Julia's desire for legitimacy. Julia enjoys the party Cifuentes throws in her honor and eventually becomes his mistress. The only gift she accepts from him is a shawl from Guatemala, an object that symbolizes her betrayal of Ulloa and that will acquire other meanings as it passes from hand to hand later in the narrative.

Isabel's daughter, Idolina, lies (supposedly) paralyzed in her room as the result of her knowledge that her mother was the silent accomplice to the murder of her father, Isidoro. Her hatred of Leonardo is such that she has been struck by a kind of hysterical paralysis and has not walked for years.

This ensures her mother's attention; at the same time, she sees Leonardo's unfaithfulness as the punishment her mother deserves (78). Idolina's paralysis strikes her at a moment when she begins to half-recognize that the model of female identity offered her by her mother is one in which being female means betrayal and humiliation. She is paralyzed by her rage, but also by her recognition of womanhood as insertion into a system of sexual desire in which women are complicitous with their own misfortune and by the possibility of her own place in that system.

Another woman who is part of this community in Ciudad Real, but not of it, is Teresa, Idolina's *nana*. Like the *nana* in *Balún Canán*, Teresa has crossed over, given her love to the child of her oppressor. But while the *nana* in *Balún Canán* was a positive maternal figure for a small child, Teresa's relation to the adolescent Idolina is more complex.[16]

> *Había entre las dos ese trato que entre ama y criada sólo establece una larga dependencia por una parte y una tierna lealtad por la otra. Su relación era un juego de concesiones e imposiciones recíprocas cuyo mecanismo había perfeccionado una intimidad exclusiva. (81)*

> There was between the two of them that behavior between mistress and maid that is only established by a long dependency on the one hand and a tender loyalty on the other. Their relationship was a play of reciprocal concessions and demands whose mechanism had been perfected by an exclusive intimacy.

Balún Canán examines the possibility of an alternative to relations of hate, fear, and dominance between Ladino and indigenous people; the love and guidance of the *nana* for the Ladina girl figures a possible mediation between the two peoples as an idealized maternal bond. While this dream of cultural dialogue is shown to fail by the end of the novel, it is important to recognize that it is also a dream of another possible relation between women, specifically, between mother and daughter. In *Oficio de tinieblas* as well, a daughter struggles with the way she is inducted into the values that order her world; the values may be enunciated by the patriarch-landowner but they are enforced by the mother, and the daughter's interpellation into that social order is mediated by her relationships with women—Isabel, Julia, and Teresa—as well as with men.

The story of how Teresa came to this situation, revealed through a conversation between Julia and Isabel, confronts the values of the *coletos* (as the inhabitants of Ciudad Real call themselves) with those of an outsider. Isabel tells how she forced Teresa to nurse Idolina. When Teresa's own child went hungry, Teresa fled, but was captured, beaten, and tied up, and her baby was taken from her. When the child starved to death, her husband beat her and blamed her for the loss. Isabel justifies her hideous actions with the *coleto* refrain: "Teresa no es más que una india. Su hija era una india también" [Teresa is nothing but an Indian. Her daughter was an Indian, too] (140). Teresa returns to care for Idolina because she has no other place to go. Like the *nana* in *Balún Canán*, Teresa makes a place for herself in the world through her mothering of a Ladina girl. In the conversation between Julia and Isabel, the clash between the two social classes of Ladinos is mediated by the absent figure of a Maya woman, Teresa, in a manner that prefigures the role the Maya rebellion will have in redistributing power among Ladinos.

As did the *nana* in *Balún Canán*, Teresa offers her charge an alternative to the parents' order through a magical way of seeing the world. However, the vision she offers is not one of harmony but of vengeance. During one of her games with the girl, the *nana* prophesies the death of Idolina's parents, the burning of the house, and their own freedom." Idolina takes this story as more than a game, though: "¿Es una promesa?" "Sí" ["Is that a promise?" "Yes"] (87). As the promise of Cárdenas does for Pedro, Teresa's promise gives Idolina a purpose; she begins to walk again in secret. A potentially dangerous alliance between indigenous and Ladina women is represented here as a model for political insurrection (burning down the house). But when Julia accidentally discovers that Idolina is now "cured" and allies herself with the girl, it soon becomes clear that Idolina's rebellion, like Julia's, comes from her desire for recognition and assimilation. When she does not need Teresa anymore, Teresa disappears.

Both Julia and Idolina want to be recognized, to be integrated into the social world of Ciudad Real's elite women, to change their marginalized condition, but not by challenging the values that are in fact the cause of their marginalization. As the town prepares for the imagined Maya siege, Julia tries to gain acceptance through lavish parties. The women come to eat her food, make a mess, and insult her. But as soon as Julia learns how to participate in their conversation, she comes to be accepted, especially when she realizes how narrow their world is. The incessant themes of their conversation are men, money, and gossip (285–289). A passage in the text that details the possible relationships with men begins with the father; it starts out in the third person, but slips into the second person when the idea of sexual desire creeps in:

El padre, que bendice la mesa y el sueño, el que alarga su mano para que la
besen sus deudos en el saludo y en la despedida.
El padre que, una vez, te sentó en sus rodillas y acarició tu larga trenza de

adolescente. Entonces te atreviste a mirarlo en los ojos y sorprendiste un brillo de hambre o un velo de turbación, que te lo hizo próximo y temible y deseable. (286)

The father, who blesses the table and repose, who stretches out his hand to be kissed by his dependents in greeting and farewell.

The father who once sat you on his knee and caressed your long adolescent's braid. Then you dared look him in the eyes and you surprised a glimmer of hunger or a veil of arousal that made him seem close and fearful and desirable.

Once more, the position of women of the privileged class as female is cast in terms of an incestuous complicity. In a reversal of the common trope of incest in nineteenth-century novels in which the real taboo is miscegenation—relations between men and women of different classes or races—Castellanos figures the exclusive possession of ruling-class women by ruling-class men as a form of incest. These women's lives are claustrophobic, literally so in the case of Idolina, who lives shut up in a dark room. Their identity is mediated through men, money, and participation in a discourse that keeps them separate and prevents solidarity and recognition of commonality. One way that this is achieved is through the discourse of racial hatred and fear. The policing of racial/cultural difference structures these women's lives in ways that both confer privilege and ensure their subjugation. The struggles of Ladina women to find a satisfactory place among the claustrophobic and harrowing options of elite society at no time in the novel take the form of imagining a solidarity with nonelite women, or identifying their own pain with other forms of oppression. Isabel does not identify with Marcela's sexual abuse or with Teresa's usurped motherhood and loss because they are Other to her— "indias," female Indians. Idolina is comforted by Teresa, but does not identify her rage or desire for revolt with Teresa's because she has the possibility of assimilation into *coleto* society, while Teresa is denied recognition even of her humanity.

In the sphere of men's actions, the national conflict between the oligarchy and other Ladino participants in the Revolution is articulated by the contrast between the land reform agent, Fernando Ulloa, and the priest, Manuel Mandujano. Both act as mediators between Ladinos and Maya. The task of both is to win the allegiance of the Tzotzil people, but to opposing systems of values: the revolutionary ideas of equal rights and the traditional colonial doctrine of racial superiority. Ulloa, an outsider from the capital, is charged with representing reforms to both *coletos* and Maya. His values make the *coletos* uneasy; they attempt to suborn him by appealing to ethnic solidarity. In a conversation with Cifuentes that echoes the exchange between Isabel and Julia, Ulloa gives voice to a counterhegemonic discourse that threatens the local elite. The confrontation between the two men dramatizes the clash between the ideology of the local landowning class and the revolutionary discourse of social justice. Cifuentes defines what it means to be *patrón*:

> Y para ser patrón, según usted, basta un palmo de tierra.
>
> ¡Qué equivocado estaba Fernando Ulloa! Ser patrón implica una raza, una lengua, una historia que los coletos poseían y que los indios no eran capaces de improvisar ni de adquirir. (149)

> And to be a *patrón*, according to you, you only need a handful of land.
>
> How mistaken was Fernando Ulloa! To be a *patrón* implied a race, a language, a history that the *coletos* possessed and that the Indians were not capable of improvising or acquiring.

This ideology posits the landowning class as the sole agents of history. Cifuentes warns Ulloa that he is stirring up trouble and that the Maya peasants will be the losers, but Ulloa is secure in the belief that he is doing his job and that his system of values is just. Ulloa's father was a poor Zapatista, and his refusal to go along with Cifuentes is motivated by loyalty to his past. He realizes that the ranchers will never concede without a struggle:

> En este momento los finqueros estaban dispuestos, con tal de tener la fiesta en paz, como decían, a conceder alguna mejoría en el trato de sus peones. Pero en lo que no iban a transigir nunca era en que los indios creyeran que habían conquistado un derecho. El patrón debería ser siempre la divinidad dispensadora de favores, de beneficios gratuitos y de castigos merecidos. El ámbito de su existencia no iba a ser violado por un juicio, por una interpelación de*los inferiores. (154)

> In that moment the ranchers were disposed, just to keep the party under control, as they said, to grant some improvement in the treatment of their workers. But where they would never give an inch was in letting the Indians believe they had conquered a right. The *patrón* must always be the divine granter of favors, of gratuitous rewards and deserved punishments. The limits of his existence would not be violated by a judgment, by an interpellation from his inferiors.

The landowners are willing to make some material changes, but will never concede that they might have to recognize themselves in the eyes of those they consider their inferiors.

Ulloa meets the same ferocious resistance in town, where he teaches math in a school located in an expropriated convent. The next generation of the elite rejects and resents his liberal values, and the other teachers, to whom he is "un reproche vivo" [a living reproach] (159), call him a Communist. Fernando is dismissed from his job when a priest complains that he has said "que todos los hombres eran iguales, que los indios eran hombres, y que por lo tanto merecían gozar de los mismos privilegios y ventajas de los Ladinos" [all men were equal, that Indians were men, and therefore deserved to enjoy the same privileges and advantages as the Ladinos] (159). The community rallies to expel the threat represented by both his discourse of equality and his actions of representing that discourse to them, a reaction he does not understand.

The only person who will consent to work with Ulloa after his dismissal is César Santiago, a young man from Comitán whose father made a fortune by illegally taking over church property. Santiago plays an important role in the narrative because he represents the rising local bourgeois class that will ally with the central government in order to displace the oligarchy. His family has never been forgiven for their humble origins; wealth is not as important to the old Ladino oligarchy as name. Santiago is the social-climbing Mestizo, resentful of the oligarchy's privilege and willing to make alliance with Ulloa, the liberal technocrat who identifies with the idea of the nation, while the other students identify only with their class and their region. Santiago himself does not like or understand the indigenous people he is supposedly helping.

Another dialogue illustrates the struggle between Ladinos over hegemony, a struggle played out through the conflict with the Maya. Later, after the uprising has begun, Ulloa seeks help for the imprisoned Tzotzil women from Virgilio Tovar, Ciudad Real's best lawyer. Tovar refuses to defend the women and points out that Ulloa himself is in danger, something he does not seem to realize:

> Lea Ud. nuestra historia: sublevaciones en 1712, en 1862, en 1872. ¿Por qué no ahora? . . . Tienen miedo. Es natural, porque siempre que han intentado rebelarse lo pagaron muy caro. Por eso recurren a sus supersticiones, a sus brujerías. Como creen que sus ídolos los protegen se lanzan a matar y a destruir. ¡Se olvidan de que nuestro Dios es más fuerte y más poderoso que los de ellos! (242)

> Read our history: uprisings in 1712, in 1862, in 1872. Why not now? . . . They're afraid. That's natural because any time they've tried to rebel they've paid dearly. That's why they turn to their superstitions, their sorcery. Since

they think their idols will protect them they launch into killing and destruction. They forget that our God is stronger and more powerful than theirs are!

Note how the Ladinos share the Maya belief in a rival god; they are no different in their superstitions from the people they despise. Tovar says he will not "betray" his people, and Ulloa replies the same: "Ciudad Real es México y en México hay leyes justas y un Presidente honesto. ¡No me iré! ¡Yo tampoco traiciono a los míos!" [Ciudad Real is Mexico and in Mexico there are just laws and an honest president. I won't leave. I won't betray my kind either] (242–243).

Ulloa thus comes to identify his cause with that of the Maya peasants, and Pedro and the boy Domingo accompany him on his tour as he listens to their woes:

> *Vienen con sus quejas como van al altar de sus santos. Y es la misma salmodia,*
> *la misma letanía de abusos padecidos, de pobreza, de enfermedad, de ignorancia.*
> *La desgracia de estos hombres tiene algo de impersonal, de inhumano; tan*
> *uniformemente se repite una voz y otra y otra. (186)*

They come with their complaints as if they were going to the altar of their saints. It's the same incantation, the same litany of abuses endured, of poverty, illness, ignorance. The misfortune of these people has something impersonal, inhuman about it, so uniformly is it repeated by one voice after another after another.

Ulloa promises to help the Maya with the law, but Santiago says, "No hay más ley que la fuerza. Y la fuerza la tienen los finqueros" [The only law is that of might. And the ranchers are the ones with might] (187). Santiago urges him to lead a real revolt, but Ulloa persists in his naïve trust in the law and fails to read the situation correctly until it is too late. He is not the reader of signs posited by the tale of San Juan Fiador (from the novel's opening) who might enable the mutual comprehension that would forge a national community between indigenous and Ladino.

The only mediator between Ladino and indigenous communities tolerated by Ladino society is the priest, Manuel Mandujano. His efforts, a continuation of colonial practices, oppose those of Fernando Ulloa. He tries to make a name for himself by uniting his parish, split along class lines, in opposition to changes from outside. He rebukes Julia at her party and exhorts his parishioners to unite against Ulloa. Mandujano shares the Ladinos' complete contempt for these *indios,* and so is dismayed when the corrupt old bishop announces to him that he is being transferred to a new post in San Juan Chamula, a move he recognizes as an effort to thwart his ambitions.

Charged with representing the doctrines of the church to his new parishioners, the priest resorts to violence when he fails to communicate in any other way. The marginally bilingual sacristan, Xaw Ramírez Paciencia, is his only link to the people, but the situation is one of total mutual incomprehension. Mandujano rejects the gifts offered him and is appalled to find that Xaw has been performing marriages and that the *brujos* have been hearing confessions. He tries to teach Xaw the catechism but they do not understand each other. Mandujano does not recognize the courteous attention intended by Xaw's interjections but sees them as signs of stupidity. When he interrupts a ceremony one night he is saved from a beating only by the intervention of Pedro. Later, he will realize that by playing on ethnic fears he will be able to unite Ladinos against Maya.

The ability to speak the other community's language is of vital importance for mediators between communities. The Ladinos who do speak Tzotzil, Leonardo and Doña Mercedes, use it as a tool for exploitation. Neither Mandujano nor Ulloa, charged with bringing the Maya over to their ways of thinking, speaks Tzotzil. Both must rely on interpreters whose understanding of the ideas they are reporting is different from that of the Ladinos. When Fernando speaks of land reform to the Tzotziles, Pedro translates both the words and the ideas:

> *Fernando habló con lentitud, como si se dirigiera a un niño, escogiendo las palabras más fáciles, repitiéndolas como si la repetición las tornara comprensibles. Dijo que él era un amigo de los indios y que había venido desde muy lejos con una recomendación del Presidente de la República para que les devolvieran la propiedad de sus tierras; cuando cada uno sea dueño de su parcela es necesario que todos trabajen, que levanten buenas cosechas, que las lleven a vender a los mercados. Con el dinero que consigan, dijo, pueden vestirse mejor, pueden comprar medicinas, pueden mandar a sus hijos a la escuela.*
>
> *Los ancianos ecuchaban y de toda la peroración no sacaron en limpio más que se les estaba exigiendo que pusieran en manos de un extraño los papeles que, de generación en generación, habían atesorado y transmitido y que para ellos representaban lo más precioso.*
>
> *Winiktón hablaba convirtiendo las palabras del ingeniero en la expresión de sus propio sueño. Decía que había llegado la hora de la justicia y que el Presidente de la República había prometido venir a arrebatar a los patrones sus privilegios y a dar a los indios satisfacción por todas las ofensas recibidas, por todas las humillaciones, por todas las infamias (182–183).*

Fernando spoke slowly, as if addressing a child, choosing the easiest words, repeating them as if repetition would make them comprehensible. He said that he was a friend of the Indians and that he had come from very far away with a charge from the president of the republic that their land be returned to them; when each one was master of his own parcel it would be necessary for all to work, to raise good harvests, which they would bring to sell in the markets. With the money they would get, he said, they could dress better, they could buy medicine, they could send their children to school.

The elders listened and the only clear thing they got out of the whole speech was that they were supposed to put into the hands of a stranger the papers that, from one generation to another, they had treasured and handed down and that, for them, represented what was most precious.

Winiktón spoke, converting the words of the engineer into the expression of his own dream. He said that the hour of justice had arrived and that the president of the republic had promised to come and seize the privileges of the bosses and give satisfaction to the Indians for all the offenses they'd received, all the humiliations, all the infamy.

What Ulloa tells them is how they will be integrated into a new economic order, one in which they will own their own land, but that still means selling through Ladino-controlled markets. Pedro interprets this speech as the promise of justice signified by the president's handshake. As before, the old men of the community respond to what touches them most directly, Ulloa's request that they give him the documents proving their title to the land. He speaks to them as if to children, but they are not as naïve as he is concerning the probable fate of their papers. Xaw, acting as translator for the priest, Manuel Mandujano, also uses his ability to speak Spanish to represent an outsider's discourse to his people, but does so in order to preserve his own position. In both cases, the Ladino mediators are outsiders trying to win the allegiance of the Maya by getting them to identify with one of the two rival Ladino discourses, but in each case they must rely on indigenous translators whose understanding of their ideas and representation of them are shaped by their own positionings.

Ulloa tries to act as a mediator between communities, to represent the discourse of one to the other, with the intention of disrupting power relations. He is tempted by the idea of using power himself, but with the best of intentions:

Poder, sí, y sin remordimientos, porque no iba a satisfacer ninguna ambición turbia ni a conseguir ninguna ventaja ilícita. ¿Ah, como lo usaría? Contra las argucias de los ricos, contra la mala fe de los que ocupaban cargos desde los que se debía defender a los atropellados, a los inermes, a los desvalidos. (244)

Power, yes, and without remorse, because he wasn't going to satisfy any clouded ambition or get any illicit advantage. Oh, how would he use it? Against the sophistry of the rich, against the bad faith of those who occupied posts from which they were supposed to defend the downtrodden, the powerless, the helpless.

What Ulloa fails to recognize is that he will not get the power he needs to enforce his promises from the governor in Tuxtla, who is disturbed by Pedro's insistence that his people receive the land they have been promised. His position is analogous to that of the well-intentioned *indigenista* intellectuals and bureaucrats whose forms of intervention are inadequate to bring justice.

Pedro is partially successful at mobilizing the young men around the idea of revenge, but he does not successfully translate the discourse of social equality to his people in a way that would make it an effective counterdiscourse against the Ladino system of racial hierarchy. Catalina is the one who is able to mobilize her people as a community. Beth Miller has pointed out that Catalina acts as a Gramscian "organic intellectual," articulating new forms of understanding and acting out of her community's own values and traditions.[17]

As *ilol*, one of those in the community using indigenous magical practices and maintaining the survival of tradition, Catalina is accorded both respect and fear. Yet she is not recognized as complete: within her belief system she is a failure because she is not a mother. Her function as organic intellectual arises from her attempts to rewrite the trope of female identity from one of reproduction to one of creation.

Catalina first tries to escape the place assigned to her because of her sterility by adopting Domingo, the child of *mestizaje*. This effort to use a child as sign for maternity is a failure, however. She resents Pedro's involvement with the Ladinos and feels abandoned when Pedro socializes Domingo into male society. Without the child himself, her fiction of motherhood collapses.

She is also frustrated when she tries to listen to the men's early talk of revolt; she compares her solitude to being buried in a cave. "Voy a pudrirme aquí, en la tumba, en la cueva" [I'm going to rot here, in the tomb, in the cave] (191). From this image arises the memory of a cave she had discovered as a child, one with three stone figures. Her pain causes others to avoid her so she searches for these stones, and when she finds them, begins to prophesy greater days ahead. Her exclusion is what motivates her search for an alternative.

Catalina's formulation of a counterdiscourse is a success. The stones are recognized by the community as the old gods, and the community takes this change in religious practice to signify liberation.

> *"Los dioses antiguos han resucitado." Este era, pues, el momento que todos aguardaban. Los ancianos, con los ojos nublados de vejez, agradecían haber vivido lo suficiente para ver el fin de sus esperanzas; los hombres, en la plenitud de sus edad, acogían el maravilloso anuncio con reverencia y alegría; las mujeres, atónitas, no comprendían nada sino que la carga del sufrimiento iba a aligerarse; y los niños se movían con facilidad dentro de la atmósfera del milagro. (209)*

> "The ancient gods have revived." This was, then, the moment all had been waiting for. The elders, eyes cloudy with age, gave thanks that they had lived long enough to see the realization of their hopes; the men, in the prime of life, welcomed the marvelous news with reverence and joy; the women, astonished, only understood that their burden of suffering would be lightened; and the children moved easily through the atmosphere of miracles.

On a metaphorical level, Catalina has given birth to a discourse that can be a liberating alternative to the foreign ideas that Pedro represents. People flock to the site where there is now an altar and offerings. Everything used there must now be made by Maya and no *caxlanes* are allowed. But Julia's Guatemalan shawl is placed on one of the stones because she is not from Ciudad Real, is the wife of their ally Fernando, and has red hair. First a sign of sexual infidelity, of betrayal, the shawl is now taken as a sign of alternative allegiances.

In the passages that tell how the people flock to Catalina's cave, different voices from the community question and answer, speak in chorus, united before the new gods in their desire for an end to their suffering.

> *de todos los puntos hemos llegado. El hilo de lágrimas que sala una mejilla se une al otro hilo de lágrimas y al otro y al otro, para desembocar aquí, para anegar el llanto, para cubrir el cerro. (210)*

> from all directions we have arrived. The thread of tears that salts one cheek joins with another thread of tears and another and another to flow out here, to drown the weeping, to cover the hill.

The people traditionally go to the church to lament, but now their cries seek another form, one as yet incoherent. The gods are reborn, but they no longer speak the language of the people; at first, they have no answers. Catalina steps into a new role as translator for her people: "Lo que calla el ídolo has de decirlo tú" [That which the idol doesn't say, must be said by you] (211). Her solitude and their expectations combined seem to provoke a fit, and when she falls down and speaks, she speaks their memory and their collective desire: "En su voz vibraban los sueños de la tribu, la esperanza arrebatada a los que mueren, las reminiscencias de un pasado abolido" [In her voice vibrated the dreams of the community, the hope stolen from those who died, the memories of an abolished past] (212). The people do not yet understand what she says, but her speech is a sign that their time of adversity is at end. She is the center of events now, "el velo tras el cual los otros vislumbraban una realidad divina" [the veil through which the others could glimpse a divine reality] (214). Like Julia's shawl on the idol, which marks a connection to Ulloa's promises, Catalina signifies a new response to an ancient oppression.

Pedro acts to link these events with the growing revolt, speaking with the men while the women care for Catalina. One who resists the new discourse is Xaw. At Tzajal-hemel, now a bustling center of trade and pilgrimage, he witnesses the ceremonies that have grown up around Catalina's fits; her speech is incoherent and she still cannot put her visions into words, but she receives visitors and exercises a kind of arbitrary power. Xaw is angry because Catalina now plays the role that used to be his when, as translator to the priest, he was still the intermediary between his people and the divine; his post has been usurped (221). Xaw betrays his community by telling the priest, Manuel Mandujano, about the new cult, setting in motion a repressive response from Ciudad Real. When the church's hegemonic discourse of religion fails to keep indigenous people in their place, the Ladinos are quick to use the means of domination at their disposal: whips, guns, fire, and prison.

The use of language in this situation is once more an instrument of domination. Manuel uses his whip to take the idols from the altar, speaking as incomprehensibly as Catalina. Back in the city, the bishop ignores his warnings of an uprising, but the civil authorities see a political opportunity. Informed by Xaw, they attack the village while the Tzotzil men are absent, rob and loot and carry off the women and children to prison in Ciudad Real. Xaw's accusations and the trial are all in Spanish, and because none of the women speak it, they do not even realize what is happening. The lawyer turns the case of idolatry into political rebellion, blaming Ulloa for stirring things up; the shawl, given yet another meaning, connects Julia and Ulloa with the rebels. Manuel tries to assert the authority of the church over matters of doctrine, but the public is not interested in these distinctions; they all agree that these Indians would be too stupid to rebel on their own. The blasphemy they recognize is not the Maya's change of religious practice but, rather, their efforts to escape social and economic control.

Without a translator, Catalina finds herself in the same situation as Marcela, caught without a proper story for what is happening to her:

¿Qué relación podía existir entre su delirio, su amor desesperado por Pedro, su anhelo de maternidad burlado por Domingo, su retorno a la infancia, su hallazgo en la cueva, su exaltación como sacerdotisa, el fervor de su pueblo y estas palabras con que ahora estaban señalándola? (237)

What relation could there be between her delirium, her desperate love for Pedro, her desire for motherhood disappointed by Domingo, her return to her childhood and her find in the cave, her exaltation as priestess, the fervor of her people, and these words with which they were now marking her out?

After the trial, the women are released, but Catalina is devastated. The women still see her as their sacred intermediary, and, although she fears the pain of responsibility, the people's expectation of a sign moves her to act. After an intense process of spiritual preparation, she begins to re-create the image of the idols, first mentally and then with mud. Catalina enacts Castellanos' ideas about female creation as formulated in *Sobre cultura femenina;* here, a woman turns to creation as a means of self-affirmation, integration into the community, and transcendence when motherhood is denied her. Through her creation, Catalina can act as mother to her people: "Catalina lo volvía a tomar de la mano, como a un niño, para conducirlo" [Once again Catalina took them by the hand, as with a child, to guide them] (250). Once more, Catalina provides the means for her community to come together, to define itself differently, but reaffirming her version of their history.

The fear of a revolt performs the same unifying function in Ciudad Real. Leonardo Cifuentes has learned of the new images through a chain of betrayals. He goes to the bishop and strikes a bargain; he will not tell the ranchers about the revival of the cult, and the bishop will send the troublemaker Manuel back to Chamula. Cifuentes' goal is to provoke the rebels even further so he can crush them later. He succeeds because Manuel wants to use the situation to further his ambitions and returns to the cave with his whip. This time Catalina breaks the whip and he is killed. The bishop absolves himself of any guilt, but the people of Ciudad Real are riled up by Manuel's sister Benita, who blames the bishop for her brother's death. A mob forms in front of the bishop's palace, and Cifuentes steps in as leader, the local *caudillo*. All feel themselves to be protagonists in their regional drama. Recalling the rebellions of the past (referred to by Tovar), they think of their future glory as the men go fetch their guns and the women lay in supplies. Ethnic solidarity does not eliminate all internal divisions. They hide their possessions, but their fears are as much of the Ladino soldiers who might sack them and rape their daughters as of the Maya rebels. They also wonder if the poor Ladinos will join the uprising, but think it unlikely because they fear the Indians will attack them as well. Cifuentes exploits the wild rumors, absence of aid from the government, and general chaos in order to install himself in power. He writes up the Ordenanzas Militares, Military Regulations, which bring order around the solution: "con los indios hay que acabar" [We must finish off the Indians] (340). All members of the Ladino community are united by the crisis.

The dramatic climax of the narrative is the sacrifice of Domingo. As the citizens of Ciudad Real prepare for what they imagine is an imminent attack, the people of San Juan Chamula prepare to celebrate Easter. This is an important time for the people to renew their relationship with the sacred forces, and the human threat recedes before this necessity. Santiago wants to stir them up by using the new cult; it was he who stole Julia's shawl and with this gift made the people trust Ulloa. Pedro cannot convince his people of the imminent danger because they feel strong with magical forces. Ulloa prefers to promote calm, realizing that for the Maya to succeed they must have more than a victory; they must have an idea, something to fight for (308).

From the Tzotzil point of view, what they need is something to fight the power of the Virgen de la Caridad, who defeated them in 1712 (305). Cuaresma, or Lent, is "el vientre del año" [the womb of the year]—this image of gestation begins the episode as Catalina goes into church with Domingo, full of hate because the people have returned to church and she cannot convince them to worship only her gods. She still views her sterility as a fault and sees Domingo as her last renunciation. Domingo is to be the sacrifice, the "Indian Christ," and the means of constituting community. He symbolizes everyone's sins and misfortunes. Already marked as child of the eclipse, Domingo is further singled out when Xaw drops the holy water and its rose petals all over him. Catalina is the one who enunciates the form the sacrifice will take. "Ellos lo clavaron en una cruz y lo mataron y bebieron su sangre. Desde entonces nadie los puede vencer" [They nailed him to a cross and killed him and drank his blood. Since then nobody can vanquish them] (309). The version she gives reads the story of Christ's Passion and the story of communion literally. While transubstantiation is supposed to be literal, or "real," the literal reading of the symbolic that the Maya perform serves to construct an alternate narrative in which causality is different from the metaphorical order recognized in the Christian myth. This "superstition" is hardly different from the lawyer Tovar's insistence that the Ladinos' God was more powerful than that of the Maya.

When Domingo passes out, Catalina revives him, for his pain is necessary.

"Va a ser la víctima, pero también el testigo, de su propia ejecución" [He will be the victim, but also the witness, of his own execution] (323). The cross is raised, but in addition to the sacrifice itself a prophecy is needed "porque nada significa lo que ha sucedido si las palabras no le dan forma" [because what has happened means nothing if words do not give it form] (324). Catalina speaks, lucidly now, saying they should resist the Ladinos and that those baptized with this blood will not die. She does not simply tell them to return to worship the images of the gods, her aim when she entered the church. The form of the ritual has merged with the events and given form to the resistance of the indigenous community.

The process of integrating the personal with the communal is shown as the interplay of two kinds of reading, literal and figurative. Domingo is a literal manifestation of the metaphor of Conquest and is treated as a literalization of the symbol of Christ through his crucifixion. While he is not literally Catalina's child, he is the child of her desire. When he is interpellated into male society, she multiplies him in the form of stone gods and later the clay images. Finally, in the closing myth that retells Catalina and Domingo's story as the *ilol* and her "hijo de piedra," her stone child, these interpretive modes are collapsed into one figure, which is then put into narrative circulation for new purposes. In each case, Domingo is a figure that is supposed to forge community through "syncretism"—as literal Mestizo, and through the cultural *mestizaje* of old religion and Christian forms—but the founding acts of violence continue to engender injustice.

In her narrative of the failure of the uprising itself, Castellanos falls back on the images of purposelessness that she noted in Pineda's account. When the Maya men prepare for war, some follow Pedro or Ulloa, but they have no real leader, no plan, no supplies, and very few weapons. During the uprising, Catalina remembers Domingo's death and falls into a state of near collapse. She is still respected as an *ilol*, but is completely ineffectual as a leader. Ulloa is unable to get Pedro and the others to organize and wishes he had tried earlier; everything has gone beyond order, morality, or reason. At first the people think that they will not die, but soon they begin to fear for their lives and are afraid to attack the city because of the power of the Ladinos' Virgin. Various acts of violence are committed against those they find in their path, but the one person they encounter who is most directly responsible for their oppression, one of the landowners, is able to shoot one man and hold the rest of them off with his words. The rebels are shown as swallowed up in the impulse, without organization, attacking the wrong people.

But if the failure of uprising is attributed to a lack of effective leadership, it is finally crushed because a series of betrayals has made it possible for the

Ladinos to get the upper hand. After the Maya have been defeated, the governor reveals to the bishop that he delayed sending troops because he had received anonymous letters about how the *coletos* were trying to use the situation to block agrarian reform. The letters also make wild accusations against Leonardo Cifuentes, saying he murdered Fernando Ulloa to get Julia, whom he has sequestered. The last accusation makes us realize that these letters must have come from Idolina, as had other letters addressed to Fernando Ulloa about Julia's unfaithfulness.

The intervention of Idolina's letters underscores how the chain of betrayals passes through the women: Idolina; her *nana,* Teresa; and Julia. Earlier in the novel, when Idolina turns to Julia for a way out of her paralysis, her *nana* Teresa flees the Cifuentes house and rejoins her people, telling them she had been imprisoned in a house in Jobel (a common-enough occurrence). She joins Marcela's family and Marcela's mother speaks out against Catalina. Teresa misses the comfort of the Cifuentes house and "her child" Idolina, whom Julia has stolen from her. She wishes she could return, but is prevented by the unrest. The following version of Catalina's release from jail that is told to her by Marcela's father, Rosendo, is significant:

> *Es una ilol. Ni los mismos ladinos pudieron dominarla. Estaba en la cárcel y de repente ninguno de los guardianes pudo mantener cerradas las puertas. Y nuestra comadre Catalina y las otras mujeres que estaban presas salieron volando hasta su paraje. (254)*

> She's an *ilol.* Not even the Ladinos themselves could overcome her. She was in jail and suddenly none of the guards could keep the doors closed. And our sister Catalina and the other women who were prisoners got out and went flying off to their place.

This account, which claims power for the rebels, will be taken up in the story Teresa tells of the events at the end of the novel.

When the family goes to the cave to see Catalina's new clay images, Teresa goes with them because she fears being seen as different and accused of betrayal. Catalina is once again the divine intermediary, but now she speaks clearly. Like Xaw, Teresa does not participate in the rituals. She returns to the Cifuentes house instead. Idolina is glad to see her, but things have changed; Idolina is able to walk, leave her room, take part in the town's fevered preparations for battle. To recapture her interest, Teresa tells her about what she has seen and that the *ilol* told her that her prophecies of revenge were going to come true. Since Idolina now walks, this means that her parents will die.

Idolina and Teresa go to see Julia and boast to her about the new idols. Julia is frightened that she will lose her precarious new social position through Ulloa's involvement with the uprising and goes to Cifuentes, putting in motion the events leading to the defeat of the uprising.

Catalina, as "organic intellectual," synthesizes the paradigms available to her as a way out of the situation in which she finds herself because of her culture's definition of the female. Idolina and Julia are both alienated within a sexual discourse as well, and their actions are also attempts to be integrated into it. Idolina's poison pen letters, like the gossip of the other town women, are her attempt to intervene in the sexual and political order: she tells Fernando of Julia's infidelity and tells the governor of Leonardo's machinations. Julia's shawl signifies the system of sexual exchange into which she entered by accepting it; it is read as a sign of ethnic betrayal by both Maya and Ladinos, although each group reads it according to different values. Catalina's signifying action is different from those of Idolina and Julia in that she takes the terms of her marginalization—the equation of woman's value with her reproductive function—and turns it into a creation. This radical act of creation is both self-creation and creation of a new means of signification out of the cultural materials available to her, a "revitalization" of her community's way of reading itself into the world that makes possible their resistance. Catalina is effective in constituting the group as an agent. Julia and Idolina, on the other hand, rather than creating a new place for themselves out of their culture's resources, seek only a more satisfactory integration into the existing order. The circulation of signs, such as the shawl and the letters, has an effect, even if that effect is not motivated by the women's intentions, precisely because they work within the system in place and also work to consolidate the ethnic identity of the group. Catalina's mobilization fails in part because Pedro and Fernando fail to connect her revitalization of the syncretized Christian-Maya myth effectively with the revolutionary discourse of human equality. The isolated actions of other women, Julia, Idolina, Teresa, and Doña Mercedes, on the other hand, feed into Cifuentes' efforts to reinforce Ladino domination; Cifuentes is able to provide his community with a discursive tool that unites ethnic solidarity with pragmatic means: the Ordenanzas Militares, which are used to crush the rebels.

In the face of competing claims on allegiance, one of the forms of action most frequent in this novel is betrayal. The word *traición,* or betrayal, is used in a number of ways to characterize situations of conflicting allegiances. The political choices of allegiance or betrayal are made acutely manifest by the social drama that is the uprising: Ladinos in Ciudad Real regard Ulloa, his ideas, and the laws he attempts to enact as a betrayal of ethnic solidarity; Xaw betrays his people in order to retain his prestige as *sacristán;* Catalina betrays Domingo's trust and causes his painful death in an attempt to reconstitute her people's destiny.

Entwined with these dramas of political allegiances and betrayals are the unequal relations of power that condition forms of sexual betrayal, ranging from marital infidelity to complicity in sexual abuse: Isabel's infidelity to her first husband, Isidoro, makes her complicit in his death at the hands of Leonardo Cifuentes, poisoning her life and that of her daughter, while Cifuentes' repeated sexual betrayals are exercises of power without consequences to him. Julia is unfaithful to Ulloa with Cifuentes out of her desire for security and respectability. Doña Mercedes is a professional traitor who lures Maya women to be raped by Cifuentes and spies on the Maya; she facilitates the oppression of women sexually and of the Maya politically. Idolina's anonymous poison pen letters betray Julia to Fernando and Leonardo to the governor, linking the sexual betrayals to the outcome of rebellion through the circulation of stories.

Ulloa is the only Ladino character who seems to act from principles of justice rather than self-interest, but he still cannot tell the Maya apart from each other and consistently fails to interpret situations correctly because of his ignorance of both Maya and Ladino assumptions about their reality. Initially, he refuses to betray the Maya and their cause because he believes in justice and the law. He does betray them in the end, though, in the mistaken belief that he can trust the Ladinos. Ulloa asks for complete amnesty for the rebels, but walks into a trap; he is taken prisoner and gives details of the rebels' situation but is then lynched by the mob. Now "order" reigns.

Ulloa thinks that the rebellion fails for lack of an idea or a goal, but this is only partially true. There are ideas and goals but they are not those articulated by the agent of nationalist integration. Pedro also acts from a desire for justice and there are parallels between the roles of the two as leaders, but they fail to communicate with each other. Ultimately, Ulloa's "betrayal" of his Maya allies is a result of his cultural illiteracy. The agent of change who might intervene successfully in this polarized society will have to know and understand the history of the conflict, the motives, fears, beliefs, desires of individuals that impel them to act as they do and to give their allegiances as they do. No such agent is represented in the novel; the space for that critical understanding, with the implications for action that it conveys in the Mexican context, can occur only in the reader's negotiations with the stories in the text.

Some Maya survive, dispersed in the mountains, after the massacres. They continue to hold onto their traditions in the form of the *oficios* and forms of worship. A cave is their center of worship (caves continue to be sacred places for the Maya as they were before the Conquest), where they think they revere the divine word, the pact that was so important to Pedro; but the book they cannot read is the Ordenanzas Militares, Leonardo's directives for their genocide. The implication is that their struggle will be advanced only when they have access to and understanding of the means used to dominate them, when they can read all of the signs. Orality is the means of preservation and cultural survival, but while it alone does not provide them with the strategy for winning their struggle, it is what enables them to continue and resist, to survive, and perpetuate their memory.

To what does Castellanos attribute the failure of the revolt? On the one hand, she does represent an indigenous attempt to act and relate their own history on their own terms in a form particular to the region; the accounts of the 1712 and 1868 revolts, as well as of the "caste war" of the Yucatán, reveal the central role of syncretic religious beliefs in these rebellions. But the implication at the end of the novel is that the revolt's failure is due to lack of planning and leadership, to lack of articulation with the national situation, and to guidance by a magical belief that the crucifixion of Domingo will render them invulnerable to *caxlán* weapons. The counterdiscourse the Maya have constructed enables them to unite and rebel, and later to survive, but it is not effective as a means for liberation.[18]

Castellanos is unable at this point to delineate the forms of indigenous political consciousness, informed by liberation theology and international solidarity as well as a radical critique of *indigenismo,* that have appeared in the last few decades and that have completely recast indigenous resistance and political action in Latin America (Bonfil Batalla). But her novel is a remarkable account of ideological struggle and ironically prophetic of events three decades later. Her version of history shows the indigenous community acting from an understanding of its past and constituting itself as historical agent through its own cultural paradigms. By inviting the reader to understand the ongoing ethnic conflict in Mexico as if from the position of the oppressed, Castellanos exposes the situatedness of contending worldviews, or modes of historical consciousness and action, of the many players in this social drama. By staging for the reader the characters' choices of allegiance in terms of dramas of interpretation, and their choices of action as acts of storytelling, Castellanos' novel moves to delegitimize the interpretive norms that the reader might share with Ladino society by rendering them visible.

Survival in the face of defeat is what Teresa's tale at the end of the novel enacts as well. All of these women—Julia, Idolina, Teresa—have been defeated, as has Catalina. The novel's last narrative act occurs after the uprising has been crushed, Julia has left town, and Idolina is enclosed once more in her room. Idolina listens to the sounds of Leonardo's triumph and Isabel's new happiness and hears the voices of the dead. Their story of defeat is conjured away with another, the "mythic" version of the events that Teresa tells her to comfort her. It is the story of the rebellion, but told now as "long ago and far away." This myth is not passed on in the Maya community, or what survives of it in the mountains. It is told instead in this space of confinement by a woman who has been rejected by and has betrayed her community to another who has done the same.

The story Teresa tells, the last version of this history, is of an *ilol* of great power who had a stone child who spoke and performed miracles. The Ladinos were afraid and sent a priest to see this son. He brought the pair to Ciudad Real, where they underwent many proofs and she broke her chains. They received offerings from both Maya and *caxlanes* but grew proud and began to devour the first-born sons of families. The people sought help but the *ilol* killed the messengers. Together the *caxlanes* and Maya fought her but her magic was strong. She was finally defeated by a trick; they wrapped the stone boy in a magic shawl and both died and spread pestilence. Only one in ten survived, and the Ladinos declared that they must do penance. Now the name of the *ilol* is banned. In this story, Catalina's three forms of mothering, her adoption of Domingo, and the figurative births of the stones gods and the clay images are conflated into a literal child of stone. Maya powerlessness at the trial is reread as power by attributing a magical causality to Catalina's release, recirculating a story that was being told just after the fact. The defeat in the uprising is also reread, not as their failure or their defeat by more powerful foes but as the fault of the evil *ilol*. Survival is ensured only by propitiation of power; this tale represents a form of penance as well, a speech act that permits the precarious survival of those who have been unable to break out of dependence, as Teresa herself has not. The last two sentences of the novel underscore both the continuity of oppression and the imperative for change: "Silenciosamente volvió a su lugar. Faltaba mucho tiempo para que amaneciera" [Silently she returned to her place. It would be a long time before the dawn] (368).

There are striking parallels between the end of *Balún Canán* and the end of *Oficio de tinieblas*. In *Balún Canán* the children try to survive the curse of their family's colonial abuse through a narrative act, a story that might enable their survival, but the girl's reading lessons have taught her to equate her own survival with guilt. In *Oficio de tinieblas* the last scene of Idolina and Teresa together also figures the continued subordination of Indian women to Ladina women, the failure of women's solidarity because of racial conflict, the failures of their revolts (differently motivated but against the same oppressors): their failure to curse the oppressors. Idolina does not escape Miranda's room; Miranda cannot yet leave Próspero's house. The guilt felt by the girl in *Balún Canán* was that she survived while her brother died, but in this version of Miranda's story the guilt assigned to Idolina's acts of survival is her failure to envision any connection between herself and Teresa. But to imagine the consequences of this connection is frightening. Throughout the novel, Castellanos' denunciation of forms of social violence frames our understanding of its victims' responses. Her nerve seems to fail her when she portrays Catalina's sacrifice of Domingo and the violence of the Maya's insurrection. Perhaps she is afraid of her own rage, the rage that comes across so clearly when Teresa and Idolina say out loud what they really want, when Teresa, like Catalina, "prophesies" the destruction of the girl's family: "La ceniza dice que se va a quemar esta casa. Dice que el marido y la mujer van a morir" [The ashes say that this house will burn. They say that the husband and wife will die] (87). To acknowledge to each other their connection, the change they desire, means burning down the house.

7

"Buceando cada vez más hondo . . .": The Dangerous Memory of Women's Lives

Con una fuerza a la que no doblega ninguna coerción; con una
terquedad a la que no convence ningún alegato; con una persistencia
que no disminuye ante ningún fracaso, la mujer rompe los modelos
que la sociedad le propone y le impone para alcanzar su imagen
auténtica y consumarse—y consumirse—en ella.
Para elegirse a sí misma y preferirse por encima de lo demás se necesita
haber llegado, vital, emocional o reflexivamente a lo que Sartre llama
una situación límite. Situación límite por su intensidad, su dramatismo,
su desgarradora densidad metafísica.

Rosario Castellanos, "La mujer y su imagen" *Mujer que sabe latín* (19)

With a strength that bends to no coercion and a stubbornness that
no argument can persuade, with a persistence that does not diminish
in the face of disaster, woman breaks the models that society proposes and imposes upon her in order to achieve her authentic image
and consummate herself—and be consumed—in it.
In order to select oneself and place oneself before others one needs
to have reached vitally, emotionally, or reflectively what Sartre calls
a "limit situation"—a situation that due to its intensity, its
dramaticism, or its raw metaphysical density, is a point of
ultimate desperation.

Trans. Maureen Ahern, *A Rosario Castellanos Reader*, 243

In the prose that Rosario Castellanos published after *Oficio de tinieblas*—the
short stories of *Los convidados de agosto* (1964) and *Album de familia* (1971)
as well as hundreds of newspaper essays—she leaves the arena of explicitly
indigenista writing although she does not abandon the framework for understanding that she developed there. Castellanos acts on the advice she gave
women writers at the end of *Sobre cultura femenina* by taking up the task of

"diving ever deeper" into her own experience and self-knowledge as a woman. In her poetry, stories, and particularly in the essays anthologized in *Mujer que sabe latín,* she abandons the rhetorical defenses that characterized her earliest tentative exploration of "*cultura femenina*" in favor of speaking frankly and clearly about women's responses to models of subordination.

Chloe Furnival reads the corpus of Castellanos' short stories as acts of exposing and demystifying the powerful constructions of social inequality, such as gender and ethnic relations, that undergird Mexican society. In "Confronting Myths of Oppression," Furnival recognizes Castellanos as a pioneer in this task, reminding us that feminist ideas that look well known from our perspective after thirty years of intense feminist dialogue and debate were in their time new and courageous. Furnival also characterizes Castellanos' feminism (and her *indigenismo*) as idealistic and "liberal-reformist," defining the latter as "a stance that advocates the idea that women need to challenge the distorting stereotypes of conventional femininity, and fight for legislation and reform in order that they might take up their rightful and 'equal' places in the linear (masculine) time of project and history" (59).

To some extent this is a fair characterization, but only up to a point, as Furnival also recognizes when she acknowledges that Castellanos' "pessimism" marks the limits of her idealism. I would argue that in her feminism as in her *indigenismo* Castellanos begins by espousing liberal goals but that through her situated practice of the "dangerous memory" of women's suffering she also performs a more radical critique. In her essays, Castellanos certainly undertook the demystification project as a public duty and also advocated publicly the extension of the rights and privileges of citizenship enjoyed by at least some men to all Mexican men and women. Yet even as early as *Sobre cultura femenina,* in a text where she was seeking admission to masculinist institutions, her suspicion of those institutions' practices led her to a more radical questioning.

Although in 1950 she had written as if "women" could be assumed to be women of a certain race, class, and cultural heritage, even then Castellanos recognized the limitations and dangers of "immasculation" for women as knowers and cultural agents. We have seen how in her *indigenista* writing Castellanos does not shy away from an acute critique of assimilationist or integrationist ideals; rather, her fiction deliberately dwells on the breakdowns of that approach. To borrow the metaphor she used in *Sobre cultura femenina,* if in her search for understanding one foot rests firmly on the ground of such utopian notions as individual freedom and choice, the other foot "gravita en el vacío," is "suspended in the void," of what she recognizes as uncharted waters: the experiences (of women, of indigenous people) that historically have been excluded from the imagination of personhood.

Her *indigenista* fiction allowed her to develop further the critical strategies she tentatively postulated in *Sobre cultura femenina*. On the one hand, she is a *contrabandista;* by investigating the mechanisms of ethnic conflict in Chiapas, she smuggles herself into and occupies fully the authorizing discursive ground of the Mexican Revolution with its promises of equality, citizenship, social and economic justice in order to put forward her claims for the disenfranchised. At the same time, her performance as "resisting reader," both of colonial hierarchies and of the state's assimilationist projects, leads her to represent the Maya's culture and history of resistance as an alternative grounding for political claims in the Mexican national context, thus challenging her readers to transform their understanding and enactment of the Revolution's promises and affirming the necessity for collective forms of structural change. These challenges and affirmations take her beyond the integrationist mode of *indigenismo* from which she begins, in large part because she is determined to account honestly for failures of solidarity. The ending of *Oficio de tinieblas* implies that only when Idolina can do what Arthur Smith begins to do—recognize and feel solidarity with the suffering of those she has been taught to despise—will she be able to understand the nature of her own suffering. This has implications for Castellanos' feminism as well as for her understanding of *indigenismo*'s nationalist project.

The first story of *Los convidados de agosto* and the last story of *Album de familia* concern the difficulties of being a woman writer. They can be read as a frame for the feminist fiction of these two collections, whose stories concern women's struggle to speak, read, or write as authorities about their own experience. The two sets of stories present coherent portraits of privileged women's oppressive socialization and the range of their responses to it. The first book, still set in Chiapas' towns, dramatizes the collective dimensions of these women's suffering by staging struggles for control over their sexuality; in all four stories young women find themselves expelled from "decent society" into forms of social marginalization. The second collection is set in Mexico City and concerns women of relatively more affluence and freedom, women who have attained the security of marriage and domesticity, which saves them from that fate, yet that very domesticity becomes the object of scrutiny and critique.

The four stories in *Los convidados de agosto,* published two years after *Oficio de tinieblas,* continue to explore the same provincial world as the novels and *Ciudad Real,* but they no longer take ethnic conflict as their principal theme. *Ciudad Real* maps out systematically the forms of oppression that regulate social relations between Ladino and indigenous sectors; *Los convidados de agosto* focuses on women of the Ladino elite and the suffocating values that shape their lives so absolutely. In effect, Castellanos sets out to describe the collective dimensions of Miranda's social location and socialization. The four stories reveal this socialization to be a destructive, dehumanizing process that demands that women of the privileged class suppress their will, agency, and sexuality to maintain the power and privilege of the men of their families. The protagonists are all young women who are punished when they do not pass successfully from the father's house to a husband's control, and the stories relate their desperate attempts to conform and to resist. Yet, as in Castellanos' other fiction up to this point, none of the characters can articulate a consciousness of another possible way of being; in each case her resistance is still enacted through such conventional plots as running off with a man, or dreaming of rescue through romance (Furnival). And, as was the case at the end of *Oficio de tinieblas* and *Balún Canán,* communication or solidarity between women, which might provide an alternative ground for understanding, is virtually absent.

"Las amistades efímeras" [Fleeting Friendships] explores class difference through the relationships of two adolescent girls who choose different avenues of self-definition; the unnamed female narrator comes to her vocation as a writer while her friend Gertrudis runs off with a man and consequently falls out of the middle class. While the story is ostensibly about Gertrudis, it is also about the failure of the narrator, the aspiring writer from a family with "decent" values, to understand the life of the friend whose story she is telling and whom in the end she abandons.

As is often the case in Castellanos' fiction, the first paragraph is the seed of the story. The nameless first-person narrator appears as a self-confident storyteller looking back on her adolescence, a time when she defined herself in contrast to her best friend, Gertrudis. Gertrudis, she says, was "casi muda" [almost mute] (11) while she herself spoke incessantly, in a kind of frenzy; their one-sided interaction is suggested by the series of verbs for which she is the only subject: "hacer confidencias y proyectos . . . definir . . . interpretar" [share confidences and make projects . . . define . . . interpret] (11). She requires a (mute) interlocutor because this self-definition through words is not a dialogue; in fact, she abandons her friend when Gertrudis starts to speak for herself and offers a different interpretation of her own story.

As the story begins, the reader seems to be learning about Gertrudis through the narrator's direct observation of her, but through the course of the story we become aware of a discrepancy between two possible interpretations of Gertrudis' character and actions, a discrepancy that is manifested in spite of the narrator's pretensions of knowledge and control. At first, Gertrudis' life seems to have been traced out for her according to the conventionally satisfying plot of small-town life: marriage to her boyfriend, Oscar, who will set up a little shop. The narrator acts as their go-between, first composing verses at Gertrudis' request, later writing letters when the couple is separated because Gertrudis' father has taken her out of school and put her to work in the store that sells to the workers on his ranch. At this point, the narrative shifts from relating what the narrator might have observed directly in her friend's life to what she could know only if Gertrudis had told it to her, or if she imagined or invented it: Gertrudis' state of mind and her motives. The exclamation "¡Qué lentamente transcurre el tiempo cuando se espera!" [How slowly time passes when one is waiting!] (12), marking the point where Gertrudis has moved away from the narrator, blends the voices of the two girls because it is both the narrator's commentary and Gertrudis' state of mind.

Gertrudis' own use of words to convey her sentiments is presented as utterly impersonal and conventional; the letters Gertrudis and Oscar send to each other on their own are copied out of a book:

> *Las cartas de Oscar estaban copiadas, al pie de la letra, del* Epistolario de los enamorados, *del que ella poseía también un ejemplar. Si por un lado le proporcionaba la ventaja de poder contestarlas con exactidud, le restaba expectación ya que era capaz de preverlas.* (13)

> Oscar's letters were copied, word for word, from the *Letters for Lovers*, of which she too had a copy. If on the one hand this offered her the advantage of being able to answer them correctly, it deprived her of expectation since she was able to predict them in advance.

This boring, supremely conventional correspondence contrasts with the letters the narrator writes to Gertrudis revealing that Oscar seems to have other plans; he is going to escape this predictable small-town life by going off to Mexico City (the standard plot of young men escaping provincial tedium to make their fortune in the capital). The narrator comments on her own gossipy letters:

> *Me gustaba escribir estas cartas: ir dibujando la figura imprecisa de Oscar, la ambigüedad de su carácter, de sus sentimientos, de sus intenciones. Fue gracias a ellas—y a mi falta de auditorio—que descubrí mi vocación.* (14)

> I liked writing these letters: sketching the imprecise figure of Oscar, the ambiguity of his character, of his feelings, of his intentions. It was thanks to them—and to my lack of listeners—that I discovered my vocation.

The pleasure she takes is in the writing itself, and, one suspects also, in the excitement of meddling and possible romantic drama. These letters can be seen as a figure for the narrator's presentation of Gertrudis in the whole story; she is inventing Gertrudis as she invented Oscar, not because she makes up what happens to her friend but because she colors in the motives and the emotions that will serve her imagination.

Immediately after this revealing commentary on the pleasures of telling other people's stories, the narrative shifts even more clearly into the realm of the narrator's imagination. In her description of the tedium of Gertrudis' life, and of Gertrudis' own consciousness of it, language on the ranch is said to be reduced to "gruñidos . . . imprecaciones . . . parloteo . . . órdenes" [grunts . . . imprecations . . . chatter . . . orders] (15): the words "Oscar" and "novia," which seemed to lay out Gertrudis' life so clearly, no longer seem to have meaning to her; the convention "cada cosa en su lugar" [everything in its place] learned in her home economics classes no longer seems to apply and she feels herself "otra" [other]. This change, described as a loss of meaning, is also signified by the fact that here she can bathe completely naked:

> Porque en La Concordia se bañaba entera, con el cuerpo desnudo, no se
> restregaba los párpados con la punta de los dedos mojados en agua tibia,
> procurando no salpicarse el resto de la cara, como en Comitán. (15)

> Because at La Concordia you bathed yourself all over, with your whole body
> naked, not rubbing your eyelids with fingertips wet with warm water,
> making sure not to splash the rest of your face, as in Comitán.

On the ranch, Gertrudis is imagined fully in her body in contrast to the shame-filled denial of the body that is the rule in town. But how does the narrator know all this when, as we learn in the next paragraph, Gertrudis hardly writes her anything?

> Gertrudis me aseguraba, en sus recados escritos a lápiz sobre cualquier papel de
> envoltura, que no tenía tiempo de contestar mis cartas más extensamente. Sus
> quehaceres . . . en realidad era perezosa. (15)

> Gertrudis assured me, in the notes she wrote in pencil on any piece of
> wrapping paper, that she didn't have time to answer my letters at greater
> length. Her chores . . . actually she was lazy.

Those three dots, the lapsus, represent the narrator's movement from description to a judgment of her friend, one offered up in place of Gertrudis' own explanation (she didn't have time).

At this point, the reader is becoming aware of how the narrator uses her own imagination to fill in the gap between the conventionally romantic language of Gertrudis' love letters and the reality of Gertrudis' actions. The narrator has presented Gertrudis as passive because she listens and does not speak, but this characterization is belied by her decisive actions: she escapes the nuns to see her boyfriend, Oscar, and later escapes the tedium and emptiness of life on her father's ranch by running away with a stranger.

The ensuing story of how Gertrudis runs off with a man seems to be told in two registers: the actions are the stuff of small-town drama, but the tone and presentation of the characters is deadpan, using neither the stylized language of popular romance nor the more sophisticated novelistic conventions of high bourgeois romance: a man arrives at the store and, after an extremely laconic conversation, Gertrudis runs off with him, taking her little sister, Picha, with her almost by accident. The next day her father, the local big shot, shows up and forces them to marry even though the man is wanted by the law and will be taken to prison, leaving Gertrudis alone. There are no romantic protestations of passion when the two leave together, no gestures of fear or surprise when they are found. The conventional threat of violence in the honor story the father invokes is dissipated by the equally conventional, matter-of-fact shotgun wedding complete with ring and dowry. The effect is comic because the characters seem to know the conventions of these stories so well that they just shrug and get on with it.

But Gertrudis' attempt to escape the rigid and stifling roles expected of her as a woman in Comitán have only led her to another, equally rigid and well-known role. The father washes his hands of all responsibility for his daughter, repeating conventional wisdom: "Ya está bajo mano de hombre" [Now she's under a man's hand] (25). First Gertrudis is forced to work as a drudge for her in-laws while her husband is in jail for cutting telegraph wires (an act with political connotations). Then, when her husband gets out of jail, he abandons her for his former girlfriend and, rather than returning to Comitán, Gertrudis goes on to Mexico City, where she works as a maid. This is not an unusual story: thousands of young women from the provinces make the move to the capital—or to the United States—in a similar fashion.

In Mexico City, the narrator and her friend are reunited, but the narrator's family reacts to Gertrudis' story with shock, not with sympathy for the girl's hard lot, but with disapproval of her sexual transgression. Here the values of class and respectability come into play; the parents forbid the girls to see each other, but the friends meet secretly "como si no supiéramos que pertenecíamos a especies diferentes" [as if we didn't know that we belonged to different species] (27). The narrator has moved to Mexico City, but her family is seeking to maintain its respectability, while Gertrudis' move to the capital is equated with a "fall" from her status as ranch owner's daughter to that of maid.

There has been another change, however; Gertrudis talks more. "Nuestra conversación era agradable, equilibrada" [Our conversation was pleasant, balanced] (27). It seems that their friendship is on a more equal footing than it was in Comitán. Yet the ending of the story belies this impression. Gertrudis weeps (the first time we have seen her show strong emotion) when she finds out that her erstwhile husband has died and that she is now a widow. The narrator does not understand this reaction; after all, she says, he abandoned her and married his former girlfriend so Gertrudis is not obliged to mourn him. But Gertrudis acknowledges the reality of their affection; while the narrator holds up convention, Gertrudis affirms experience and the bond between two people: "A veces era cariñoso conmigo. ¡Necesitaría yo no tener corazón para no llorarlo!" [Sometimes he was affectionate toward me. I'd need to be heartless not to cry for him!] (28). Gertrudis does not see herself as immoral or sinful. She is still profoundly conventional in her understanding, yet she throws herself into the risks of action and feeling, and thus removes herself completely from the social class to which she belonged.

The story ends in a surprising fashion. When they arrive at the movie, the narrator suddenly tells her friend that she'll be right back, then walks out on her, never to see her again. She goes home to write, but finds that she is unable to do so. She attributes her crisis to her impression that Gertrudis lacks the capacity for "la memoria humana y la eternidad de las palabras" [human memory and the eternity of words] (29) that are so important to her; she blames Gertrudis for enjoying the movie when she's just learned of her husband's death, yet her own advice had been for Gertrudis to discount her feelings and not to mourn. The narrator's abandonment of her friend stands in ironic counterpoint to the story's epigraph, a fragment of a Nahuatl poem on the transitory nature of life and the value of friendship: "aquí sólo venimos a conocernos, sólo estamos de paso en la tierra" [here we have only come to know each other, we are only passing through on earth] (11).

The narrator projects her guilt at her own betrayal of their friendship onto Gertrudis. She seems to share the hypocritical values of her parents, who acknowledge the need for charity but are horrified by the messiness of the lives of people like Gertrudis. The story ends as it begins, with the narrator asserting a definition of herself in contrast to her best friend, but this time her arrogant certainty fails her: "Tal vez, me repetía yo con la cabeza entre las manos, tal vez sea más sencillo vivir" [Maybe, I told myself with my head in my hands, maybe it is easier to live] (29). She writes; Gertrudis lives. Gertrudis has resisted, tried to escape, has moved on while the narrator struggles with guilt. This association of guilt and writing echoes the end of *Balún Canán*, but with a crucial difference: now the adolescent narrator, unlike the little girl, is altogether too practiced at telling stories using the lessons in hypocritical social norms she has learned. Being a writer does not guarantee self-knowledge, nor is it necessarily an adequate tool for understanding another's story.

The narrator's crisis of confidence occurs because the convenient dichotomy she asserted in the beginning (her speech, Gertrudis' muteness) has broken down: her interpretation of Gertrudis' personality and actions collides with Gertrudis' own explanation of her tears. One of the ways that the reader becomes aware of this discrepancy is that our familiarity with the conventions of Gertrudis' story makes evident the contrast between the very different ways the two girls frame Gertrudis' experience. Each knows the kind of story Gertrudis is living, just as they knew by heart the letters in the *Epistolario de los enamorados;* they know what the proper actions, emotions, and speech should be for such a story. But while the narrator's competence in the conventions of bourgeois fiction allows her to tell a story about her friend, it is inadequate to represent Gertrudis' feelings or experiences and dictates their separation. The narrator's bourgeois values make her insist on Gertrudis' passivity and voicelessness even as Gertrudis acts and takes risks; and the narrator herself abandons the friend who is no longer mute, even as she blames the friend for lacking loyalty. The ambiguity of the story's ending obliges the reader to question the narrator's understanding of the story she has told; in this way, Castellanos approaches obliquely the limits of her own vision and capacity to tell.

The next story, "Vals 'Capricho'" [The Caprice Waltz], is about a young woman like Gertrudis who acts for herself and is punished for it. It is also another story of failed solidarity between women. The girl's aunts, in collaboration with the priest, try to educate her to be a proper young lady, to make her into a proper sex object. She internalizes the town's hierarchy of scorn, but her efforts to conform fail to win her acceptance or a place in Comitán's close and narrow Ladino society. The ruling class recognizes and constitutes itself through its policing of sexual and racial difference, and its women collaborate ferociously in their own oppression.

The story begins with a hint at what is at stake for each Ladina woman of the propertied class: "La palabra señorita es un título honroso . . . hasta cierta edad" [The word Miss is an honorable title . . . up to a certain age] (30). To be a *soltera,* an old maid, in this world is a horrible fate (a theme developed in Castellanos' poems "Jornada de la soltera" [Spinster's Journey] and "Kinsey report" as well as in the many portraits of spinsters in her fiction). Furnival points out that in Castellanos' writing spinsterhood is "paradigmatic for the confined status of women in general" (59), and that this story in particular shows the construction of spinsterhood as a form of social control: "The equation is made explicit in this story: the preservation of male domination in such communities implies the confinement or social death of women" (61). There are three unmarried women in the story, two spinsters and the girl they try to save from that fate. Natalia Trujillo and her sister Julia maintain a precarious respectability despite their spinster status because they serve the social pretensions of their class. Natalia gives piano lessons and considers herself an artist while Julia sets the fashion as dressmaker for the best families. The tone of the story gently mocks the elaborate rituals of Natalia's piano performances:

Era un privilegio—y una delicia—ver a Natalia acercarse al piano, abrirlo con reverencia, como si fuera la tapa de un ataúd. (30)

It was a privilege—and a delight—to see Natalia approach the piano, open it with reverence, as if it were the lid of a coffin.

The image of piano as coffin hints at her "social death" in the respectable values that confine her, while the slightly extravagant descriptive language parrots ironically the characters' clichés: "La civilización, que todo lo destruye, minó aquel prestigio" [Civilization, the destroyer of all, undermined that prestige] (31). Like the niña Nides in "Cuarta vigilia," the sisters are from the Ladino sector in decline; they are poor but cling to the signs of rank and respectability that are left to them. In fact, they live by selling those values to the class in ascendancy, the new postrevolutionary bourgeoisie.

Their scandalous brother has made his fortune but lives a decidedly unrespectable life on his ranch. Because he is a man, he does not have to respect sexual conventions, as do his sisters. He sends his daughter, Reinerie, to them to be polished and the rest of the story is a grotesque Pygmalion narrative in which the sisters succeed in "civilizing the savage" but fail utterly to win her social acceptance by any means, and in the process lose their own social safety.

One of the first things they try to do to this wild child is to rename her: they like the names Claudia and Gladys while the priest likes María. They try to get her to wear shoes, all because of their fear of gossip. When the pompous priest criticizes her behavior, the two aunts withdraw into the oratory for a secret conversation; in this scene their delightful, lively voices in dialogue are an unexpected contrast to the syrupy gentility of the narrative voice's characterization of them. In private, they speak another language, but only in private. And Reinerie is so different it is as if she speaks another language too:

Las conversaciones entre las jóvenes comitecas y la recién venida de la montería eran tan difíciles y sin sentido como las de los manuales de idiomas extranjeros. (42–43)

The conversations between the young women of Comitán and the new arrival from the highlands were as difficult and meaningless as those found in foreign-language manuals.

Reinerie is lonely, so the sisters try everything to help her fit in: the newest styles from New York, proof of her legitimacy, a dowry, her first communion, lavish displays of her father's wealth. Reinerie chooses Alicia as her new name and throws herself into her own transformation, but her social isolation continues. What makes Reinerie inadmissible to this society is that she knows about sex, and talks about it, that she responds to male advances in the streets by hauling out a pistol (42). She unmasks the social game; she is not ignorant or helpless and so they punish her for upsetting the order of things. The townspeople call her "india revestida" [dressed-up Indian] and think of her as corrupt, but it is her "civilizing" that corrupts her. She embraces the project of her transformation, even to the point of wishing her mother (an Indian) would die.

"Reinerie se declaró vencida ante el boicot" [Reinerie declared herself defeated by the boycott] (48), yet she remains rebellious. She stops going out, shuts herself in her room. Books provide no refuge, nor do her aunts' distractions—new furniture, new hats, watching the airplanes take off and land. The three women go down to the field to watch the planes, but when the pilot tries to speak to them they are like "tres estatuas de sel" [three salt statues] (52), paralyzed in a dream of flight. They are so caught up in the provincial values that dictate their social isolation that they cannot respond to the possibility of change through escape to the big city.

Junto con su sobrina, Julia y Natalia dejaron de frecuentar el templo y la abrumaban de cuidados, de mimos, para compensarla, para protegerla. Gladys, Claudia, se sentía aplastada por aquel cariño como por la losa de una tumba. María experimentaba las torturas del Purgatorio; y en cuanto a Alicia se había borrado como si nunca hubiera nacido. (55–56)

Together with their niece, Julia and Natalia stopped going to church and smothered her with doting attention, to compensate, to protect her. Gladys, Claudia felt pressed down by that affection as if by the slab of a tomb. María experienced the torments of Purgatory, and as for Alicia, she had vanished as if she had never been born.

The other names represent other people's expectations of her and their efforts to shape her identity; her own choice (Alicia) has disappeared, and her own name has been utterly rejected. Reinerie begins acting in ways that seem mad to everyone else, and one morning she disappears. That she leaves "descalza" [barefoot] signifies a return to the highlands, where going barefoot means being Indian. In Comitán, there is no way for her to be herself, no support or recognition, even from her aunts, except as negation. It is not that they do not see what she is; it is, rather, that she is a threat so great that no efforts at change or assimilation, no amount of money will buy her acceptance. In the end, the social body expels her as a threat to its order because her origins are impure (her mother is Indian), because she knows too much (about sex), and because she acts for herself. The story displays the terrible frustration of women who do everything to conform only to find that it will never be enough because the price of acceptance is the renunciation of all autonomy, all capacity for action, all claims to being a person. In this world female subjectivity is dangerous when it knows itself, and this danger or fear is of the same order as the fear of an Indian uprising, which we saw so carefully delineated in *Ciudad Real*. It is one thing to imagine the Mestizo as the figure of Mexican national identity, and another for a Mestiza to be recognized and treated as an equal.

The third story, "Los convidados de agosto," is another exemplary tale of a woman's desperate attempt to live within the prescribed social norms for women of her class, only to find that any desire, any half-conscious urge for autonomy will be met with extreme forms of social violence. The spinster Emelina does not manage to do what Gertrudis or even Reinerie was able to do—leave the house of her confinement. The story's epigraph, verses by Lope de Vega, sums up the honor code that is played out here: "Blanca me era yo cuando fui a la siega / dióme el sol y ya soy morena" [White was I when I went to the harvest /I was struck by the sun and now I'm dark] (57). The sun's natural action and a woman's venture out of the house are coded so as to equate sexual dishonor with a fall from racial privilege.

The action takes place on a festival day in Comitán, a day of carnival when a degree of escape from order and prohibitions is allowed, as signaled by the musical frenzy in the streets. Everyone laughs, but the different degrees of freedom for men and women are demonstrated by men's freedom to give open expression to their pleasure while women hide their laughter behind their shawls. All women wear these shawls, but their different social status is marked by the different kinds of cloth.

The protagonist Emelina is a spinster whose dreams become a nightmare, as underscored by a series of emblematic images such as the "campanada fúnebre" [funereal tolling] (59) of church bells that wake her up from a dream of being alone with a man. Emelina is socially confined not just because she is a woman, but by the particular conditions of her class position. She has power over others: she can be served in bed by a maid, and has been raised

183

to recognize the difference between "indizuela" [a little Indian girl] and "se-ñorita decente" [a decent young lady]. But there is nothing for her to do and she is afraid of coming to resemble her unmarried sister, Ester, who is bitter about working for the enemy (the revolutionary government) and jealous of Emelina's "pequeños placeres" [little pleasures] (72); she mocks Emelina's desire to go to the fair at age thirty-five.

Emelina is very conscious of the examples of women who have been "lost," who have been with men without being married. She shares the general cen-sure of these women; her fear of hardship and ostracism is a powerful bar-rier. But Emelina still takes pleasure in her body, her senses. In her bath she abandons herself "al peligro y al placer" [to danger and pleasure] (78), the danger being that she might drown if she doesn't watch out. Emelina has not given up yet; she is still waiting "al margen" [on the edge] (67) for her chance to live the romance that she knows only through her mother's stories of ser-enades and suitors. And if she does not take a chance, she'll be like the ca-nary, afraid to leave the cage when the door is opened (69).

Her daydreams take on more focus; every year the big thrill of the festival comes when the makeshift stands for the bullfights collapse, a moment when all can permit themselves some collective license. The carnival gives her a chance to put a face on her vague dream, linking it to an older dream about her brother's friend Enrique, who never was quite a suitor (80).

The town's nickname for Emelina and her friend Concha, "las dos de la tarde" [two in the afternoon], mocks their spinsterhood. They pass up the games and lower-class flirtations and go straight for the bullfights. The bull-fighting scenes are, not unexpectedly, all about Emelina's sexual desires. The first bull is afraid, tries to avoid its fate by jumping out of the ring, as she'll try to do later. She has come for that moment when the stands collapse, as they do every year, and disorder—contact between strangers—is permissible. Only by positioning herself as a victim is she permitted sexuality outside the house. When the ring collapses and Emelina faints, she is revived by a stranger who gives her brandy; this encounter is her dream made reality. She goes with him to an open-air bar, at first without thinking but then in open defi-ance of convention. She knows she's defying the norms by talking compul-sively with a stranger and drinking in public with him. When her brother Mateo and Enrique arrive and take her away by force, she tries to resist both the hands of the crowd that bear her away and her own nausea. To Enrique's insults, she protests: "No me iba a hacer nada malo. Sólo me iba a enseñar la vida" [He wasn't going to do anything bad to me. He was only going to show me life] (95). The story ends with Emelina giving voice to her pain, shame, and rage in a wordless howl, while Enrique enters a brothel.

In these three stories women are made outcasts when they act out of their sexuality, giving form to an inner sense of selfhood even as they try to conform to what others expect of them. Gertrudis jumps without hesitation into the role of "fallen woman" because the alternative is so bleak, but she does not find romantic love, or escape poverty and hardship. Reinerie is the wild child everyone tries to rename, to reshape, to break, and by the end she is broken, but not broken in. Emelina tries to do what Gertrudis did, to take a chance at some kind of freedom, as pitiful as it might be, because her house is a prison and her life a form of social death. Yet not one of these women sees her life from a perspective outside the powerful norms that punish them for having bodies, desires, for wanting to be persons to even the most minimal degree.

The unconscious acts of resistance that Castellanos presents here take the form of visceral reactions, healthy reactions to a sick society, but ones that are punished with extreme cruelty. In her earlier fiction Castellanos gives examples of an alternative, indigenous historical consciousness that makes possible collective resistance and rebellions, but in these stories none of the women are able to see their own experience or reactions as valid, as potentially normative, that is, as an alternative to the norms with which they are bombarded from every side. There are no other examples of speech or action that might authorize their attempts to act out another way to be. None has available a language that would make it possible for her to see herself as other than marginal or deviant.

The stories give voice to a crescendo of inarticulate rage and pain, unmitigated by any shared recognition with others. Gertrudis is almost mute, and when she does speak for herself she is rejected by the (articulate) narrator; Reinerie retreats into another language that to her aunts signifies only madness; Emelina howls like an animal, a madwoman.

The last and longest story, "El viudo Román" [The Widower Román], deliberately rejects the idea that marriage might provide a defense against this fate; these women's voicelessness is not only the result of their marginal social position as unmarried women. In this story the main female character is not poor or marginal in any way. She's a popular and beautiful young woman from the best family who marries the most eligible man in town and is socially destroyed by him.

"El viudo Román" reworks the themes of a Golden Age honor drama, a genre obsessively concerned with the power of speech and the containment of women's agency, through some of the conventions of gothic mystery. This is most evident in the dénouement where Don Carlos Román returns his bride, Romelia, to her family the day after their wedding, asserting that she is not a virgin, and the family chooses to believe him despite Romelia's offer to show the bloodstained sheets as proof. The word of the "man of honor" and a property owner counts; the word of a woman does not.

Through the play of narrative voice and point of view in this story, Castellanos shows how this double standard of authorizing speech acts is enacted. As in "Las amistades efímeras," at a certain point in the story the reader realizes that her understanding of events and motivations has been as limited and mistaken as that displayed by the gossip of the characters. Midway through the story we are obliged to reevaluate our interpretations, to reread the story, as we become aware of Castellanos' skillful manipulation. While in the beginning of the story the reader is led to believe that Don Carlos is an honorable man emerging from a decade of mourning after the death of his first wife, Estela, by the end we have discovered that he is a man obsessed, whose machinations culminate in a monstrous revenge on the Orantes family and the social death of Romelia.

Eleven years earlier, on the night of his wedding to Estela, an anonymous person sent Don Carlos a packet of letters from Estela to an unidentified lover, letters revealing that she had agreed to marry Don Carlos, whom she despises, only in order to continue seeing her lover. She falls ill and dies mysteriously; a few days later, Rafael Orantes (the brother of Don Carlos' second bride, Romelia) dies in what is said to be either suicide or a hunting accident. Part of Don Carlos' elaborate plot, culminating in the marriage and public repudiation of Rafael's younger sister Romelia, involves obtaining textual proof that Rafael was Estela's lover—proof in the form of a note from Rafael that Romelia carries in her locket and that contains the same words used by the person who sent Don Carlos Estela's letters. When justifying his actions to the priest, Don Carlos insists that he has proof, that he knows it was Rafael, but in the end, "proof" and "knowing the truth" are shown to matter only insofar as they can seem to uphold Don Carlos' obsession and provide the means for his vengeance. Certainly Romelia is the victim of both Don Carlos and of her family in their collusion to maintain the fictions of masculine "honor."

The reader, like Don Carlos, tries to solve a mystery: Did Rafael kill himself or was he murdered? Was he Estela's lover? Did he or someone else send Don Carlos those incriminating letters? But, like the priest, we have relied on Don Carlos' narratives for our information. The priest realizes too late that he has been manipulated into participating in Romelia's degradation, and the reader is positioned so as to understand how Don Carlos has grounded the authority of his story in social privilege rather than the values of honor and integrity that he invokes (and her family upholds) to legitimize his cruelty.

The story is a graphic illustration of the ways in which privileged women have to play by certain rules or suffer a disgrace that condemns them to a life as outcasts while men do not. Even honorable marriage and obedience do not make a woman safe from the kind of punishment we've seen meted out to other women in these stories. The story's ending shows that a woman's word means nothing, that a man's lie means more. As was so consistently demonstrated in Castellanos' *indigenista* fiction, the grounds that authorize a given speech act, despite appeals to truth, science, or justice, are in fact socially constructed positions of power and hierarchy.

While Castellanos portrays many forms of oppression and brutality toward women in her fiction, it is striking that Don Carlos is perhaps the only male character who seems to act out of sheer woman-hating. Because of his social position as doctor and property owner, Don Carlos is able to act with complete impunity. He is able to manipulate the very values that subordinate women to destroy more women. The class basis of the honor plot is laid out in the first scenes of the story, where Don Carlos asks his housekeeper, Doña Cástula, why she does not harbor resentment against the man who wronged and abandoned her in her youth. She reacts with incomprehension; out loud she answers that she is a woman and vengeance is men's business, repeating the conventional script of the honor drama. What she does not say aloud is the irrelevance of that script for her life; as a poor woman who has to work every waking minute, she does not have the time or the energy to give to such nonsense. The story's epigraph is a phrase of Sartre's: "El pasado es lujo de propietario" [The past is a luxury of property owners]. This baroque story of obsession, of revenge plotted over years, and the particular form it takes of dishonoring an entire family, is possible only within the discourse and values of Comitán's elite social class.

In fact, Doña Cástula's story is another version of what happened to Gertrudis, and is marked by the same matter-of-fact attitude; a young Ladina girl runs off with a man, is "ruined" and abandoned, but survives and makes her way in the world. Doña Cástula is Gertrudis in the provinces twenty years later. Upper-class Ladina women like Emelina, Romelia, and her sisters may not have to work, but outside of marriage they are condemned to lives of enforced enclosure, celibacy, and bitterness. Working-class women (or women whose unsanctioned sexual activity removes them from the privileged class) like Doña Cástula and Gertrudis do not reject the norms of the conventional scripts, but they do get to have some form of sexual life.

The first paragraph describes three objects in Don Carlos' place of seclusion, his study, whose emblematic significance is apparent only toward the end of the story:

> *un título borroso dentro de un marco, un juramento de Hipócrates ya ilegible y una reproducción en escala menor, de ese célebre cuadro en que un médico—de*

bata y gorros blancos—forcejea con un esqueleto para disputarle la posesión de
un cuerpo de mujer desnudo, joven, y sin ningún estigma de enfermedad. (96)

a faded diploma in a frame, a Hippocratic oath, now illegible, and a scaled-
down reproduction of that famous picture in which a doctor—in white coat
and cap—wrestles with a skeleton for possession of a woman who is young,
naked, and has no visible sign of illness.

The medical diploma that confers such status on Don Carlos is as meaningless as the illegible oath; he has abandoned his practice, is indifferent to suffering, and may even have killed his first wife. The allegorical struggle of
Medicine and Death is already sexualized by the patient's representation as a
naked, apparently healthy young woman; what is in fact at stake for Don Carlos is assertion of his rights as *propietario:* possession of Estela after her death,
and a possession that is deathlike for Romelia. The obsessive center for both
women's stories, as Don Carlos narrates them to the priest, is the ritual of
wedding-night consummation, and the social law that entitles the husband
to the complete and utter social and sexual possession of his wife.

The male property owner's possessions confer status only through public
recognition, but that also renders him vulnerable. Gossip as a form of knowledge and social control organizes much of the action in the story. The third-
person narration reports the thoughts of the characters almost as a form of
gossip. We learn through Doña Cástula's thoughts, for example, that after
Estela's death, Don Carlos "no volvió a frecuentar a nadie" [no longer associated with anybody] (103), but also that if he no longer practiced medicine,
he was very involved in his ranch and knew everything that went on on his
property, primarily through the gossip she reports back from the marketplace. Clearly "nadie" here means nobody of his social class. But we are invited to believe (because that is the popular explanation) that his grief is the
reason for his withdrawal from "society." A first inkling that something is
not quite right, that this publicly accepted story is wrong, comes when Don
Carlos himself reflects on the reasons for his isolation:

La proximidad de los demás despertaba en él una alarma que ningún razona-
miento podía reducir. Temía su compasión tanto como su indiferencia. Lo
asqueaba ese guiño cómplice con que los hombres querían hacerle saber que
estaban en el secreto de la mañas que se daba para sobrellevar su condición de
solitario. Porque no era concebible que alguien, como don Carlos, en la plenitud
de la edad y de la fuerza viril, guardase una continencia a la que ni aún los
sacerdotes, tascando el freno de una religión de que él carecía, eran siempre
fieles. Le irritaba esa inoportuna solicitud de las matronas que se desvivían por

*poner fin a la irregularidad de su situación proporcionándole lo que la natura-
leza pide y la ley de Dios manda: una compañera. Sí, esa araña, inmóvil en el
centro de la tela, esa hija, esa sobrina, esa recogida, que reunía en su persona
todas las virtudes y se embellecía de todos los adornos y cuya única misión en el
mundo consistía en hacer feliz a don Carlos, acogedora su casa y numerosa su
prole. (110)*

The proximity of others awakened an alarm in him that no reason could
calm. He feared their compassion as much as their indifference. He was
disgusted by the complicitous wink with which other men wanted to let him
know that they were in on the secret of the ways he contrived to endure his
bachelor condition. Because it was inconceivable that someone like Don
Carlos, in the prime of life and virile energy, should keep to a celibacy that
even priests, reined in by a religion that he lacked, were unable to maintain.
He was irritated by the importunate solicitude of the matrons who were
dying to put an end to the irregularity of his situation by supplying him
with what Nature asked and God's law demanded: a female companion. Yes,
that spider, immobile in the center of her web, that daughter, that niece,
that poor relation, who united in her person every virtue, was adorned with
every beauty, whose only mission in life would be to make Don Carlos
happy, his house welcoming, his offspring numerous.

Don Carlos' experiences of disgust with his own sexuality and his fear of women
are here shown as the obverse of his status, a response to gossip and public
scrutiny of his sexual life.

When Don Carlos emerges from his social isolation, having maneuvered
the priest into arranging this marriage with Romelia, it is ostensibly to fulfill
the community's expectations. But the reader learns, when Don Carlos explains his actions to the horrified priest, that he really wanted to get his hands
on Romelia's locket and take revenge on her family. And apart from revenge
he is motivated just as much by the need to destroy something in her that he
describes the first time he mentions her to the priest:

*Yo la vi una vez. Y me dio la impresión de un ser tan ávido de vivir . . . Pero no
con esa avidez que envilece, no, sino con esa otra que exalta. Lo que le sale a la
cara no es hambre, es necesidad de plenitud. (142)*

I saw her once. And she gave me the impression of a creature avid to
live . . . but not with that avidity that coarsens, no, rather with that other
kind that ennobles. What her face reveals is not hunger but a need for
fulfillment.

As in a fairy tale, Romelia is the youngest and most beautiful of three daughters. Her marriage represents the pinnacle of social success and is supposed to be the realization of every woman's dream, but the account of their utterly impersonal courtship and supremely theatrical wedding makes clear what a farce the whole marriage is; the formulae are devoid of the sentiments they rehearse. Indeed, Don Carlos' image of a wife as a spider is not far off from Romelia's fantasies of her marriage as a series of dutiful postures designed to manipulate her husband. Yet she is almost entirely ignorant and powerless in the entire matter of her marriage, and he punishes her for doing exactly what is expected of her. Romelia may be a foolish young girl who channels her desire for fulfillment into the conventional and distorted plots available to her, but by the end of the story she has joined the ranks of outcast women.

None of the female characters whose suffering is represented and explained to the reader in *Los convidados de agosto* can name her own suffering. It is Castellanos who performs that act by putting the "dangerous memory" of women's suffering into words. But in her essays she did write about women who succeeded where her characters failed:

> *Cada una a su manera y en sus circunstancias niega lo convencional, hace estremecerse los cimientos de lo establecido, para de cabeza las jerarquías y logra la realización de lo auténtico.*
>
> *La hazaña de convertirse en lo que se es (hazaña de privilegiados sea el que sea su sexo y sus condiciones) exige no únicamente el descubrimiento de los rasgos esenciales bajo el acicate de la pasión, de la insatisfacción o del hastío sino sobre todo el rechazo de esas falsas imágenes que los falsos espejos ofrecen a la mujer en las cerradas galerías donde su vida transcurre.* ("La mujer y su imagen," Mujer que sabe latín, 20)

> Each one in her own manner and circumstances rejects convention, shakes up the foundations of established custom, turns hierarchies on their head, and is able to realize authenticity.
>
> The feat of *converting one's self into what one is* (a feat reserved for the privileged few of whatever sex or condition) demands not only the discovery of one's essential traits spurred on by passion, dissatisfaction, or boredom, but above all the rejection of those false images that false mirrors offer women within the closed galleries where they lead their lives.

As in all her books of fiction, characters struggle with their situations from different states of awareness. Some struggle merely to survive (Modesta Gómez, the Bolom men) or use others to satisfy their needs or ambitions (Héctor, Enrique, Manuel Mandujano). Others try to flee (Gertrudis, Reinerie) or to break out of unsatisfactory lives (Evelina, Matilde). Some try to name both their suffering and their struggle with the words and paradigms available to them, coming to a degree of consciousness of their roles as agents of change (Felipe, Pedro, Catalina, Ulloa, the three outsiders in *Ciudad Real*). But whereas we see some characters attempt a political analysis of the racism and injustice of their situation in Chiapas, we do not see, either in the novels or in the first two collections of stories, female characters who attempt an analysis of their circumstances based on gender. Individual women often resist without thinking, even if only by attempting suicide or by going mad; they try to escape their suffering, to make changes in their lives. But in each case those few women who do not act in complicity with the systems of male domination and the ideology of racial superiority are frustrated or severely punished.

In the collection *Album de familia* Castellanos gives us for the first time female characters in the situation of "toma de conciencia" [consciousness raising/coming to consciousness], characters who move toward the capacity for self-analysis that informs her own poetry and fiction. In her essay "Satisfacción no pedida" [Unsought Satisfaction] (*El uso de la palabra*, 227–231) Castellanos performs her own reading of *Album de familia* just after its publication, distancing herself from the *indigenista* label and placing women at the center of her writing (see Chapter 3). She emphasizes the shift in setting from Chiapas to Mexico City, the focus on middle-class women's lives, and the issue of consciousness and action that she deals with here in a new way. In contrast with the dramas of *Los convidados de agosto*, the moments of consciousness in these stories do not arise from "momentos privilegiados" [privileged moments] (230), she claims; rather, they are moments of "nada pura" [pure nothing], trivial moments such as choosing a menu, a Sunday gathering with friends, a day in the life of a widowed granny. And the last and longest story speaks directly of the dilemmas facing professional women writers in Latin America.

Where unmarried women were the subject of *Los convidados de agosto*, *Album de familia* concerns women in three stages of marriage: in "Lección de cocina" [Cooking Lesson], the narrator is a bride about to cook her first meal for her husband; Edith, the protagonist of "Domingo" [Sunday], is a well-established married woman with children and a lover; and "Cabecita blanca" [White-haired Granny] is about a widowed grandmother. The chronological progression of stages in married life represented in these stories corresponds to an inverse movement in stages of consciousness regarding the roles each woman is called on to play: the first story takes us through a woman's moment of coming to a new consciousness, a moment of lucidity about her situation, leaving her poised on the threshold of choice as to how she will live her marriage; Edith is unsatisfied with the shell of her seemingly happy

191

married life, but has made her accommodations within it; Señora Justina lives out a stereotyped ideal of motherhood, ignorant of the extent to which this ideal is hollow and of just how unhappy her children are. Castellanos says of her, "Habita esa especie de limbo que constituye el ideal que persigue la educación femenina en nuestros días" [She inhabits that kind of limbo that constitutes the ideal pursued by feminine education in our time] ("Satisfacción no pedida," 231). The title story moves us out of the domestic sphere and into the lives of women who write, returning us to the image of the adolescent writer at the end of "Las amistades efímeras," and to the problems of solidarity among women.

One of the textual strategies Castellanos develops in these stories involves what Magdalena Maíz has called the use of "el paisaje doméstico" [the domestic landscape] as an instrument of self-knowledge and transformation (64). The book opens with "Lección de cocina," whose title recalls at least two of Castellanos' poems, "Lección de cosas" [Lesson in Things] and "Economía doméstica" [Home Economics], poems in which a woman's controlled evocation of the norms of domestic femininity by which she has governed her life barely masks her anger and pain over their cost. But the story could also have taken the title of the poem "Meditación en el umbral" [Meditation on the Threshold] because the narrator is poised on what she recognizes as the threshold of her life. In this story, for the first time, the flashes of ironic and corrosive humor that surfaced occasionally in Castellanos' earlier fiction and that are given free rein in her later poetry, her essays, and *El eterno femenino* become the dominant mode.

The cooking lesson is also a reading lesson; the narrator is trying to learn to read a recipe, to be the kind of wife her husband and society expect her to be, but she is a resisting reader as well.[1] At first the narrator mockingly attributes her resistance to her domestic "incompetence" but by the end of the story she has achieved a state of lucidity that enables her to read deliberately from an alternative position she defines for herself.

The story plays off the counterpoint between the bride's activities in the kitchen, cooking a piece of meat, and her reflections on her new marriage; her attention moves back and forth between the piece of meat as it is transformed from a frozen, unrecognizable package to a charred, ruined lump that must be thrown in the garbage, and her own transformations in the passage from educated spinster to "happy" housewife. From the outset, the narrator observes herself observing, comments on her own process of reading or interpretation. She is aware that choosing interpretative modes also entails choosing a place; in the first sentence she both announces her contemplation of the blinding whiteness of the never-before-used kitchen and selects from an array of available cultural associations the ones that make her most comfortable for the moment: the whiteness should be contemplated, described, evoked, she says, according to its associations with cleanliness and virginity (as opposed to use, marriage, sex) rather than its other, more repellent, associations with hospitals, illness, and death. This is because, she declares, "mi lugar está aquí" [my place is here] (7). From her many literary allusions, quotations in other languages, and use of erudite rhetorical terms, we know that the narrator is a clever, highly educated woman, but she has the wrong kind of education for her new post; all of her training in reading will not serve her here. Instead, recognizing that she must learn new lessons from history and society, she invokes the "espíritus protectores" [protector spirits] of the cookbooks; her new teachers will be the voices of the housewife and tradition, the Angel of the Hearth. Yet she is angry at the idea that, because she is a woman, she is supposed to know already how to be the ideal reader for this text, to know the rules: "Parten del supuesto de que todos estamos en el ajo y se limitan a enunciar" [They start with the assumption that we're all in the know, and simply make pronouncements] (7). Because she does not know what she is supposed to know, she feels as if she is in the kitchen under false pretenses; the danger is that her husband will find out that she is not a "proper woman."

The marriage has begun a process of change: "en el contacto o colisión con él he sufrido una metamorfosis profunda: no sabía y sé, no sentía y siento, no era y soy" [in contact or collision with him, I've suffered a profound metamorphosis: I did not know and now I do, I did not feel and now I do, I was not and now I am] (12). Socially, her previous existence as a spinster was defined as waiting in the wings for her entrance into real life as a woman—that is, as a married woman—and her sense of self is also being transformed by the relation with the other, by sexuality, by the new expectations that confront her.

But much of what she feels is anger. What she cooks up instead of dinner is a series of reflections that first recall earlier experiences of fear, loneliness, and anxiety about her place as a woman (feelings that marriage is supposed to replace with security and competence), and then she subjects those memories to an analysis that gives them a new meaning. For example, her description of the meat's redness—"como si estuviera a punto de sangrar" [as if it were about to bleed]—serves as transition to her memory of the sunburn she got on her honeymoon; this leads her to think about her place during lovemaking (on the bottom whether it hurts or not) and then moves her through a series of increasingly negative associations—self-sacrifice, the tortures of Cuauhtémoc—that she finally rejects angrily as "Mitos, mitos." [Myths, myths.] (9).

Now, in the kitchen, her anger connects with her honeymoon memories and allows her to understand them differently: her wedding night insomnia and the sensation that something is wrong become an affirmation of selfhood and consciousness in the face of her husband's indifference: "Yo también soy una conciencia" [I too am a consciousness] (10). And the moment in the hotel lobby when she was being paged under her new married name and absolutely failed to recognize that she was being publicly identified as (someone's) wife is now connected to the failure of the cookbooks to interpellate her effectively.

Like the female characters in the other stories, the bride narrator knows all about the conventions of femininity, but unlike them she questions them directly. She contrasts her interpretations (her feelings) with the conventional ones that she assumes her husband will share, making a sarcastic mental list of all the things she is supposed to thank her husband for, but then turning the question back on him: What should he thank her for? Only her virginity, which means completely different things to both of them. She's embarrassed that she's not spontaneous, sporty, knowledgeable about sex, that she freezes up in a "gesto estatuario" [statuary gesture] that he can read as "hieratismo" [hieratism] or "pasividad" [passivity] but that he cannot read properly as fear and ignorance. She resents the experience with sex permitted to him as a man, while the very virginity he prizes so highly has been for her a source of inadequacy. His sexual experience is compared to a stone covering her (his body), inscribed with the dates and names of all the other women he has slept with; she is one of many, and would like to assert her own name, yet her identity is supposed to depend on his, be derived through him: "Soy yo. Pero, ¿quién soy yo? Tu esposa, claro" [I am myself. But who am I? Your wife, of course] (14).

Nothing in literature or in popular culture has prepared her for sexual intimacy or for these confused feelings. In this sense, she *has* learned to read "as a woman," at least enough to know what the myths are, but not enough to live out the surface text and suppress her consciousness of the gap between romance and reality. The dawn scene in *Romeo and Juliet* is the only kind of story about sex she has been allowed to read so far, so she does not know how to act when they wake up in bed together. The only name she has for sexual pleasure is "transportes como se les llaman en Las mil y una noches" [transports, as they are called in The Thousand and One Nights] (16). She knows there is supposed to be some pleasure for her, too, but sexual experience is shrouded in euphemism; these are stories she, as a woman, is not supposed to know how to read.

In a rapid counterpoint between the meat browning, cooking, shrinking, burning, she imagines possible future roles and identities for herself—in one scenario she sees herself as a sophisticated career woman, meeting a man who wants to have an affair. But even as she tries to imagine the dialogue of seduction, she begins to edit her own romance; she cannot just give herself up to this kind of stereotypical fantasy without being critical. The whole fantasy ends with her divorce, and the meat is burned because she has been so absorbed in her thoughts. Her exasperated exclamation recognizes that no one taught her to be a proper piece of meat: "A esta carne no le enseñó su mamá que era carne" [This piece of meat's mother never taught it that it was meat] (18).

Now she is faced with choices about what to do, how to select the menu for her life. She can throw the meat (her old self) away, pretend it never existed, and go out to dinner, looking frivolous but not "tarada" [crazy]. Or she can let her husband see the burned meat, the "mujer inútil" [useless woman] (19) that he will imagine her to be, allow herself to be chided indulgently while she protests that she was watching all the time! The transformation of the meat got out of hand; she didn't stop it in time, and the danger is that it will disappear altogether, like her self. At this point, our narrator exercises her intellectual training ("Recapitulemos" [Let us recapitulate], 20) and moves through a very logical exercise in ontology (what is the nature of the meat's existence through its stages of transformation?), concluding that the meat still exists in her "conciencia," her consciousness. She recognizes that this is a key moment, that it is up to her to choose her path, hypocrite or ditzy dame, but in either case, she recognizes that the marriage will be played out as a kind of struggle of wills in disguise. She rejects both options as inauthentic. Should she step into the "lugar común" [the common place, the commonplace], accept her place as a certain kind of female reader, the place reserved for her in the stories she knows even before she is called on to play her part in them? If she asserts her own version of what happened she knows he'll be suspicious and uncomfortable. She does not expect him to want to read the recipe from her position.

The end of the story does not tell us what the narrator chooses. She protests that she expected to make sacrifices in the Grand Moments, not in such trivial acts (what Castellanos called "nada pura" [pure nothingness] in her essay "La mujer y su imagen"). The last words are "Y sin embargo . . . " [And yet . . .], the same phrase used in *Sobre cultura femenina* to open up a space of protest, where the ellipsis stands for the powerful yearning named in the poem "Meditación en el umbral": "Debe haber otro modo de ser."

In marked contrast to the high dramas of sexual frustration and repression recounted in Castellanos' earlier tales of provincial women's lives, the next story, "Domingo," presents a Mexican bourgeoisie whose city sophistication can accommodate homosexuality and infidelity for women as well as for men. The protagonist Edith has tremendous possibilities for pleasure and satisfaction by comparison with the provincial women in Ciudad Real, but this is still a man's world. The story parallels "Lección de cocina" in that it shows a woman reflecting on the need to make a vital choice in a moment of domestic routine, but the ending suggests that the character will choose both continued dependence and an evasion of consciousness.

When the story begins, Edith reflects on why she is dissatisfied with her life. Unlike the bride in "Lección de cocina," she has mastered her cooking lessons, but she also recognizes that her marriage is a performance from which she has to steal moments when she can be herself. Poised on the verge of a realization and a decision, she observes her friends at her weekly Sunday party as they make sophisticated conversation and play at being tolerant and bohemian. But although she recognizes their unhappiness, she also seems to share the barely concealed misogyny and bourgeois class prejudices they express; when one friend, Vicente, insults his lover on the phone because she has had an abortion, Edith reminds him that he never would have forgiven her if she had not done it, yet she also shares his contempt for his many girlfriends.

Castellanos is able to convey the limits of Edith's awareness, and the connection between those limits and her material circumstances. Her life with Carlos may be an unsatisfying series of stereotypical gestures, but she lacks the nerve to act, knowing she will probably lose her children, and the money, security, and social position she enjoys as a married woman. For all her intelligence, her education, her privileges, being a wife is her job: "Nunca he pretendido ser más que una burguesa. Una pequeña, pequeñita burguesa. ¡Y hasta eso cuesta un trabajo!" [I never aspired to be more than a bourgeoise, a modest, petty bourgeoise. But even that is hard work!] (45). She also acknowledges that all the labor of wifely performance is not enough for her to retain that social position; she cannot be a middle-class wife without a husband (44). Edith's life represents one of the possible paths for the narrator of "Lección de cocina." She has some awareness of her own disappointments, but chooses the safety of hypocrisy, of compartmentalizing her self.

In "Satisfacción no pedida," Castellanos qualifies Edith as "perezosa, frívola . . . " [lazy, frivolous] (231), observing that if her painting were to become demanding, she would abandon it: "Y la figura amorfa de su cuadro inconcluso será ella misma" [And the amorphous figure in her painting would be herself] (231).

The third story in the collection is another of Castellanos' savage portraits of motherhood, an indictment of both gender prescriptions and women's accommodation to them. The title "Cabecita blanca" refers to the role to which the Mexican wife and mother is supposed to aspire, the position of respect achieved after having fulfilled one's destiny as a woman, another of the myths that Castellanos mocks:

Como por arte de magia en la mujer se ha desarraigado el egoísmo que se suponía constitutivo de la especie humano. Con gozo inefable, se nos asegura, la madre se desvive por la prole. Ostenta las consecuentes deformaciones de su cuerpo con orgullo: se marchita sin melancolía; entrega lo que atesoraba sin pensar, oh no, ni por un momento, en la reciprocidad.

¡Loor a las cabecitas blancas! ¡Gloria eterna "a la que nos amó antes de conocernos"! Estatuas en las plazas, días consagrados a su celebración, etc., etc. ("La mujer y su imagen," Mujer que sabe latín, 16)

As if by magic arts, the egoism that is supposed to be constitutive of the human species has been rooted out in women. With ineffable joy, we are assured, mothers live for their offspring. They display the resulting bodily deformations with pride: they wrinkle without melancholy, give up what they treasure without a thought, oh, no, not for a moment, of reciprocity.

All hail the dear little white-haired grannies! Eternal glory "to those who loved us before they knew us"! Statues in the plazas, days dedicated in their honor, etc., etc.

This story illustrates the form of monstrous egoism that results from the hypocrisy of such systematic, enforced abnegation without reciprocity. This woman's complicity in her own self-deformation and allegiance to oppressive gender codes has had terrible consequences for her children and has led to an unhappiness she cannot understand. She is the extreme case implied by Edith's choice to remain in a safe but unsatisfying marriage; she trades compassion, love, and freedom for physical and psychological comfort.

Señora Justina is reading a recipe in a magazine, but she's an expert recipe reader. She has absorbed the lessons of hypocrisy; a recipe for her is one of a woman's strategies for dealing with a husband (unexpected guests, grand occasions, the mother-in-law, lovers, etc.). If her place is in the kitchen, his is "en su trabajo, la cantina, o la casa chica" [at work, in the bar, or the girl-friend's place] (49). She insults her daughter Lupe almost as if out of obligation, invoking the name of the dead father. Yet to herself she is quite clear about why she is glad to be a widow; if a husband is indispensable to a marriage, as Edith remarks, widowhood gives you the husband in the past tense. Without her husband she has the social position, a pension, a role, but she doesn't have to put up with him anymore.

One of her memories sketches how a woman like her might have been socialized into accepting this double standard. In her own youth she put up the expected defenses against men's sexual advances, but the one time she almost yielded, the man looked on her with scorn. She knows that Juan Carlos married her because she couldn't compete with him; her ah! of admiration throughout their married life "nunca fue interrumpido por una pregunta, por un comentario, por una crítica, por una opinión disidente" [was never interrupted by a question, a commentary, a criticism, a dissident opinion] (32). Like the narrator in "Lección de cocina," she arrived at her marriage in a state of sexual ignorance and knew that what was expected of her was silence, submission, and a decent martyrdom. In this system of values, she can represent his lust as a form of madness that makes his affair with his secretary a relief. Society elevates her motherhood into the achievement of her life, but her children are unhappy and she is now alone. Although she is a rather horrible woman, her behavior illustrates what it might be like to live according to the "cooking lessons."

In "Lección de cocina" a woman embarks on married life with a new, bitter recognition of its potential cost in terms of selfhood. "Domingo" and "Cabecita blanca" represent two stages in the acceptable path for married women of the comfortable middle class, two stages in an evasion of consciousness, two examples of negotiation with myths, clichés, and norms. None of these women have to worry about the poverty facing Modesta Gómez, Gertrudis, or any of the Maya women in Chiapas. But the stories show the powerful constraints that are the price of that comfort. The opportunity for some small degree of freedom from material anxiety brings the fear of losing it; the privilege that is the trade-off for having a husband, producing children, and accepting one's only allotted place demands stifling the internal voice of protest or dissatisfaction.

Marjorie Agosín has called Castellanos a liminal writer because of her attention to women on the verge of transformations. These three stories tell us ways that middle-class Mexican women's identities are structured through marriage and domesticity by narrating an individual's engagement with—or evasion of—self-awareness and action. "Album de familia," the last and longest story, takes on the dilemmas faced by intellectual women for whom writing or cultural activity is not an evasion, as it is for Edith, but a profession and a vital necessity; to choose to live as a writer means confronting head-on the conflicts between self-affirmation and domesticity displayed in the preceding stories.

Whose family album is this? There are no men in this story, and it takes place in a hotel, not a home. This a group portrait of *contrabandistas,* a presentation of those women who, in spite of all the external prohibitions and internal doubts, cross the border and write anyway. It stages a debate over the social and spiritual constraints women negotiate as they face the imperatives of doing the writer's work. The women are brought together for a reunion of the famous Mexican writer Matilde Casanova with three former students, all published writers themselves, on the occasion of her receipt of an international prize; Matilde's secretary-companion, Victoria, has organized the gathering at a beachside hotel and invited two students from the university, Cecilia and Susana, to present their "homage" as well. But their lunch, ostensibly to celebrate the public recognition of one woman's professional and artistic success, turns into a series of confrontations and quarrels revealing the fears that come with the territory. The price of success for these women writers seems to be life behind a mask, a fearful clinging to a myth that is both imposed and self-created: Matilde is the seer; Josefa, the devoted wife and mother, Aminta, the femme fatale, and Elvira, the woman of moderation. The masks these women cling to do not resolve their fear of failing to live up to the terrible exigencies of vocation, or their fear of being judged not a real woman, and especially not the fear that self-discovery and speaking the truth will reveal those fears and compromises.

The story explores in dramatic form many of the ideas that Castellanos dealt with more analytically in *Sobre cultura femenina:* the *ninguneo,* or negative prescriptions, that tell women they cannot or should not write; the ambivalence women feel about their identity as defined through motherhood; the terrible forms of narcissism that are substitutes for self-knowledge and diving into the deep, facing the monsters in one's self. This group does not set out deliberately to do the work of consciousness-raising, yet it prefigures the kind of consciousness-raising groups that were to be such an important mechanism for constituting a women's movement out of individual women's self-explorations in the seventies. In a series of theatrical scenes, the women debate the nature of their roles, defend their choices, quarrel jealously, break down their defenses, strip away their masks.

In contrast to *El eterno femenino,* Castellanos' brilliantly mordant and funny play in which myths and stereotypes of Mexican womanhood are parodied, sent-up, debunked with confident humor and irony, this story emphasizes pain and self-doubt. But there is also an enormous difference from all the previous portraits of women's pain we can read in Castellanos' fiction because in this story the women are successful professionals; they work, publish, read other women's work, talk to other women about their situations, wrestle with the myths. That they do so with anger, hypocrisy, fear, and jealousy makes this story somewhat terrible to read at times. Yet I find it remarkable precisely because in it Rosario Castellanos has the courage to show just how hard this kind of work is: a critique of myths and of the men who benefit from them is hard and necessary work, but it is still much easier than examining the forms of complicity with women's oppression that women share. These women live lives that are not exclusively defined by domesticity, but Castellanos shows as well the tremendous difficulties of creating a public space where women might work without fear. Some women have to be the first ones to cross the threshold and serve as public examples to others, but once inside they face the risks, frustrations, and failures inherent in such mythologizing.

"Album de familia" reworks a dramatic piece Castellanos published almost twenty years earlier (in 1952) in *América: Revista Antológica,* as "Tablero de damas."[2] The earlier version also stages a gathering of women writers as a ferociously unhappy encounter with stereotypes, fears, and prejudices. In the later version Castellanos changes some names and drops any male characters, but the story retains many of the structuring elements of drama: the events unfold in a series of scenes marked by the entrances and exits of characters; the two students, Cecilia and Susana, are positioned as reluctant spectators to these scenes; exposition and character presentation are accomplished primarily through dialogue.

The opening and closing sections, before and after the reunion, frame this as Cecilia's story. Cecilia and Susana are two university students, the younger generation of women intellectuals poised to step into the space opened up for them by the writers they will meet that day; at the story's end, Cecilia is faced with making a choice about her own future, whether to place her relationship with a man before her education and potential as an intellectual. The scenes she has witnessed will serve as example or instruction as she decides about her own future as a writer.

The story opens with Cecilia disturbed by a dream of a menacing sea that threatens to sweep her away. The language concentrates images of liminal states: Cecilia moves between sleeping and waking, between night and day, thinks of the relation of the water and land. The ocean waves "se detenían en ese límite" [were poised at that limit], between going forward and retreating; they disturb Cecilia because of the idea that if the waves do not stop, they will sweep away what lies in their path (the hotel where Cecilia sleeps). Later, the horror and fascination of the sea will be entwined with images of the writer's vocation as the imperative to cross over a threshold into the unknown, an image of power but perhaps also an image of the dangers of Matilde's madness.

In contrast, Cecilia feels safer during the daylight, when the sea becomes not a vast presence but an object of contemplation, "un espectáculo que podía contemplarse desde la terraza" [a spectacle that she could contemplate from the balcony] (65). This observer's posture, linked to the image of the waves falling back, to the safety of being spectator rather than actor, will be associated with the safety of hierarchies and norms that the women cling to in their confrontations. The two younger women are astonished that they have been invited to this "Olympus," since they are not in the same category as the professional writers also in attendance. They are being allowed to go behind the barriers erected to defend the famous writer from her public, whose demands have left her "agobiada . . . asediada . . . acechada . . . perseguida . . . rodeada" [overwhelmed . . . besieged . . . hunted . . . pursued . . . surrounded] (66). But by crossing this threshold, they are witness to the behavior behind the public mask.

The first thing they see is not Matilde herself but a dialogue between the gatekeeper, her secretary, Victoria Benavides, and a cynical and persistent woman journalist, collaborators and antagonists in the operation of the myth machinery. Their conversation over the terms of access to Matilde is also a debate about what it means to be a woman writer in Latin America. The dialogue describes the dimensions of a problem: Once women have won some access to the institutions of writing, publication, and success, what difference will it make? The reporter and Victoria understand the politics of an international culture industry that locates Latin America as peripheral, and the reporter sarcastically enumerates the dogmas of Mexican nationalism to which she is expected to subordinate her story (themes Castellanos examines in detail in her essays). The two women also understand how misogyny continues to condition the reception of women's work. The reporter has done a survey of reactions to Matilde's prize; male writers take nationalist pride in her award, but also react with indifference because a woman is, by definition, not their equal and therefore not a rival. She renders their misogyny with the phrase "Una mujer intelectual es una contradicción en los términos, luego no existe" [A woman intellectual is a contradiction in terms, therefore, she doesn't exist] (71), a bitter summary of the discourse Castellanos examines in *Sobre cultura femenina*.

Yet if Victoria and the reporter agree to a large extent about the nature of the discourses and institutions in which they work, they disagree vehemently about what they should do about it. The reporter denies being a feminist and claims that women have already arrived; now they must play by the rules of the game. Victoria justifies the sacrifice of her own literary aspirations to Matilde's with the idea that Matilde's myth will help make it possible for other women to go where she cannot:

> *Ya que hemos hecho un mito que por lo menos nos sea útil; que abra perspectivas nuevas a las mujeres mexicanas, que derribe los obstáculos que les impide avanzar, ser libres.* (76)

> Now that we've made a myth, at least let's make it a useful one; let it open up new perspectives for Mexican women, overthrow the obstacles that keep them from advancing, from being free.

Victoria has retained enough idealism to think it essential to open up a space, to help women cross the threshold, yet here is this young woman reporter who has moved into that space only to tell her that feminism is passé, that women are already liberated, and who is willing to sell out her work and pander to the worst clichés. What then would constitute real change for women as writers? Clearly, it is not enough for women to be able to cross the forbidden threshold and drink at the bar,[3] or to work as professional writers if they then continue to act as ventriloquists for misogyny.

Victoria had hoped to enlist the reporter in presenting a subversive model of female solidarity as an example for younger women like Cecilia and Susana, spectators to this debate, to admire and imitate. But the reporter refuses her solidarity with this effort, and the two younger women will soon be witnesses to the fact that this solidarity does not yet exist. The description of Matilde's entrance returns us to the images of liminality (noises off, a passage from darkness to lightness) from Cecilia's dream, but now Matilde embodies both the promise and the threat of crossing the threshold. Cecilia and Susana watch with horror as Victoria struggles to contain Matilde's ravings about her "guilt." The successful prizewinner is "en la cresta de la ola" [on the crest of the wave], the moment before the wave crashes down; she obsessively rehearses her emotional pain with metaphors of crime, secrets, and sterility—a child not born. In the figure of Matilde, Castellanos simultaneously mocks the popular reading of Gabriela Mistral's poetry as compensation for frustrated maternity and acknowledges the pain that women writers experience when forced to imagine their creativity as a poor substitute for a femininity defined for them as motherhood. Castellanos also mocks her own public myth when she describes how Matilde has acquiesced to a romantic myth that she is a descendant of Indians when in fact she is from an upper-class family; like Castellanos, Matilde cast her allegiances with the underdog, yet this gesture is not sufficient to resolve her own internal conflicts.[4]

Susana, the practical one, wants to leave, saying these women are all crazy and hysterical; she voices the option of retreat and acceptance of norms, while Cecilia is fascinated with what might be entailed by continuing to go over the edge. They witness the arrival of three other successful women writers, former students of Matilde's. Each of the three has also chosen and maintained a myth in an attempt to reconcile her writer's vocation with the available recipes for womanhood, and each defends her choices and compromises by attacking the others.

Josefa Gándara prides herself on being wife and mother, although she is disappointed that all three of her children are girls. She supports her family with commercial writing and bad poetry (the others sneer at her "flores naturales" [wildflowers]. Her self-sacrificing posture and her moralistic and prudish attitudes are the masks behind which she tries to conceal the fact that she has had to write commercial trash in order to support her husband and children. The flamboyant Aminta Jordán is the polar opposite of Josefa; her aggressive narcissism and publicity seeking have become her professional mask. She throws herself into her role as excessive manic-depressive, manipulates her sex scandals for publicity, and wants to be the only famous woman writer. She claims her poetry is pure, "un cultivo" [a cultivation] (92) as opposed to Josefa's "flores naturales." Neither Josefa nor Aminta recognizes Victoria as one of their university friends, and their catty and abusive behavior serves to show up their chosen identities as "women writers" as painful attempts to conform to contradictory and crippling notions of womanhood. As with Matilde, Castellanos is simultaneously ruthless and compassionate with these characters, displaying their viciousness but also the causes of their fear and pain.

Elvira Robledo's choice of moderation in writing as in life is presented as less destructive than the attitudes of the two others—she is the only one to address Cecilia and Susana as individuals or to recognize Victoria as a classmate from university days—yet she is also painfully aware that this safety has limited her art. Her more honest engagement with her vocation is represented by her decision to leave the marriage that stifled it, yet the public perception of that action, voiced by Josefa and Aminta, is that she has failed as a woman.

All of the writers' self-delusions and public manipulation cannot mask the work itself. Up to now, Cecilia and Susana have been silent witnesses to the three writers' dialogues, but when Elvira obliges them to speak up as readers and critics of these women's writing, Cecilia is brutally honest and says that Aminta's work is abominable. When Matilde appears, she outdoes her students in insecurity and arrogance, humiliating Victoria by ordering her to prepare *arroz a la mexicana* with her own hands, but her talent and vocation are recognized by all the women present as a reality.

When Susana asks why they write, if not for fame (104), Matilde launches into a monologue about the writer's vocation as a kind of "enfermedad mortal" [mortal illness] (101), about poetry as an all-absorbing fate, a form of martyrdom. The problem is how to make a life out of it. Writing involves moving between the experience of the sublime and the quotidian, and she is trying to survive in the face of madness, the fear of being buried alive by the desires of others, by their images of her. As if to illustrate her words, Aminta and Josefa jockey for favor, while Elvira observes.

At the moment when Elvira begins to question Matilde's actions, Victoria announces that the meal is ready. Matilde escapes the need to respond to Elvira by pitching a paranoid fit, claiming they're all out to poison her, to get her, denying that she ordered Victoria to make this particular dish. Victoria says: "Tengo testigos Matilde" [I have witnesses, Matilde] (117). Perhaps the function of the reunion has been to get others to witness her situation in order for it to be real; she wants them to see "los pies de barro del ídolo" [the idol's feet of clay] (119).

After Matilde finally allows Victoria to put her to bed, the women turn on each other in order to feel safe from the sight of genius as madness, but in doing so they also begin to speak honestly for the first time. In this process, Elvira serves as the guide. What they reveal about their lives does not match the myths they have maintained, but it is not false either. First the women give the usual kind of sexist names to Matilde's crisis: menopause, drugs, frustrated chastity, lesbianism. Josefa then turns on Elvira, asserting that "vale más un mal matrimonio que una buena separación" [a bad marriage is better than a good separation] (123). As they begin to remember together their classes with Matilde, whose mode of teaching they call a spiritual trance, they also have to remember that their nickname was not "las vírgenes fuertes" [the strong virgins], as Victoria claims, but, rather, "las tres parcas" [the three fates], and she was left out. Victoria remembers how badly they were treated by the male students and teachers, and Elvira begins to name the conditions that forced Aminta and Josefa into their extreme paths. But rather than seeking to blame the women for their situations, Elvira recasts their stories as forms of heroism. Her own story is that her husband was her prince charming, their marriage looked like the union of two equals but was really the attempt to annihilate each other. When she went back to writing she recognized her limitations (134). She rejects the solutions of both Aminta and Josefa: "Debe haber, tiene que haber otra salida" [There must be, there has to be another way out] (135).

One way out is Victoria's choice of refusing the writer's vocation altogether. When Victoria returns and offers to be Matilde's intermediary to help them, Elvira tries to name the reality behind Matilde's myth: that Victoria acts as Matilde's will but is treated like a maid. Victoria explains how she's taken on this role out of fear of crossing that threshold (141), and when Elvira calls her a coward, Victoria replies that none of them have had the courage to surrender completely to their vocation either, to give up the comforts of normal life. None of them wanted to exhibit themselves in their naked truth as abnormal. When she says, "Porque querían nadar y guardar la ropa" [Because you wanted to swim and keep your clothes on] (148), we return to the image of the dangerous attraction of the ocean waves and also recall the image of the woman of letters as sea serpent in *Sobre cultura femenina*. And Elvira's response also echoes Castellanos' final statement in that essay where she recommends "diving ever deeper": "Y yo sostengo que para tener acceso a la

autenticidad es preciso descubrir la figura que nos corresponde, que únicamente nosotros podemos encarnar" [And I maintain that to have access to
authenticity it is necessary to discover the face that is our own, that only we
can embody] (151).

The conversation transforms itself from blind attacks to an exchange of
images as each one reveals how she sees herself and the others, stripping away
defenses; in Aminta's description, "este Juicio Final en el que cada una de
nosotras fue alternativa o simultáneamente defensor, juez y verdugo, pero
siempre reo" [this Final Judgment in which each of us has been alternately
or simultaneously defender, judge, and executioner, but always the accused]
(152). In spite of themselves, the women have crossed a threshold together
into a kind of truth telling that Castellanos offers as the necessary condition
for the life and the work to come together.

And, despite the awful quarrels, the women eat lunch together. After almost eighty-five pages of dialogue, of dramatic confrontation and revelation,
Castellanos gives us only two brief paragraphs to describe the meal and conversation that they share, to give us a glimpse of the solidarity that Victoria
wanted to represent to the world before it existed:

> En el comedor charlaron aún con las frases entrecortadas por la masticación. Y
> rieron mientras bebían vino rojo. Y echaron sal, hacendosamente sobre el mantel
> cuando se derramó una copa.
>
> La discusión se prolongaba, en sordina, durante la sobremesa bostezante. Y
> tal vez alguna quiso llorar—tal vez porque era la más fuerte—pero la sofrenaba
> el desvalimiento de las otras. Y las otras se aprestaron en vano a restañar esa
> herida invisible que nunca abrió los labios. (153)

In the dining room they chatted even as their sentences were broken by
chewing. And they laughed as they drank red wine. And they threw salt, like
efficient housewives, on the tablecloth when a cup spilled.

The discussion went on, muted, yawning through the postprandial
amenities. And maybe one of them wanted to cry—maybe because she was
the strongest—but held back because of the helplessness of the others. And
the others prepared themselves in vain to stanch that invisible wound that
never opened its lips.

When Cecilia and Susana return exhausted to their room, Cecilia reads a
letter from her boyfriend, who has accepted a scholarship to go to Europe for
a year. She wishes she could be he so she could go somewhere, "pero Cecilia
no era él, era nada más ella, no sería jamás nadie más que ella" [but Cecilia
wasn't he, she was only she, would never be anyone else but herself] (154).

This recognition is also a horrified recognition that she has discovered her "centro de gravitación" [center of gravity] (154), that she too will be a writer. Practical Susana replies without hesitation to her question of whether it is worth writing a book: "Creo que no. Ya hay muchos" [I don't think so. There are already plenty] (154). Refusing the call is one path, but Victoria stands as cautionary example. Like the narrator of "Lección de cocina," Cecilia set off on her own path, and none of them will be safe or easy. Like Cecilia, the reader who has been the witness of the work of "dangerous memory" in these women's lives is left to imagine other possibilities.

8

Public Writing, Public Reading:
Rosario Castellanos as Essayist

Hay, quizás, una tierra de nadie—esta página—en la que ambos,
un momento, podemos coincidir.

There is, perhaps, a no-man's land—this page—in which both of us,
for a moment, can come together.
Rosario Castellanos, "El escritor como periodista," *El uso de la palabra* (18)

Queda, por último, el lector, esa hipótesis de trabajo de quienes escriben.

We are left, in the end, with the reader, that working hypothesis
for those who write.
Rosario Castellanos, "Natalia Ginzburg: La conciencia del oficio,"
El mar y sus pescaditos (49)

In an extraordinary passage from "Simone de Beauvoir o la plenitud" [Simone de Beauvoir, or Plenitude] (*Juicios sumarios*, 247–259), an essay on the second volume of de Beauvoir's memoirs, the vision that Castellanos gives of the relationship between the French writer's life and her work becomes an impassioned declaration of her own aspirations as a writer:

Pero como es usual que suceda, el libro desborda, y con mucho, los propósitos
expresos o iniciales de su autora. No es únicamente el descubrimiento de una
vocación estética ni su encarnación en obras. Es también la conquista de una
libertad personal; la integración de una ética congruente; el análisis de los
elementos que componen una conciencia; el afán por dar una estructura a los
fenómenos dispersos y contradictorios del mundo; la adquisición de un método
de conocimiento eficaz y seguro; la naturaleza, experimentada como obstáculo;
la contemplación de las imágenes; la actitud crítica y vigilante ante los prejui-
cios; los titubeos que preceden a la acción; el repentino relámpago con que
aparece ante el yo la presencia turbadora del otro; los conflictos entre el egoísmo

y la solidaridad; la disyuntiva entre la convivencia, siempre ardua y el aisla-
miento, siempre insuficiente; la agonía continua en busca de formas y, al fin, la
plenitud, cuando se asume por entero la voluntad de existir, el respeto por la
existencia de los demás y el fortalecimiento del lazo que une entre sí a todos los
hombres: la urgencia de ser libres. (*Juicios sumarios*, 247–248)

But, as usually happens, the book overflows, greatly, the initial aims expressed by its author. It is not only about the discovery of an aesthetic vocation or its incarnation in books. It is also about the conquest of personal
freedom; the integration of a congruent ethics; the analysis of those elements that make up a consciousness; the desire to give structure to the
dispersed and contradictory elements of the world; the acquisition of a sure
and efficient method of knowing; Nature, experienced as an obstacle; the
contemplation of images; a critical and vigilant attitude toward prejudice;
the waverings before action; that sudden flash with which the disturbing
presence of the other appears before the self; the conflicts between selfish-
ness and solidarity; the disjuncture between living with others, always ardu-
ous, and isolation, always insufficient; the continual agony of a search for
form, and, finally, the plenitude of assuming completely the will to exist,
respect for the existence of others, and the strengthening of the ties that
unite us all: the urgency of being free.

Each phrase in this passage expresses an aspect of Castellanos' own work;
the experience of reading gives rise to the flood of images that define a relationship between the woman and her writing, and between the woman who
writes and the woman who reads. I find this movement of sympathetic identification a compelling image of Rosario Castellanos as essayist.

Between 1960 and her death in 1974, Castellanos published hundreds of
essays in Mexican newspapers. For many of those years in a weekly column
for *Excélsior*, the newspaper with the widest circulation in Mexico, her voice
and ideas were heard in a mass forum. As a newspaper essayist she spoke to
a public that might never have read her poetry or fiction. Four anthologies of
these essays have been published.[1] *Juicios sumarios* [Summary Judgments]
(1966) collects book reviews and literary criticism, as does the volume Castellanos finished editing shortly before her death, *El mar y sus pescaditos* [The
Sea and Its Little Fishes] (1975). *Mujer que sabe latín* [A Woman Who Knows
Latin] (1973) is a collection of pieces on women that brings together many
of Castellanos' feminist ideas. *El uso de la palabra* [The Use of the Word] (1975),
a posthumous anthology of *Excélsior* columns published between 1963 and
1974, was edited by her close friend the poet José Emilio Pacheco. Pacheco

groups these sixty-five pieces around the recurring themes of Castellanos' essay writing: literature, the roles and responsibilities of intellectuals, racism and injustice in Mexico and Latin America, the lives and work of women, and one important section made up of twenty-three essays classified as "Notas autobiográficas" [Autobiographical Notes]. These autobiographical essays represent one of Castellanos' most important public gestures as a writer, the exemplary use of the daily events of her own life as woman and mother to create and affirm public recognition of the value of women's experience.

Through her fiction and poetry Castellanos explores the lives of women in Mexican society, but it is in her essays that she speaks in her own name as critic and advocate. Not all of her essays are about women, but as a body they perform three important feminist functions: those that talk directly about women make Mexican women's lives visible; those with other themes offer a feminist critique of the clichés, prejudices, norms, and myths that define and constrain Mexican society; finally, the essays as a body are themselves exemplary because with them Castellanos performs publicly, in a mass forum, as a female intellectual and as a legitimate, active participant in Mexican cultural production. During the sixties and early seventies she was one of very few women whose public writing in a forum of mass communication provided a space in Mexico for the resonance of feminist ideas.

Journalism has a long history as a significant mode of expression for male Latin American writers, but we are only now beginning to recognize the extent to which journalism has been a major sphere of women's writing as well. With the growth in women's literacy in the nineteenth century, many educated women either edited their own publications or wrote for newspapers and journals to promote their ideas. This journalism created a wide, international discussion in the Spanish-speaking world about women's lives and women's rights as well as about other social and political issues. Recent scholarship has brought to our attention the connections between Latin American women's journalism and women's involvement in movements for social change—as socialists, communists, conservatives, unionists, peasants, teachers, professionals, and as feminists.[2] In its groundbreaking study on Latin American women's journalism, the Seminar on Women and Culture in Latin America concludes:

> For Latin American women, periodical literature has constituted the chief form of participation in public dialogue, in contrast with women in the United States, who drew upon their Protestant heritage and the precedent of abolitionists such as the Grimke sisters to claim access to the public podium. (174)

This assertion is amply substantiated by the Seminar's extensive bibliography listing 377 women's periodicals (which they define as periodicals published by women, written by women, or written for women) that have appeared in Latin America since the eighteenth century; 151 of them have been published since 1980, and many of them are feminist (184). Mexico has had the second highest number of women's periodicals (after Argentina), with a total of 55. The pattern of publishing activity in Mexico parallels that of Latin America as a whole in that the most intense periods occur in the mid-nineteenth century and from 1921 to 1940; between 1941 and 1960, publication of women's periodicals drops off dramatically all over Latin America. Thus while Castellanos' work as essayist should be contextualized in an existing tradition of women's public writing, her journalism began to appear at a moment when public awareness of that tradition had all but disappeared; the few women's voices that reached the public were heard as isolated individuals.

Ahern has said that in her essays Castellanos "writes her self" (*Rosario Castellanos Reader,* 39); in doing so, she builds on the persona projected through her poetry and fiction. Castellanos stages her own life and reflections as those of an exemplary woman, whose struggles, doubts, and achievements might provoke recognition in a community of women readers. Through the act of writing a woman's life and voice into the public space of Mexican intellectual dialogue, Castellanos anticipates and creates a space for the "feminist public sphere" (Franco, *Plotting Women,* 184–187) that reemerged in Mexico after 1968. Feminism in Mexico has a rich and vigorous tradition, but at that time it had gone through a period of relative invisibility. In *La nueva ola del feminismo en México* [The New Wave of Feminism in Mexico] Ana Lau Jaiven marks the period of 1970–1976 as the resurgence of Mexican feminism as a visible social movement, due in part to the example of the women's movement in the United States and to the social spaces that opened up as the Mexican state tried to recover some of the social cohesion lost in its brutal repression of the student movement in 1968. In 1973, the woman-centered essays of *Mujer que sabe latín* found an eager audience among Mexican women beginning to define their social struggle as feminist. The title, the first half of the proverb that ends "no tiene marido ni buen fin" [(a woman who knows Latin) will have neither a husband nor a good end], speaks to the dilemmas of the educated woman. Like some of the mass-audience feminist books of the sixties in the United States, this book acted as a focal point for those Mexican women who, along with other sectors of Mexican society, were seeking ways to understand their yearning for personhood, full citizenship, and social justice in Mexico.

It is in her essays that Castellanos articulates her ideas about what Nadine Gordimer calls the writer's "essential gesture as a social being" (285–300).

Also a powerful essayist, Gordimer, as a white South African who has chosen integrity over loyalty and who publicly affirms that her task is to write in solidarity with the struggle for Black liberation in her country, is another Miranda who has renounced her allegiance to Prospero. In *The Essential Gesture* Gordimer talks about the ways the writer is "held responsible" (286), must negotiate the tension between the creative act—"the urge *to make* with words" (285)—and the demands and expectations that confront every writer as a person born into particular historical circumstances. Through her exploration of the values guiding her conception of the writer's responsibility, Castellanos makes her newspaper essays the public space where she performs that essential gesture as a Mexican woman.

José Emilio Pacheco gives one definition of Castellanos' "essential gesture" as a writer in his prologue to *El uso de la palabra* (see Chapter 1, pages 45–46), when he declares that Castellanos made her consciousness of her "double condition as woman and as Mexican" the material and organizing principle of her work. Pacheco goes on to recognize that the effect of that gesture, the fostering of an interpretive community that might recognize the values her work entails, involves learning how to read with her ("no supimos leerla" [we didn't know how to read her]).

Castellanos herself defined the relationship of the writer to her reading public in ethical terms. She returns frequently in her essays on literature to the idea of writing as *oficio* [office], a term she uses to combine the ideas of vocation and service. One of her many declarations about the writer's responsibilities (written to define the standard by which she judged a writer who failed in her eyes) begins with the idea of teaching the public how to understand:

> . . . *crear una conciencia colectiva o mantenerla alerta o vigilante; iluminar aspectos de la realidad; mostrar las leyes subyacentes en las relaciones humanas; revelar lo oculto, desmitificar, señalar lo contradictorio entre los dogmas que solicitan nuestra obediencia, denunciar la inoperancia de los prejuicios a que nos adherimos, la falacia de las doctrinas en que nos sustentamos. Función de tábano, de meto-me-en-todo cuya única recompensa adecuada es la cicuta.* ("Claude Roy, defensor oficioso," El mar y sus pescaditos, 36)

> . . . to create a collective consciousness and keep it alert and vigilant; illuminate aspects of reality; show the underlying laws of human relations; reveal the hidden, demystify, point out the contradictions between the dogmas that call for our obedience, denounce the uselessness of the prejudices to which we adhere, the fallacies of the doctrines by which we sustain ourselves. To function as gadfly, busybody, whose only adequate recompense is the cup of hemlock.

The writer's office should be that of "witness, judge, and guide" ("El escritor y su público," *Juicios sumarios,* 406). She returns constantly to this theme in her essays, as a premise for book reviews, or as a basis for more extended examinations of Mexican literary history and cultural politics.

Castellanos writes as an ethicist or moralist, obeying the imperative enunciated in her poetry, "Debe haber otro modo de ser" [There must be another way to be]. She insists on the task of cultural critique and both examines how other writers perform that task and provides her own examples. In her reviews or essays of literary criticism she almost always focuses on how writers in their lives and/or work engage in these searches for meaning, look for answers to these questions in their particular moment and circumstances.

Certain key words that recur as anchoring values in her reading are *inteligencia, lucidez, generosidad, solidaridad, plenitud* [intelligence, lucidity, generosity, solidarity, plenitude]. Castellanos writes repeatedly of *inteligencia* as the faculty for knowing that is given form through writing. A privileged form of *inteligencia* is *lucidez,* which she frequently opposes to irrational mysticism on the one hand and the power of habit, cliché, and self-interest on the other. Writers she admires are lucid; they see clearly and act on their perceptions. But lucidity is more than a clarity of vision, it is also a way of living and being. In her frequent definitions of the term, lucidity as a way of knowing does not demand the division of subject and object (object as other) that is evoked with so much pain in her poetry. Rather, *inteligencia* and *lucidez* aspire to a form of relatedness that she sometimes names *generosidad* and other times *solidaridad,* and that arises from recognition of the personhood of others. Despite the incoherence, injustice, and emptiness we might experience, Castellanos affirms a state of being she calls "plenitud" as both origin and goal, a kind of joyful attention to being in the world. In her essays on Woolf, Weil, de Beauvoir, Heine, Mann, Akutagawa, and many others, quite often Castellanos describes the way that lucidity leads characters (and writers) to despair or suicide, but even in those instances, lucidity allied with generosity and solidarity makes it possible for the writers to perform their essential gestures as writers.

Castellanos presents these values to her readers in one form or another in most of her essays, but two essays in particular, "La corrupción intelectual" [Intellectual Corruption (1969)] and "El escritor como periodista" [The Writer as Journalist (1972)], are worth a closer look because they exemplify the two rhetorical stances that define the wide range of voices Castellanos adopts in her essays. The first employs the magisterial tone of Castellanos as philosopher and professor of comparative literature, speaking as an expert with all the authority missing from *Sobre cultura femenina* (see Chapter 2); the second, written from Tel Aviv, where she was serving as ambassador, looks back on her debut as columnist after years of success, but uses the intimate, self-deprecating, and tremendously ironic voice that also harkens back to *Sobre cultura femenina.*

"La corrupción intelectual" appeared in 1969 in *La corrupción,* a collective effort by seven Mexican intellectuals denouncing corruption in Mexican society as a betrayal of the Revolution and effect of global capitalism's inequalities; the introduction invokes the example of Cuba to call for a new social revolution. Castellanos' argument here lays out systematically many of the values that knit together the body of her work. In a manner reminiscent of the philosophical argumentation in her master's thesis, she first describes what it is that intellectuals do (or should do) in order to discuss forms and causes of corruption, that is, how they do it badly. Intellectual life (when it is not corrupt) receives a tradition or past knowledge, but then sorts through it critically; the activities of interpreting and ordering require discipline and flexibility and, above all, respect for language. Teaching is creative when it is Socratic and active, but corrupt when placed in the service of dogma or uncritical rhetoric. Science involves testing knowledge and becomes corrupt when carried out in the service of commercial interests or personal ambition, but also when the scientist claims no responsibility for the uses to which that knowledge is put. Equally reprehensible are lawyers in the service of the powerful or doctors, journalists, or artists who subordinate their work to an ideology. If, in Castellanos' view, the writer's task requires taking moral and ethical stands, being engaged with the world and performing public acts of judgment, she also asserts repeatedly that this task will be corrupted if carried out in the service of particular dogmas or interests. The act of judgment, the exercise of *inteligencia,* should be a free exercise of reason.

"La corrupción intelectual," with its abstract and categorical language and logical exposition, exemplifies Castellanos' magisterial stance in the essays. But Castellanos could also be self-mocking about her pretensions to change society. In "Consultorio sentimental" [Advice to the Lovelorn] she describes her response to an invitation to be on television as Pavlovian salivation. Eager to work for "la elevación del nivel cultural" [raising the level of culture], she finds out instead that she is supposed to give advice à la Dear Abby. Instead of the didactic mode that is one rhetorical pole in her essays, Castellanos here uses a strategy of self-deflation; by inviting the reader to identify with her naïveté, pretensions, and embarrassment, she skewers the same mass media sexism and inanity that she attacks directly elsewhere.

"El escritor como periodista" exemplifies another characteristic rhetorical stance from which Castellanos speaks as a "professional reader," the intimate voice and the autobiographical persona. Pacheco made this essay the "involuntary prologue" to *El uso de la palabra* because in it Castellanos describes

213

her essay writing to her readers. Claiming that what distinguishes her newspaper writing from the rest of her work is a new relationship to her readers, she outlines the evolution in her awareness of her public, of what it meant to be read. Her early poetry she says, rather ruefully, was little more than a monologue because her poems were so bad and so few people read them. With the success of her fiction, she was shocked to find out that some readers were angry with her at "being used" in her stories; people were recognizing themselves, quite literally, in her work. But she still had trouble imagining these angry Chiapas neighbors as "readers." Only when Julio Scherer García, the editorial page director at *Excélsior*, asked her to contribute a regular column to the paper did she realize that she was guaranteed a reading public, and that those readers would know her in a new way: "iba a escribir para que me leyeran" [I would be writing in order to be read] (15).

Some of those people for whom she was writing would be women. In the same essay she claims she missed her only chance to be a serious reporter because when sent to interview an important woman, the two of them ended up chatting about recipes, children, and husbands. She presents this as the story of her failure to become a serious journalist, and yet her anecdote gently rejects the way that young women reporters are relegated to writing for the "women's page," the assumption being that, after all, two women talking together could hardly be "news." Her anecdote also suggests indirectly that this conversation between women might be a model for a different kind of relationship with the reader that she wants to create in her journalism: these essays make a space for a dialogue between a woman clearly speaking as a woman and a reader who might also be a woman. She shows herself in the role of the timid fledgling reporter interviewing the important woman, and as that important woman herself.

Quite often Castellanos calls attention to her relationship to the reader through her familiar tone and direct address, as we see again in her account of her initiation into writing as a journalist:

Julio me tuvo paciencia y me estimuló y me aconsejó y acabé por agarrar el paso y ahora me siento de lo más cómoda platicando con usted de esto y de aquello y de lo más allá. Y comentamos los acontecimientos e intercambiamos puntos de vista, y, ¿lo ve usted?, somos amigos, antes puntuales ahora intermitentes, pero siempre amigos. (17)

Julio was patient with me and urged me on and advised me and I ended up getting the hang of it and now I feel completely comfortable chatting with you about this, that, and the other. We comment on what's happening and we exchange points of view, and—you see? we're friends, formerly regular and now intermittent, but always friends.

The informality of the verb "platicar" used here to characterize her essay writing, the direct address to the reader and the use of "we," the display of women's "domestic" concerns along with a "feminine" tone of ironic, self-deprecating complicity, are some of the strategies Castellanos uses in many of these essays to authorize her introduction of women's experiences and perspectives into the arena of public intellectual life in Mexico. She has come far from the ambiguously double-voiced rhetorical strategies of *Sobre cultura femenina*, where she had to write first of all to please and impress a committee of powerful male philosophy professors. Now she is able to posit women as among her community of readers. And indeed, her readers talked back to her: the feminist play *El eterno femenino: Farsa* came about because two readers of her columns, the director Rafael López Mirnau and actor Emma Teresa Armendáriz, asked her to collaborate with them (Ahern, *A Rosario Castellanos Reader*, 54).

Castellanos uses personal experience or an ironic voice to challenge the authority of received notions and powerful interests. And she is also willing, as an ardent defender of the power of reason, to present her judgments with great authority and erudition. In dozens of essays of literary criticism, Castellanos performs in public as a "professional reader." *Juicios sumarios* and *El mar y sus pescaditos* are both collections of literary essays, and many of the essays in *Mujer que sabe latín* concern women writers or female literary characters. In a literary review, a writer presents his or her judgments as those of a professional or an expert, someone qualified in some way to pronounce literary judgment. The voice of the essay is a personal voice—the voice of that particular reader—but one that assumes the authority of experience, of taste, of perception. This kind of piece offers us the chance to witness the writer in the act of reading and thinking, in the act of reflection and judgment. Part of the implied contract with the reader is that the persona in the essays refers us back to a real person who presents opinions and judgments to us with the intellectual authority of an expert.

Castellanos' book review essays show an impressive, even astonishing, range of reading in the literatures of the Americas and Europe, as well as in philosophy and history. In her didactic mode, Castellanos very often frames her approach to a specific text or figure with a larger question, often casting her nets very wide. In quite a few of the literary essays in *El mar y sus pescaditos*, Castellanos castigates writers for not living up to what she sees as their responsibility. She mocks Claude Roy because he talks about literature as companion, distraction, nurse, and because he assumes common moral values. She rejects François Mauriac's bourgeois conviction about the "natural order of things" and his naturalization of human suffering, and calls the work of Graham Greene morally escapist and overly propagandistic. She is disappointed with Erich Maria Remarque's later work because she finds that he describes but does not interpret; in each of these reviews she speaks to her conviction that the writer must interpret and judge, not merely reflect. These writers, and others she reviews elsewhere, are guilty in her eyes of a failure of engagement that is, in effect, a failure of imagination.

The act of imagination is inseparable for her from the ethical relationship to readers. In "Arte y destinatario" [Art and Its Audience] (*El mar y sus pescaditos*, 195–199) Castellanos quotes Sartre—"¿Para quién se escribe?" [For whom does one write?] (197)—to ask what difference there is between writing for the "masses" and for the elite. Using an insipid children's book as an example, she answers that when the writer thinks the reader is stupid, the result is terrible writing; inferior texts produce bad taste. Writers who accept their privileges in a country of high illiteracy and refuse to use them in a way that will be of use to others are guilty of "mala fe" [bad faith] ("La novela mexicana contemporánea" [The Contemporary Mexican Novel], *Juicios sumarios*, 113). What emerges from the accumulation of assertions about the writer's critical task is the notion that the writer's relation to the reader is a pedagogy. Teaching her readers how to read critically is a civics lesson, not so different, perhaps, from Teatro Petul.

For the most part, Castellanos speaks specifically about the political context of her declarations about Mexican literature and intellectual life. In "Sublevación por la injusticia" [Uprising because of Injustice] published in 1970, she points out how the censorship of Oscar Lewis' *Los hijos de Sánchez*, a case in which a national outcry arose over an unflattering analysis of Mexican social dynamics, was a harbinger of the political crisis of 1968. She holds up Elena Poniatowska as an example of someone who defied the very real political risks with her book *La noche de Tlatelolco* [translated as *Massacre in Mexico*], and exhorts writers and journalists to follow her example, not to fear telling the truth, to oppose a false patriotism.

The clichés of national chauvinism were a favorite target for Castellanos, whether she found them in the mass media or in the pronouncements of intellectuals. In "El mejor de los mundos" [The Best of All Worlds] (*El uso de la palabra*, 135–138), she mocks the rhetoric of Mexican progress and success as the equivalent of seeing the world through Dr. Pangloss' glasses. In "PRI, cocina, paz, ingenio, amor" [PRI, Kitchen, Peace, Ingenuity, Love] (*El uso de la palabra*, 170–173) she ridicules the idea that Mexico should imitate the United States with her own parody of a rather silly article in *Time*. The result is a hilarious list of Mexican nationalist clichés that defensively assert Mexican superiority but rationalize inequality: teaching is a vocation, so teachers do not need decent pay; *pulque* is as good as meat for the poor; chiles have plenty of vitamins; Mexican workers can make anything out of scraps; "como México no hay dos" [there is nothing else like Mexico].

Castellanos deflates more sophisticated pronouncements on Mexican national character in "La tristeza del mexicano" [The Sadness of the Mexican] (*El uso de la palabra*, 174–177). She stages her essay as a response to a reader's challenge that she, like Octavio Paz, explain the Mexican nation and its problems. She demurs, insisting (ironically) that although she has intuitions about this problem she may not be capable of discerning an underlying law of Mexican national character (she will not be as presumptuous as Paz in *El laberinto de la soledad*). Instead, in keeping with her usual aims, she would rather "poner en crisis una serie de lugares comunes" [to throw into crisis a series of commonplaces] (175), that is, examine clichés about Mexicanness, a task in which she implicates her reader: her "corresponsal" (correspondent) is "corresponsable" (coresponsible) for the effort (175).

First she describes what she sees as the standard mechanism by which intellectuals turn a defect into a national quality: they take some fact, explain it through reference to a pre-Columbian myth or the colonial past, then assert something aesthetic about it, such as, for example, that "el mexicano es triste" [the Mexican is sad]. She then breezes through a version of Mexican history as if it were the answer to the question of why the Mexican is sad, in a hilarious send-up of popular, sentimentalized myths. What she proposes instead is that "nos aceptamos, no como una imagen predestinada sino como una realidad perfectible" [we accept ourselves, not as a predestined image but rather as a perfectible reality] (177).

Sometimes Castellanos uses a child's viewpoint, as she did in *Balún Canán*, to denaturalize the ways an individual learns her place by learning to read social norms. In "Aplastada por la injusticia del mundo" [Flattened by the World's Injustice], she tells of an incident that occurred when she was a girl in Chiapas that illustrates conflicts between class allegiances and other lessons about justice and citizenship. An election (in which women, of course, could not vote) was to be held, during the period when the oligarchy was in turmoil over President Cárdenas' land reforms and the state's anticlerical measures. When the town drunk, el Panchón, protests the arrest of the independent candidate, she takes her civics lessons seriously and brings him home to get her father's gun so that together they can fight this injustice. The political injustice is only compounded because she does not understand either his drunken invective or her subsequent punishment.

"El alba de los pueblos ayer" [The Dawn of Time, Yesterday] (*El uso de la palabra,* 190–193) assumes the reader's familiarity with the stories she has told in her fiction and essays about growing up in the provinces; here, she uses her son, Gabriel's, question (Were there dinosaurs when she was a child?) to reflect on her own childhood experience and perspective; to him, her provincial childhood seems as distant as the age of dinosaurs. From this vantage she recalls the juxtaposition of twentieth-century technology and medieval values: electric light and the honor code, the first radio and talking movies, the first two-story building: "Los dinosaurios éramos nosotros" [We were the dinosaurs] (193).

In a group of essays on the picaresque novel and travel writing, Castellanos examines a genre that provides a partial parallel with her own critique of colonialism. In "Sobre la picaresca" [On the Picaresque] (*Juicios sumarios,* 190–203) she contextualizes the Spanish picaresque novel as a response to changes produced by Spanish colonialism, the accumulation of capital from the American mines that shook up feudal social structures, and an industrialization that did not absorb unemployed labor. She reads the picaresque, including later variants in Spain and the Americas, from the premise that what is at stake is how social norms dictate who gets to be "una persona humana" [a human person] (190). Her treatment of the *pícaro* as marginalized observer whose vantage point reveals structures of power and inequality stands in counterpoint to her acid review of Saul Bellow's *Henderson the Rain King.* She reads this novel as a variation on the tired Western literary trope of the "peregrinación a las fuentes" [pilgrimage to the source]; the privileged individual from a rich country journeys to a non-Western place, accumulating stories about his spiritual renewal in an exotic setting, but failing to see his implication in colonialism (*El mar y sus pescaditos,* 90). By contrast, she identifies with Doris Lessing in her writing about her return to Rhodesia ("Doris Lessing: una mirada inquisitiva" [Doris Lessing: An Inquisitive Gaze], *Mujer que sabe latín,* 88–93); she sees Lessing as a reporter, not an exoticist, because she speaks to the ways that "color" and race mystify the economic motives of exploitation (91), and she understands the White liberal as paternalistic. Like Castellanos, Lessing returned home having rejected the values of her family and attempts to model a new way for Miranda to read her family's story.

Castellanos wrote often about Chiapas in her essays, not just as the setting for events in her life, but as *indigenista* social critic, with the same reformist zeal and consciousness of the limits of reform that appear in her fiction. In *El uso de la palabra,* Pacheco groups essays that revisit the themes of racism and *indigenismo* in Chiapas under the rubric "México: el dedo en la llaga" [Mexico: The Finger in the Wound]. "Teoría y práctica del indigenismo" [Theory and Practice of Indigenism] (1964) still reflects her faith in the INI's efforts to change social relations, but warns at the same time that outsiders' theories will fail; changing the Indian will not help Indians when the prevailing attitude is that Indians are not human. "Difícil acceso a la humanidad" [Difficult Access to Humanity] (1968) gives voice to her outrage at a report that Mestizos in Colombia excused their hunting of Indians in the jungle because they "didn't know it was illegal to kill Indians." The essay gives a history in which to understand their response: "¿Desde cuándo los indios son personas?" [Since when are Indians people?] (157). "El padre Las Casas y la agonía del indio" [Father Las Casas and the Agony of the Indian] (1966) describes efforts to change this kind of thinking in Chiapas, pointing out that today's oligarchy would reject Las Casas' ideas as vehemently as did the oligarchy of his own day. Her warning in this essay echoes what she illustrated in *Ciudad Real*: while members of the ruling class should, and sometimes do, reject the hierarchy of master-slave, those feelings will not themselves effect social change. As elsewhere, Castellanos asserts the need to create "una conciencia colectiva" and her faith in the effective use of language:

Si algún poder tiene la palabra, si alguna función tiene la teoría, si algún jugo ha de exprimirse del conocimiento, es éste de dar un nombre a las cosas. El nombre verdadero y exacto, aparte de producir un placer estético, mueve a la acción, a la conversión y a la corrección." (146)

If there is any power in the word, if there is any use for theory, if we can squeeze some juice out of knowledge, it is that of giving things their name. The true and exact name, besides producing aesthetic pleasure, can move us to action, to conversion, to correctness.

Her faith in the power of consciousness-raising is tempered by her warning that there will be four hundred more years of injustice if we do not work to destroy the brute forces that have not responded to appeals for charity, equality, or reason.

"Discriminación en Estados Unidos y en Chiapas" [Discrimination in the United States and in Chiapas] (1965) compares homegrown Mexican racism to the ideologies of the Ku Klux Klan or the Nazis, challenging the good liberal reader to ask: If plunged into that context, what would be "our" reaction? Out of her own painful experience, she predicts that most would echo the outburst of Doctor Salazar in "El don rechazado," become disillusioned and then angry when the needy are not grateful for charity (see Chapter 4).

Castellanos connects her faith in the task of critique, of naming reality, with her goals of solidarity, generosity, fraternity. "Divagación sobre el idioma" [Digression on Language], "Modito de hablar" [Our Little Way of Talking], and "Notas al margen: El lenguaje como instrumento de dominio" [Notes on the Margin: Language As an Instrument of Domination] (*El uso de la palabra*) all give examples of what she sees as a particularly Mexican problem with language. "Divagación" presents her "theory" that Spanish in Mexico has been shaped by its history as the language of the colonial elite; it is a language for shouting at God, a monologue before "un auditorio reducido al silencio por la estupefacción, por el respeto, por la fuerza" [an audience reduced to silence by stupefaction, respect, force] (162). Yet if rigid social hierarchies are manifested and maintained through the use of language, then renewing and renovating our use of the language might have power as well.

Mujer que sabe latín pulls together feminist essays that, like her fiction, demystify the prescriptive social roles and norms for women. In "La mujer y su imagen" [Woman and Her Image], one of the key essays in the collection, Castellanos outlines her understanding of the processes of interpellation that shape women's subjugation, much as she historicized racism in Chiapas (see Chapter 7): history, as written by men, converts women, or "lo femenino," into a monotonous series of myths or projections, an always-binary struggle. The mythified woman is not a person but, rather, a series of figures in the stories of masculine triumph over the material and the concomitant fear of uprising by the subordinate. Elevating women, when women are not being oppressed in all the usual ways, becomes a form of propitiation of that fear, but these forms of elevation—anorexia, crippling shoes, and so on—are also debilitating: the myths convert a being into a thing. Recalling Virginia Woolf's Angel of the House, Castellanos says that notions of feminine purity really require a radical ignorance of self, and that education has generally worked to shape women for their prescribed roles of waiting and serving others; maternity is converted into pain and self-sacrifice. The end of this essay defies the inevitability of this history, declaring that women do (and should) defy the traditional arguments about their incapacity, and because they are women, not myths, they have the possibility of making an alternative system of values, of breaking out of these stories to arrive at their own images.

"Otra vez Sor Juana" [Once Again Sor Juana] (*Juicios sumarios*, 1966) posits three particularly Mexican views of femininity: the Virgin of Guadalupe is a positive model of self-sacrifice; Malinche serves as a negative model of female sexuality; Sor Juana is admired as a genius, but is considered scandalous because she was a female genius. In her *Respuesta* Sor Juana clearly declared that she chose to become a nun because it was the only decent alternative to matrimony that would allow her to pursue her intellectual vocation, yet critics such as Ludwig Pfandl could only read her desire for autonomy as hysterical.

The characters in "Album de familia" rehearsed the issue of women crossing the threshold into the professions and social spaces that were denied Sor

Juana. This essay on women's participation in formal education elaborates on the idea that while access to education is a necessary first step in changing women's lives, simply letting women attend school is not the solution. She points out that the laws may have changed to make education obligatory for girls as well as boys, and in theory women can pursue an intellectual path, but she then goes on to list ways that ideals of womanhood and fear of marginalization continue to deny personhood to women ("Otra vez Sor Juana," 23). Women's access to education still depends on economic status, marriage, family attitudes, social prejudices, and internalized sexism. Ironically, the disintegration of the family is often what opens this door for women, but women continue to struggle in isolation. The alternative Castellanos envisions is a new consciousness, defined as "vivir con lucidez lo que ahora únicamente se experimenta como malestar" [living with lucidity that which right now we only experience as uneasiness] (38).

The way those feelings are learned is the subject of "Costumbres mexicanas" [Mexican Customs], which distills many of the ideas developed in *Album de familia* about marriage and the power of mass media clichés. "Las mujeres no elegimos" [We Women Don't Choose] (27) is the refrain to her account of middle-class courtship and marriage: not only the rituals are prescribed but also the emotions that women are supposed to feel at each stage; custom is reinforced through the mass media. "Y las madres, ¿qué opinan?" [And the Mothers, What Do They Think?] asks why, in the debates on population explosion, nobody bothers to ask mothers what they think. If maternity is a value, all the more reason not to impose it on women.

Mas para proceder de esta manera se necesitaría, previamente, considerar a las mujeres no como lo que se les considera hoy: meros objetos, aparatos (por desgracia, insustituibles) de reproducción o criaturas subordinadas a sus funciones y no personas en el completo uso de sus facultades, de sus potencialidades y de sus derechos. (47)

But to proceed in this manner it would be necessary, beforehand, to consider women differently from how they are considered today: as mere objects, apparatuses (unfortunately irreplaceable) for reproduction, as creatures subordinated to their functions, but as persons with complete use of their faculties, of their potential and their rights.

But does Castellanos simply assert the authority of women's experience? To some extent, this is her strategy. Yet she marks the limits of that authority through scrupulous attention to her "(ambiguously) non-hegemonic" status (see Chapter 1, note 5). The essays about marriage, motherhood, and divorce are, for the most part, about middle-class women, women like herself, women who have material possibilities and choices available to them that poor women lack. Beginning in 1970, Castellanos addresses the issue of class conflict between Mexican women and spells out the consequences for feminism of the "(ambiguously) non-hegemonic" status of women of privilege, that is, how the privilege of some women contributes not only to the oppression of others but to complicity in their own oppression. Three essays relate her own dependence on maids. She tells the story of her relationship with María Escandón, her *cargadora* and her servant until her marriage, and makes public her shame when Gertrudis Duby de Blom points out that she had never taught this woman how to read. She makes herself the example of the contradiction. She vows to do better with Herlinda, her husband's *nana,* who now takes care of their son, Gabriel. But she recognizes that when Herlinda's consciousness regarding her relationship with her employers changes it is not as a result of Castellanos' efforts but rather through contact with other workers at the five Latin American embassies in Israel, as she describes in "El frente doméstico" [The Domestic Front]: "Ay, Herlinda y yo estamos en plena guerra de clases, cada una en su respectiva trinchera. Y yo sé que la razón histórica es suya" [Oh, Herlinda and I are in the middle of class war, each one in her respective trench. And I know that history is on her side] (*El uso de la palabra,* 251).

Another essay, "La liberación de la mujer, aquí" [Women's Liberation, Here], draws the connection between her personal experience and its political consequences. She takes note of a feminist march in the United States that demanded public attention to the issues of objectification of women and domestic work and asks why Mexican women are not doing the same; it is as if women's liberation in the United States were happening on another planet. Are women in Mexico so satisfied, or so afraid of ridicule? They are taking notes, she says, but "cuando desaparezca la última criada, el colchoncito en que ahora reposa nuestra conformidad, aparecería la primera rebelde furibunda" [When the last maid disappears, that bolster on which our complacency rests today, then we'll see the first furious rebel] (60). In this essay, she publicizes feminist concerns, dismisses with humor the antifeminist responses she anticipates, and speaks directly to an audience of women who she assumes share her dissatisfaction and desire for change. And finally, she includes herself in her illumination of class privilege and complicity. Yet, despite her attention to divisions of class here, Castellanos still is unable to imagine the maid as the potential feminist.

For the most part, however, Castellanos worked hard at bringing to her readers' attention figures of women who might provide positive examples.

"La mujer ante el espejo: cinco autobiografías" [Women in Front of the Mirror: Five Autobiographies] groups five autobiographical portraits, by Santa Teresa, Sor Juana, Simone de Beauvoir, Virginia Woolf, and Elena Croce, reading them as models of five ways of making one's own image, five women outstanding for their acute awareness and exemplarity. Ahern calls these women "feminine mentors," the women with whom Castellanos identifies and whose stories she relates as examples of living with lucidity (*A Rosario Castellanos Reader*, 40–41).

Along with Sor Juana, Simone Weil, and Simone de Beauvoir, Virginia Woolf is a figure Castellanos returns to often. She looks to Woolf for a model for reading. In a discussion of Juan Rulfo's novel *Pedro Páramo*, Castellanos addresses her reader directly: "Let's talk about literature the way Virginia Woolf did":

> *El ejemplo de Virginia Woolf consiste en partir de un hecho dado—real o imaginario—y desarrollarlo hasta lo que serían sus últimas consecuencias. Ella se preguntó qué habría ocurrido en el hipotético caso de que Shakespeare hubiera tenido una hermana dotada también del genio expresivo del escritor. Y la coloca en las situaciones que la habrían correspondido y nos dibuja la figura de una muy perfectamente anónima ama de casa.* (El mar y sus pescaditos, *115*)

> Virginia Woolf's example consists in starting from a given fact—real or imaginary—and developing it to what would be its ultimate consequences. She asked herself what might have happened in the hypothetical case in which Shakespeare had a sister with the same expressive gift as that writer. And she places her in situations she would have encountered and traces for us the figure of a perfectly anonymous housewife.

Castellanos picks up on Woolf's idea of the "common reader" as model for her own practice, the reader open to the book, able to situate herself in a tradition, to choose her models well whether among her own contemporaries, in the past, or in other languages.

In the prologue to *Meditación en el umbral*, an anthology of Castellanos' poetry, Elena Poniatowska points out how Castellanos became important as a public figure and example for other women precisely because she spoke of herself and explored herself in her work:

> *Tuvo el atrevimiento de explorarse a sí misma, desgarrarse y salir de los papeles estipulados. En la literatura se liberó. Aunque nunca se expuso en la vía pública ni empleó el lenguaje feminista nos dio el mayor alegato de nuestro tiempo mexicano. Su discurso en el Museo Nacional de Antropología e Historia el día*

15 de febrero de 1971 es clave en la causa de la mujer porque por vez primera a nivel nacional, Rosario denunció la injusticia en contra de la mujer y declaró que no era equitativo ni legítimo que uno pueda educarse y el otro no, que uno pueda trabajar y el otro sólo cumpla con una labor que no amerita remuneración, que uno sea el dueño de su cuerpo y disponga de él como se le da la real gana mientras que el otro reserva ese cuerpo no para sus propios fines sino para que en él se cumplan procesos ajenos a su voluntad. Rosario, ese día, fue ciertamente la precursora intelectual de la liberación de las mujeres mexicanas. (21–22)

She had the daring to explore herself, to tear herself open/away and leave behind stipulated roles. In literature she liberated herself. Although she never went out into the streets or used a feminist vocabulary she gave us the best plea/brief of our time in Mexico. Her speech in the National Museum of Anthropology and History on February 15, 1971, is key in the cause of women because, for the first time at the national level, Rosario denounced injustice to women and declared that it was neither just nor legitimate that some could be educated and others not, that some could work and others could only carry out tasks that deserved no compensation, that some were masters of their bodies and disposed of them as they saw fit while others reserved their bodies not for their own purposes but so that in them processes could be carried out against their will. Rosario, that day, was certainly the intellectual precursor of the liberation of Mexican women.

To understand what a tremendous change has occurred in the conditions of possibility for Castellanos' public declarations, we can compare this public gesture with Castellanos' very first essay, published in 1950 at the beginning of her writing career. In *Sobre cultura femenina* she had to begin by asking if there was even such a thing as "cultura femenina," if women were even capable of producing culture, and described those women who did actually write in the face of crushing prohibitions as "contrabandistas," as smugglers. A major difference between this highly ambivalent academic exercise and her journalism after 1960 involves the conditions of authority for her voice as a woman writer and thinker; when she wrote *Sobre cultura femenina* she wrote as a woman who did not yet have the social status conferred in Mexico by marriage or motherhood, from a position her society defined for her as freakish, abnormal, the product of frustration. She was performing a narrowly codified intellectual exercise in an institutional space where a female presence was still an anomaly. For all the privilege she derived in Chiapas from her social origins as non-Indian and daughter of the provincial landowning oligarchy, and in Mexico City from her access to a university education, she herself experienced her critique of misogyny in philosophy as a form of trespassing. Although she was questioning the virulently misogynist philosophical discourse that negated the capacity of women to write or produce culture, she still took the terms of that discourse extremely seriously. This essay consequently oscillates between a subversive double-voiced discourse and a kind of ventriloquism in which Miranda mouths the words and values of Prospero's books without managing to undermine them completely. As Elena Urrutia reminds us, writing ten years after Castellanos' death in *fem*, the feminist journal that represents the renewal of Mexican feminism in the public sphere:

> *¿Quién, en México, en 1950, tenía una idea clara del feminismo como podemos tenerla en esta medianía de los ochenta, luego de un proceso de concientización, de análisis, de militancia feminista desarrolladas propiamente en la década de los años setenta, y más particularmente en su segunda mitad? (284)*

> Who, in Mexico, in 1950, had the kind of clear idea of feminism that we can have in the mid-eighties, after a process of consciousness-raising, of analysis, of feminist militance, all developed in fact in the seventies, and more precisely in the second half of the decade?

As confused as it sounds to us today, Castellanos' first essay initiates a gesture toward something else; it anticipates many of the future ideas Castellanos would work through in her fiction and poetry and, finally, in her essays. She questioned the material conditions and the roles, myths, and discourses that construct the social location of women in Mexican society, especially middle-class women. Her writing both maps those places and enacts dislocations: her strategies of re-vision include engendering the writing voice as female, placing female experiences at the center of the work, and using an array of strategies of double-voiced discourse. But, however crucial *Sobre cultura femenina* might be to our understanding of Castellanos' work and however significant it is as an early document of feminist thought in Latin America, it did not reach a wide audience on its publication in 1950, and therefore could not generate a current of feminist inquiry or be received by women as an articulation of their concerns.

Ten years later, Castellanos was able to take advantage of her social recognition as a prizewinning and successful writer, as a professor of comparative literature, and as a wife and mother, to speak with authority. She no longer has to write as a smuggler, but has been invited by Julio Scherer García to enter the almost exclusively masculine preserve of the opinion page of *Excélsior.*

She may still be speaking to potentially disapproving readers, as in the past, but her essays derive authority from the fact that she is riding the "nueva ola del feminismo en Mexico" [the new wave of feminism in Mexico]. As an exemplary figure, a feminist mentor, when Castellanos performs as a woman reader or makes her own life the starting point for a feminist critique, she is serving as a public point of resonance for a much larger social movement. Both in essays explicitly concerned with gender issues and in those that are not, she performs as "the common reader" who also "reads as a woman."

Afterword

*El sentido de la palabra es su destinatario: el otro que escucha, que
entiende y que, cuando responde, convierte a su interlocutor en el
que escucha y el que entiende, estableciendo así la relación del diálogo
que sólo es posible entre quienes se consideran y se tratan como iguales
y que sólo es fructífero entre quienes se quieren libres.*

Rosario Castellanos, "Notas al margen: el lenguaje como instrumento de dominio,"
Mujer que sabe latín (180)

The meaning of a word is its addressee: the other being who hears it,
understands it, and who when he answers, converts his questioner
into a listener and understander, establishing in this way the
relationship of dialogue that is only possible between beings who
consider themselves and deal with each other as equals. And that is
only fruitful between those who wish each other to be free.

Trans. Maureen Ahern, *Rosario Castellanos Reader* (253)

In Castellanos' *indigenista* novels, the responses of the daughters of privilege
to the social inequality of women and of indigenous people is shaped by their
"(ambiguously) non-hegemonic" position, one that I have compared to the
figure of Miranda in *The Tempest*. The girl in *Balún Canán* and Idolina in *Oficio
de tinieblas*, the two characters analogous to Miranda, both struggle with that
situation but remain caught in its contradictions, still identifying themselves
as Prospero's daughters and unable to see alternatives to the discourses of
gender and race that structure their own oppression and the oppression of
others. Both of these girls turn to writing in their desperate attempts to cope
with the intolerable nature of the demands placed on them: the girl in *Balún
Canán* writes, but what she writes is her brother's name, out of the guilt she
assumes as the inescapable condition of being female and bearing the Argüello name; in *Oficio de tinieblas,* Idolina writes poison-pen letters that rewrite
events around her both literally and figuratively—she rewrites her story and
her letters change the course of events. Writing is a form of action for both, but
without a political consciousness of the causes of their pain, writing reinscribes

them in their painful situation: the girl writes her brother's name, not her own, which we never learn; Idolina's letters reinforce rather than break the power of her stepfather and she remains shut away in her dark room. In *Oficio de tinieblas*, the woman who acts to change her life is not Ladina but Maya. Catalina's mobilization of her people's resistance through alternative cultural paradigms is also an attempt to "revitalize" motherhood as female identity. But despite the power of the desire Catalina embodies, none of the women characters in the two novels, indigenous or Ladina, comes to more than a partial consciousness about the nature of oppression in their world, or sees the Revolution's promises as a real possibility for change in their lives as women.[1]

Miranda represents a position in a story about relations of domination, not a model for action. I have been reading Castellanos' prose as the work Miranda must do to write herself out of that story. But she does not directly represent in her fiction the kind of consciousness she herself struggled to achieve, the kind of consciousness toward which the novels gesture as they enact alternative ways of reading. The space in which that consciousness emerges is in the poetry, drama, and essays. Is the absence of a model for effective female action in her fiction a failure of imagination on Castellanos' part? It could instead be called her own form of lucidity: in speaking her own truth, her words hypothesize a community of readers who can read new stories, who can together affirm alternative values. She guides us to thresholds, but reminds us that each of us must do the work of getting across.

Notes

PREFACE

1. The term comes from Rachel Blau du Plessis and has been elaborated by Margaret Homans. See Chapter 1 here for discussion.

1. PROSPERO'S DAUGHTER

1. Both of these translations of *cultura femenina* are possible; see chap. 2 for discussion. All translations from the Spanish are mine unless otherwise noted.

2. In Mexican Spanish, el ninguneo is the noun that describes the act of ningunear, that is the social act or attitude of minimizing, discounting, slighting or putting down. Coined from the Spanish pronoun for "nothing" or "nobody," it refers to the treatment meted out to persons whom the speaker literally considers to be "nobody" or "nothing" (Ahern, *Rosario Castellanos Reader,* 22).

3. See Ana Lau Jaiven, *La nueva ola del feminismo en México* (1987) for a detailed account of feminist organizing and debate after 1968.

4. Two books that provide rich frameworks for answering this question and that consider the work of Rosario Castellanos are Franco, *Plotting Women,* and Schaeffer.

5. In "Her Very Own Howl," Margaret Homans elaborates on this idea, specifically as it involves privileged women's relations to writing and power: "The most useful term for the complicity that in these novels differentiates gender-based from other kinds of linguistic exile comes from an essay written semi-collectively by Rachel Blau du Plessis and others . . . They introduce the term '(ambiguously) non-hegemonic' to describe one aspect of the uniqueness of women's marginality. Unlike other disenfranchised groups, most women writers have in the past tended to give allegiance simultaneously to the ruling class and race and to other women, who are always among the ruled. True, a structural description of women's revolt against patriarchal discourse will resemble descriptions of other groups' revolts, but if we consider how content may shape form, women's historical experience as an '(ambiguously) non-hegemonic' group can be seen to distinguish this revolt from any other" (199–200). Homans is looking at women writers in the United States, but thinking about these

complex interactions through the figure of Miranda might be useful for reading the work of many relatively privileged women writing out of a variety of colonial contexts (neo- and post-): Doris Lessing, Nadine Gordimer, Olive Schreiner as white women writing in southern Africa; Jean Rhys or some Francophone Caribbean writers; and many women writing in Latin America.

6. See chap. 3 for an extended discussion of *indigenismo*.

7. A number of outstanding feminist studies of Latin American women's writing have appeared in the last few years. For thorough discussions of the particular strategies of Latin American women writers, see *Talking Back* by Debra Castillo, Amy Kaminsky's *Reading the Body Politic,* and the essays in *Latin American Women's Writing: an Anthology* by Sara Castro-Klarén, Silvia Molloy, and Beatriz Sarlo.

8. And yet the recent debates between Wole Soyinka and Ali Mazrui in the journal *Transition* about the place of Islam and who can claim to be a "black African" demonstrate that this distinction is not as clear as many would like to think.

9. I prefer to use the term "Indian" (equivalent to the Spanish *indio*) only when referring to the category as it was created and deployed by European colonialism. In other instances, when I am referring to people who identify themselves as native to the Americas, I prefer to use the English words "indigenous" or "indigenous people(s)" as corresponding to the Spanish *indígena*.

10. Houston A. Baker refers to these new readers as "debunkers" and describes their use of the Tempest trope: "Language, writing, ideology, race, and a host of other Western signs are conveniently given resonance and force (in the office of a definition of *civilization*) by the simple iconography of the conquering magician Prospero and his enslaved and 'deformed' island subject Caliban" (190).

11. In his 1929 essay "Discourse Typology in Prose," Bakhtin defines "double-voiced discourse" as a "doubly oriented discourse in which a relation with another speech act is the essential factor." He calls this orientation a "hidden polemic."

12. For a concise discussion of the historical role of the Latin American writer as social critic/Caliban in response to the thesis of Prospero, see Braulio Muñoz, "The Novel and the Dream," in *Sons of the Wind: The Search for Identity in Spanish American Indian Literature,* 1–31.

13. Raymond Williams' chapter on hegemony in *Marxism and Literature* elaborates on the distinction made by Antonio Gramsci between "rule," or domination, manifested in political institutions and the use of force, and "hegemony," or the social and cultural practices that shape the relations between classes or groups in a society: "The true condition of hegemony is effective *self-identification* with the hegemonic forms: a specific and internalized 'socialization' which is expected to be positive but which, if that is not possible, will rest on a (resigned) recognition of the inevitable and the necessary" (118).

14. Some of the most significant works that valorize Caliban as figure of the colonized include Aimé Césaire; Frantz Fanon, *Peau noire, masques blanches;* Lamming.

15. See Houston Baker for an example of the use of the Caliban analogy by an African American critic from the United States.

16. Braulio Muñoz points out that the Spanish colonizer regarded colonial culture in Spanish America as an extension of Spanish culture, but that "the hegemonic claim,

however, was never more than that; it hid the existence of alternative cultures throughout the colonial period, particularly Indian, but also that of black slaves, mulattos and mestizos" (3). He goes on to argue that, while the anticolonial dream of *mestizaje* as cultural unity (Caliban's dream) is powerfully liberating, it still contains the contradiction of the hegemonic claim in that it excludes alternative cultures. See Williams, *Marxism and Literature* (108–128) on hegemonic, alternative, and oppositional practices.

17. For a discussion of the editorial tradition regarding Miranda's speech, see William Shakespeare, *The Oxford Shakespeare: The Tempest*, 16–17.

18. See Jacobus for a discussion of figures of women in theoretical exchanges between men. Similar ideas are developed in Sedgwick and in Luce Irigaray's "Des marchandises entre elles," translated in *New French Feminisms: An Anthology*, eds. Elaine Marks and Isabelle de Courtivron, pp. 107–110.

19. Jehlen explores this dilemma. What feminist cultural critics are attempting to perform is the equivalent of lifting the world with a lever: theoretically posssible, but where do we stand?

20. I am borrowing from Althusser's definition of the term "interpellation" for a key idea: the way the subject is hailed, called on to recognize himself or herself through certain categories, beginning with the category of Subject. For interpellation to be successful, this recognition function must work. Althusser elaborates this notion as part of how ideologies operate, and we can also see it as part of the mechanism of the hegemonic that Williams calls "self-identification."

21. In *La Malinche in Mexican Literature: From History to Myth*, Sandra Messinger Cypess reviews the multiple meanings, negative and positive, projected on the figure of La Malinche in Mexican culture. She discusses Castellanos' re-visionary presentation of Malinche in her play *El eterno femenino* and in her poem "Malinche" as examples of critique of patriarchal paradigms and giving voice to the silenced.

22. For information on Rosario Castellanos' life, the following sources have been useful to me: Calderón; Carballo, "Rosario Castellanos"; Cresta de Leguizamón; Dybvig; Megged; Poniatowska, ¡*Ay vida, no me mereces!*; Schwartz; Solana et al.; Vásquez.

23. In an interview Castellanos told Rhoda Dybvig why she changed studies: "Yo buscaba en las obras literarias algo más profundo: la respuesta a todos los problemas; una concepción ideal y una orientación estética. Como esto no estaba analizado en la carrera literaria, me decidí por la filosofía." [I was searching in literary works for something deeper: the answer to every problem, an ideal conception and an aesthetic orientation. Because this was not being analyzed in literary studies, I chose philosophy] (18).

24. Solana et al. Some of those in this group are Wiliberto Cantón, Emilio Carballido, Ernesto Cardenal, Sergio Galindo, Miguel Guardia, Luisa Josefina Hernández, Jaime Sabines, and Dolores Castro.

25. Gordon.

26. While in Israel she wrote of her relations with Herlinda Bolaños, the woman who had raised her husband and who now cared for her son, Gabriel, and of her attempts to change the nature of a relationship she described only half ironically as one of class struggle. Castellanos, "El frente doméstico," *El uso de la palabra*, 248–251.

27. About these early efforts, Castellanos was rather harsh:

Un poema larguísima en el que quería abarcar el universo entero y conferirle un sentido gracias a la única perdurabilidad posible que, a mis ojos, era entonces la de la creación estética. Usaba el verso libre y abusaba de las imágenes a un grado que, con frecuencia, se perdía el hilo del discurso. En resumen, podría afirmarse que esta Trayectoria del polvo *era tan ambiciosa que fallida.*

No me sirvió siquiera para aprender ni la brevedad ni la sobriedad. Todos sus excesos y sus defectos se repitieron en el poema siguiente Apuntes para una declaración de fé, *al que le añadía, como toque original, el uso deliberado de lugares comunes y prosaísmos para pintar un panorama negro del mundo contemporáneo y terminar en una apoteósis esperanzada, y absolutamente gratuita, de un futuro mejor que tendría su desarrollo (¿cómo no?) en las ubérrimas tierras americanas.* ("Una tentativa de autocrítica," Juicios sumarios, 430)

A very long poem in which I tried to take on the whole universe and give it meaning by means of the only permanence possible, which, in my eyes, was at that time aesthetic creation. I used free verse and abused images to such an extent that often the thread of discourse was lost. In sum, one could affirm that this *Trayectoria de polvo* was as ambitious as it was flawed.

This didn't help me even to learn brevity or sobriety. All this poem's excesses and defects were repeated in the next poem, *Apuntes para una declaración de fé,* to which were added, as an original touch, the deliberate use of clichés and commonplaces to paint a black picture of the contemporary world ending with an apotheosis, hopeful and absolutely gratuitous, of a future that would unfold (how not?) in the fertile lands of the Americas.

28. Castellanos, *El rescate del mundo,* and *Poemas (1953–1955).* Two of the dramatic pieces she wrote in the early fifties were not published until later as *Salomé y Judith.*

29. For explorations of the evolution of Castellanos' feminist consciousness in her poetry, see Calderón; de Beer; Beth Miller, *Rosario Castellanos;* Yvette Miller; Rivero, "Paradigma de la poética femenina hispanoamericana y su evolución"; Schwartz.

2. CASTELLANOS AS RESISTING READER: *SOBRE CULTURA FEMENINA*

1. Castellanos cites Virginia Woolf's *Three Guineas* in her essay, but she did not read Simone de Beauvoir's book until after she had completed her essay; during a year of study in Spain, funded by a fellowship, she traveled to Paris where she met de Beauvoir.

2. Soto gives a richly detailed account of the dimensions of Mexican women's social and political activism before the Second World War while Jaiven recounts the resurgence of feminism in Mexico in the seventies.

3. See "Translating Gender" in *Reading the Body Politic* by Amy Kaminsky for an

important discussion of the conceptual implications of translating a feminist vocabulary between English and Spanish.

4. Henry Louis Gates, Jr., speaking of African American and African writing, points out that "philosophers and literary critics, such as Hume, Kant, Jefferson and Hegel, seemed to decide that the presence of a written literature was the signal measure of the potential, innate 'humanity' of a race." The allegations that a people had no literature have always compelled writers to respond in their writing to refute this claim; in Gates' words again, "allegations of an absence led directly to a presence, a literature often inextricably bound in a dialogue with its harshest critics" ("'What's Love Got to Do with It?'" 347–348).

5. See Margarita García Flores' interview with Adelina Zendejas for both an account of that history and an acknowledgment of contemporary feminists' ignorance of it; in Mexico, as in the United States, it would take a "second wave" of feminism for most women to rediscover that history.

6. The longing for another way to be for women is also central to Castellanos' play *El eterno femenino* (The Eternal Feminine).

7. Nahum Megged has read these passages as evidence that Castellanos accepted these judgments entirely: "En su ensayo sobre la cultura femenina estaba dispuesta a aceptar la inferioridad femenina como fenómeno indiscutible" [In her essay on feminine culture she was ready to accept the inferiority of women as an indisputable phenomenon] (94). This reading disregards the very irony that Megged celebrates in Castellanos' later work. Elena Poniatowska also seems to take Castellanos entirely seriously in this section: "en sus tesis *Sobre cultura femenina* (1950) sustenta nada menos que la mujer es inferior al hombre, que ella misma es inferior, y pide perdón por atreverse a pisar un terreno que no es el suyo. Algunas de sus ideas erizan los cabellos y uno tiene que frotarse los ojos repetidas ocasiones y preguntarse '¿Lo dice en serio?'" [In her thesis *Sobre cultura femenina* (1950) she sustains nothing less than that women are inferior to men, that she herself is inferior, and she asks pardon for daring to tread on ground that is not hers. Some of her ideas make your hair stand on end, and you have to rub your eyes and ask yourself, "Is she serious?"] (¡Ay vida, 85). Although she acknowledges Castellanos' irony a few paragraphs later, she too feels that at this point in her life Castellanos believed this discourse. Perla Schwartz, on the other hand, reads the essay as a rebuttal of misogyny and as a call for the creation of a new feminine culture; she characterizes this project as "feminismo integracionista" (integrationist feminism) (43–44).

8. This skeptical stance is implicit in her first epigraph, one of two passages from Unamuno's *Del sentimiento trágico de la vida*: "Nuestras doctrinas no suelen ser sino la justificación a posteriori de nuestra conducta o el modo como tratamos de explicárnosla para nosotros mismos" [Our doctrines are usually nothing but the justification after the fact of our conduct, or the way we try to explain it to ourselves] (9). She signals here that the pronouncements she examines are rationalizations, thus authorizing her own questioning stance.

9. Miller is glossing a passage from Luce Irigaray's *Ce sexe qui n'en est pas un* that focuses on the ambivalence of women's *relation* to language and suggests a strategy of double discourse for women, but also some of its pitfalls:

Il n'est, dans un premier temps, peut-être qu'un seul "chemin," celui qui est historiquement assigné au féminin: le mimétisme. Il s'agit d'assumer, délibérément, ce rôle. Ce qui est déjà retourner en affirmation une subordination, et, de ce fait, commencer à la déjouer. Alors que récuser cette condition revient, pour le féminin, à revendiquer de parler en "sujet" (masculin), soit à postuler un rapport à l'intelligible qui maintient l'indifférence sexuelle.

Jouer de la mimésis, c'est donc, pour une femme, tenter de retrouver le lieu de son exploitation par le discours sans s'y laisser complètement réduire. C'est se resoumettre—en tant que du côté de "sensible," de la matière . . .—à des idées, notamment d'elle, élaborées dans/par une logique masculine, mais pour faire "apparaître," par un effet de répétition ludique, ce qui devait rester occulté: le recouvrement d'une possible opération du féminin dans le langage. C'est aussi "dévoiler" le fait que, si les femmes miment si bien, c'est qu'elles ne se resorbent pas simplement dans cette fonction. Elles restent aussi ailleurs: autre insistence de "matière," mais aussi de "jouissance." (71–2)

There is, in an initial phase, perhaps only one "path," the one historically assigned the feminine: that of *mimicry*. One must assume the feminine role deliberately. Which means already to convert a form of subordination into an affirmation, and thus to begin to thwart it. Whereas a direct feminine challenge to this condition means demanding to speak as a (masculine) "subject," that is, it means to postulate a relation to the intelligible that would maintain sexual indifference.

To play with mimesis is thus, for a woman, to try to recover the place of her exploitation by discourse, without allowing herself simply to be reduced to it. It means to resubmit herself—inasmuch as she is on the side of the "perceptible," of "matter"—to "ideas," in particular to ideas about herself, that are elaborated in/by a masculine logic, but so as to make "visible," by an effort of playful repetition, what was supposed to remain invisible: the cover-up of a possible operation of the feminine in language. It also means "to unveil" the fact that, if women are such good mimics, it is because they are not simply resorbed in this function. *They also remain elsewhere:* another case of the persistence of "matter," but also of "sexual pleasure." (Trans. Catherine Porter, *This Sex Which Is Not One,* 76)

In describing the task of the feminist reader/writer, Irigaray plays "le féminin" against "les femmes." She points out the risks of, on the one hand, maintaining the duality of inside/outside and the posture of "l'indifférence sexuelle," and, on the other hand, of a "*mimétisme*" that would too well reproduce a discourse of dominance. The mimetic practice that she advocates in the second paragraph is a practice of "les femmes" (and not "le féminin"), a practice of repetition that inscribes difference because it is done by female subjects. Implicit in Irigaray's suggestion of "jouer de la mimésis" is the feminist reader who can read this double practice.

10. See also her essays "La palabra y el hecho," *El uso de la palabra,* 52–55, and "Y las madres, ¿Qué opinan?" *El uso de la palabra,* 44–47.

11. Keller describes the strikingly similar dilemma facing the woman scientist. If we substitute "writing" for science and "writer" for scientist in the following statement, we have a clear description of Castellanos' dilemma in *Sobre cultura femenina:*

In a science constructed around the naming of object (nature) as female and the parallel naming of subject (mind) as male, any scientist who happens to be a woman is confronted by an a priori contradiction in terms. This poses a critical problem of identity: any scientist who is not a man walks a path bounded on one side by inauthenticity and on the other by subversion. Just as surely as inauthenticity is the cost a woman suffers by joining men in misogynist jokes, so it is, equally, the cost suffered by a woman who identifies with an image of the scientist modeled on the patriarchal husband. Only if she undergoes a radical disidentification from self can she share masculine pleasure in mastering a nature cast in the image of woman as passive, inert, and blind. Her alternative is to attempt a radical redefinition of terms. Nature must be renamed as not necessarily female, and accordingly, recast with a more inclusive subjectivity. (174–175)

This observation resonates powerfully with Castellanos' more overtly feminist projects in her later writing, culminating in the publication of *Mujer que sabe latín* and the play *El eterno femenino: Farsa*, where she does propose more radical redefinitions of terms.

12. Welch explains the ways that the term "dangerous memory" is used by liberation theologians to mean the practice of recounting the memory of oppression and suffering, of conflict and exclusion, as a critique of existing institutions and discourses (such as the church and theology), particularly as they claim to speak in universal terms (35–39).

3. CASTELLANOS AND *INDIGENISMO* IN MEXICO

1. Although the word *indigenismo* comes into common use as a name for these practices in the twentieth century, Luis Villoro extends the concept to consider the colonial and early Independence periods as well.

2. *Struggle and Survival in Colonial America*, a collection of essays that reconstruct the lives of ordinary people in the Americas under colonial rule, is an especially valuable resource for understanding these dynamics.

3. For a fascinating history of the thesis that Columbus "discovered" America, see O'Gorman.

4. See Ferrari. This issue is entirely devoted to essays on *indigenismo*.

5. "During most of the nineteenth century, the sedentary Indian tribes, which included the majority of the country's population, were in revolt throughout Mexico" (González Navarro, 147). This was also true in Peru and the Andean regions, where the revolt led by Tupac Amaru in 1780 marked a period of revolutionary activity in which ethnic revolts were put down quite savagely.

6. See Rama on the importance of "originality" to the trajectory of literature in Latin America. Braulio Muñoz shows the relationship of the Spanish American "dream of sociocultural unity" (2) to a discourse of *mestizaje* and, specifically, to *indigenista* writing.

7. On "passing," Julio de la Fuente states:

En lo que toca al pase del indio en México, dicho pase es un hecho diario y se efectúa decantando el lenguaje y la indumentaria indígena, principalmente, o una suma de rasgos culturales habitualmente considerados como indios. Sin embargo, en muchos casos no es necesario eliminar nada, ya que el indio no se ha considerado como tal, o ha aprendido ya a considerarse un campesino, un trabajador, o un nativo de una región determinada. El curso de los acontecimientos en México parece señalar que, tanto los indios como los no-indios, están interesados en que aquellos pasen a ser no-indios y que tal paso es relativamente fácil. Esto significa, en gran medida, la desaparición de la indianidad. ("Definición, pase y desaparición del indio en Mexico," Relaciones interétnicas, 72)

Concerning "passing" by Indians in Mexico, this "passing" is a daily fact and is carried out by decanting the indigenous language and dress, mainly, or the sum of cultural traits that are usually considered indigenous. Nevertheless, in many cases it is not necessary to eliminate anything, given that the Indian does not consider himself to be such, or has learned to think of himself as a peasant, a worker, or a native of a particular region. The course of events in Mexico seems to indicate that both Indians and non-Indians alike are interested in having Indians pass over into being non-Indians, and that such a passage is relatively easy. This means, in great measure, the disappearance of Indianness.]

8. For details on the function of the Chiapas Center, see Alfonso Villa Rojas, and de la Fuente, "Resumen de la acción indigenista." For an excellent evaluation of *acción indigenista*, in particular as it concerns the problem of language, see Heath.

9. For a fascinating discussion of *indigenismo* in the context of the broader history of theories and practices concerning rural Mexico, see Hewitt de Alcántara. She looks at the paradigms that orient different approaches used by scholars and bureaucrats from urban centers in their efforts to understand and change the conditions of rural people in Mexico. One important conclusion of her work is that many saw "folk culture" or indigenous culture in negative terms and postulated modernization and incorporation into the nation-state as a solution to problems of poverty, while others saw that incorporation as the cause of more exploitation rather than less. Both of these positions have been held by *indigenistas*.

10. We can see the INI's efforts as the attempt to develop what Gramsci called "organic intellectuals." In their introduction to the section of *The Prison Notebooks* called "The intellectuals," Gramsci's editors, Quintin Hoare and Geoffrey Nowell Smith, state:

The central argument of Gramsci's essay on the formation of intellectuals is simple. The notion of "the intellectuals" as a distinct social category independent of class is a myth. All men are potentially intellectuals in the sense of having an intellect and using it, but not all are intellectuals by social function. Intellectuals in the functional sense fall into two groups. In the first place there are the "traditional" professional intellectuals, literary, scientific and so on, whose position in the interstices of society has a certain inter-class aura about it but derives ultimately from past and present class relations and conceals an attachment to various historical class formations. Secondly, there are the "organic" intellectuals, the thinking and organising elements of a particular fundamental social class. These organic intellectuals are distinguished less by their profession, which may be any job characteristic of their class, than by their function in directing the ideas and aspirations of the class to which they organically belong. (3)

11. In both of her novels, but especially *Oficio de tinieblas*, Castellanos has characters who act as catalysts of change. In *Balún Canán* Felipe Carranza Pech returns to his community with new ideas about his people's participation in national affairs, as does Pedro González Winiktón in *Oficio de tinieblas*. Both are received with distrust at first, and both transform the promise of change, symbolized as a handshake with Lázaro Cárdenas, into their community's own terms of justice—resistance to exploitation and the demand for land.

12. A key book in the elaboration of official Mexican *indigenismo* is Gonzalo Aguirre Beltrán's *Regiones de refugio*. Since 1968, a group of anthropologists has attacked *indigenismo* as ethnocide. Their views are represented in Bonfil Batalla et al., and Materne. For an excellent summary of the points of contention, see van Zantwijk.

13. "El indigenismo, sobre todo, en sus sucesivas olas desde el siglo XVIII aludido, ha sido bandera vengadora de muchos nietos de gachupines y europeos, aunque lo que en realidad éstos hicieron desde la Emancipación, llegada la hora del cumplimiento de las promesas, no les acredita blasones nobiliarios" [Indigenism, above all, in its successive waves since the eighteenth century as referred to before, has been the avenging banner of many of the grandsons of Spanish settlers and Europeans, although in reality what they have done since Emancipation, at the hour of fulfilling promises, does not confer on them honors of nobility] (Rama, 120).

14. Angel Rama's work explores these contradictions in the Latin American literary enterprise. In *Transculturación narrativa en América Latina* he describes succinctly the interplay among three impulses that have directed the progression of literary production in Latin America in varying doses—"independencia, originalidad, representatividad" [independence, originality, representativeness](11–20)—in terms of movement between the poles of center and periphery, but he does not lock these poles into the (European) terms of European center and Latin American periphery. Following Cuban anthropologist Fernando Ortiz, Rama analyzes Latin American literary development (and its theorization) as a process of transculturation: the selection, rejection, and invention that occurs when two cultures come into contact, and literary transculturation as occurring in languages, in literary structure, and in "cosmovisión," or the site of values and ideology. Even as he reads texts as products of this process, or as spaces of cultural conflict, Rama reminds us that literature and literary historiography are ideological projects; in Latin America, the history of colonialism forces to the surface the political contradictions of an aesthetic doctrine that holds literature to be somehow autonomous or "useless."

In his discussion of *indigenismo* in the Andean region, Antonio Cornejo Polar considers *indigenista* texts to be privileged sites of the transculturation that Rama describes. These texts both represent and enact the conflict of European and indigenous cultures and symbolic systems, of written culture and an oral culture, of different ways of understanding and representing history and identity.

15. Other essays in the same collection on the topic of the writer's role in Mexico are "Problemas de la novela" [Problems of the Novel], "Ideología y literatura" [Ideology and Literature], "La novela mexicana contemporánea" [The Contemporary Mexican Novel], and "La novela mexicana y su valor testimonial" [The Mexican Novel and Its Testimonial Value].

4. BALÚN CANÁN AS PALIMPSEST

1. Victor Turner defines a social drama as an "event . . . which is cross-culturally isolable and which exhibits, if it is allowed to come to full term, a characteristic processual structure" (141). He describes the structure as follows: "social dramas, 'dramas of living' as Kenneth Burke calls them, can be aptly studied as having four phases. These I label breach, crisis, redress, and *either* reintegration *or* recognition of schism. Social dramas occur within groups of persons who share values and interests and who have a real or alleged common history" (145). Turner considers social dramas the grounds for some narrative genres that in turn provide models or frames for the experience of social dramas as they "feed back into the social process, providing it with a rhetoric, a mode of emplotment and a meaning" (149).

2. A number of articles on Castellanos' novels avoid an "either women/or Indians" approach by treating the link between forms of oppression as a problem of language and power. Harrison-MacDonald lays the foundation for this approach, examining Castellanos' development of her ideas about language and culture in her essays and novels in terms of the ways oppression is codified and maintained through language use but also in terms of the ways women and indigenous people try to use language to redefine an oppressive reality. Fiscal states this problem as that of the "incapacidad de mujeres e indígenas para valerse del lenguaje, incapacidad que se traducía en una situación de debilidad y desventaja" [the inability of women and indigenous people to avail themselves of language, an inability that is translated into a weak and disadvantaged situation] (25). Schlau examines how continued oppression is reinforced by language as well, but rather than implying that some kind of characteristic of these groups results in an inability, she talks about the limited access of women and indigenous people to effective discourse as a question of power (46). And Cypess' reading of *Balún Canán* provides an excellent example of how Castellanos shows these relations of power through the workings of discourse.

3. For an interesting psychoanalytic perspective on Castellanos' family relations and their impact on her work, see Franco Leñero.

4. In the traditional psychoanalytic account offered by Franco Leñero, the guilt Rosario feels about her brother's death stems from feelings of sibling rivalry. However, it is clear that the child was witness to her family's attempts to redirect the force of a curse from her brother to her.

5. For example, "La espada de la injusticia, dice Simone Weil, es una espada de

dos puntos y hiere tanto al que la empuña como al que se encuentra en el extremo contrario" [The sword of injustice, says Simone Weil, is a sword with two points that wounds he who grasps it as much as whoever finds himself on the other end] (*Juicios sumarios*, 126). Another aphorism that Castellanos cited frequently is "Esa distancia que, según Simone Weil, es el alma de lo bello" [That distance that, according to Simone Weil, is the soul of the beautiful] (*Juicios sumarios*, 224).

6. See Villoro for an extremely useful account of the history of the ideological "conceptuación de lo indígena" (conceptualization of the indigenous) in Mexico from the Conquest to 1950.

7. See chap. 5 for a more extensive discussion of *Ciudad Real*.

8. This kind of dramatic presentation is a direct descendant of the missionaries' use of dramatic forms to accomplish a similar project, that of interpellating the Indians into Christianity.

9. Some of the critics who treat Castellanos' novels specifically in terms of ethnic conflict include Mario Benedetti, John S. Brushwood, María Luisa Cresta de Leguizamón, Emma Godoy, Alfonso González, Luis Leal, Marta Portal, Phyllis Rodríguez Peralta, and Joseph Sommers.

10. An example is Luis Leal's brief evaluation of Castellanos' narrative: "Lo importante en las novelas de Castellanos es que presenta a un indio humano, inteligente, conciente de sus problemas y de que puede resolverlas sin ayuda externa. Todo ello dramatizado artísticamente, lo que da valor permanente a esta obra narrativa" [The important thing in the novels of Castellanos is that she presents an Indian who is human, intelligent, conscious of his problems and that he can solve them without outside help] (*Breve historia*, 290).

11. Essays that represent her views on this subject include "Ideología y literatura," "La novela mexicana contemporánea," and "La novela mexicana y su valor testimonial," in *El uso de la palabra*, 76–130.

12. León-Portilla, 356, gives a Spanish translation of a Tzeltal story on the discovery of corn transcribed by Marianna C. Slocum: El origen del maíz según los tzeltales contemporáneos [The Origins of Corn according to Contemporary Tzeltales]:

Te voy a decir otra cosa. La oí. Los ancianos hace mucho me la contaron. Ellos decían así: De este modo apareció la primera semilla de nuestro maíz. Allí estaba una hormiga negra grande, como las que vemos que andan y hacen sus casas en la tierra. La hormiga llevaba a cuestas maíz. Cuando ellos vieron que era maíz lo que llevaba a cuestas, la agarraron. Le preguntaron dónde cogía el maíz. Entonces la amarraron, la apretaron mucho por el miedo.

I'm going to tell you something else. I heard it. The old folks told it to me a long time ago. This is what they said: This is the way that the first seed of our corn appeared. There was a big black ant, like the kind we see walking around, making their houses in the ground. The ant was carrying corn on its back. When they saw that it was carrying corn, they grabbed it. They asked it where it got the corn. Then they tied it up, they squeezed it tight to frighten it.

13. For an example of this approach, see González, "La soledad y los patrones de dominio en la cuentística de Rosario Castellanos" (107–113).

14. Again, to quote Margaret Homans, "there is a specifically gender-based alienation from language that is characterized by the special ambiguity of women's simultaneous participation in and exclusion from a hegemonic group (with the qualification that while a hegemonic group usually refers to white, ruling class men, it can also refer in context to men of any woman's own race or nationality, who are hegemonic relative to her" (205).

15. Two otherwise favorable views cite the child's narration as the novel's major problem: "If only Señora Castellanos had been able to solve her story-telling problem she might have written a masterpiece. Unfortunately she puts most of it into the mouth of the seven-year-old Argüello daughter—herself, presumably—who narrates away in the breathless historic present, like an all seeing eye. There are occasional monologues by adults and patches with no narrator. The effect is inevitably one of maddening dissociation" (Maurice Richardson, NS July 25, 1959, pp. 115–116, cited in Foster, 241); and "It would have been a still better novel had it been all written from the child's viewpoint: the sudden change of narrator takes away from both the pace and the pathos of the story; it is almost as if the author felt she couldn't keep it up, that relating a whole revolution, even as experienced by one family, on one hacienda, from a seven-year-old's point of view, was too complex an undertaking" (Anne Fremantle, *Saturday Review* June 11, 1960, 38, cited in Foster, 242).

16. Cited in Cypess.

17. "The novel can be defined as a diversity of social speech types (sometimes even a diversity of languages) and a diversity of individual voices, artistically organized . . . Authorial speech, the speeches of narrators, inserted genres, the speech of characters are merely those fundamental compositional unities with whose help heteroglossia can enter the novel" (Bakhtin, *The Dialogic Imagination*, 262–263).

18. Laura Lee Crumley de Pérez shows how this child's voice is also the reader's access to another set of silenced voices, those of indigenous people. She compares this aspect of *Balún Canán* to Arguedas' use of a (male) child narrator in *Los ríos profundos*. In *Balún Canán* the vision of the Indian world has value for the girl because she receives it through the loving mother figure of her *nana*.

19. See Castellanos' essay "El idioma en San Cristóbal de las Casas" in *Juicios Sumarios*, 131–137.

20. See Wolf, 205, for an explanation of how the institution of *trabajo baldío* came about; under colonial rule, when haciendas took Indian land they would then lease it back to them for their own use in return for labor on the rest of the hacienda land.

21. This could be a reference to the kind of hybrid codexes produced by Indian writers in the sixteenth and seventeenth centuries, which told Indian stories in their own languages along with illustrations. See Lienhard, "Las huellas de las culturas indígenas."

22. This is reinforced in the account of Matilde's childhood. After the death of her parents she is reared by her older sister and remembers everyone's comments to the effect that she has no family because there is no man in the house.

23. Castellanos, "La participación de la mujer mexicana en la educación formal," *Mujer que sabe latín*, 21–40.

5. *CIUDAD REAL:* THE PITFALLS OF INDIGENISTA CONSCIOUSNESS

1. These stories were published in 1960, the year after the Cuban Revolution and not long after the U.S.-sponsored coup against the Arbenz government in Guatemala, when the United States was in fact training Cubans for the Bay of Pigs invasion in the area.

2. Given the parallels between Alicia's situation and Castellanos' own on her return to Chiapas, the story might be read as a version of her own painful disillusionments.

3. See Annis for an examination of why evangelical Protestantism has become so successful among the Maya in recent years.

6. VERSIONS OF HISTORY IN *OFICIO DE TINIEBLAS*

1. A portion of the work in English did appear as "Office of Tenebrae," translated by Anne Fremantle and Christopher Fremantle, in Fremantle, 72–79.

2. For details on the 1712 uprising, see Wasserstrom.

3. For the historical background of ethnic conflict in Chiapas, see Wasserstrom (127–168).

4. Castellanos uses this incident in the novel but Bricker's oral accounts by both Ladinos and Indians, collected over one hundred years after the events, mention it as well. In an oral Ladino account of the 1869 uprising, the teller reports the role of the Virgin in defeating the Indian uprising of 1712 and also attributes the Ladino victory of 1869 to her. See Bricker (321).

5. Two primary sources for the events of the uprising are Molina and Pineda. Molina's account is contemporary while Pineda's was written twenty years later.

6. The "talking cross" or talking saint statue as a way of representing spiritual and political action is still part of Mayan life and was a major part of the Maya rebellions known as the Caste War of the Yucatán. See Reed and Bricker for details.

7. This idea informs Gonzalo Aguirre Beltrán's notion of "regiones de refugio" (*Regiones de refugio*).

8. For an excellent discussion of the way in which ideas about history are related to the assumption that history is written, see Mignolo.

9. Bricker provides texts of oral histories of caste wars in Chiapas as told by both Maya and Ladino informants, in Maya and in Spanish.

10. Bricker accepts the account of the crucifixion while Rus and Wasserstrom claim it is apocryphal.

11. Letter published in "Diorama de la cultura," *Excélsior* (August 11, 1974), 4.

12. While the sophisticated calendar of the ancient Maya is no longer used in its original form, many Maya communities have retained important elements from it, both as a means of reckoning the passage of time and as a means of understanding the

symbolic importance of events. See Dennis Tedlock's introduction to his translation of the Popol Vuh.

13. Laura Lee Crumley de Pérez suggests that we look at the way the word *regazo* (lap) works as a figure in *Balún Canán;* the figure of the maternal is associated with a Maya woman for the Ladina girl, while, within the Maya community itself, sterility is associated with the lack of communication between men and women.

14. The *atajadoras*, or "black widows," as they are called by Morris are no longer allowed in the marketplace of San Cristóbal (18).

15. The account of how he signs the contract, hiding his Maya name and becoming anonymous among the others without the prestige and recognition of his own community, how he is tricked into more debts, is like the first story in *Ciudad Real*, "La muerte del tigre."

16. The essays "Herlinda se va" and "Frente doméstico" (*El uso de la palabra*) elaborate on Castellanos' own experiences with her *nana*.

17. See chap. 3, note 10.

18. This fear is echoed by Fanon: "The African people and indeed all underdeveloped peoples, contrary to common belief, very quickly build up a social and political consciousness. What can be dangerous is when they reach the stage of social consciousness before the stage of nationalism. If this happens , we find in underdeveloped countries fierce demands for social justice which paradoxically are allied with often primitive tribalism" ("Pitfalls," 204).

7. "BUCEANDO CADA VEZ MÁS HONDO . . .": THE DANGEROUS MEMORY OF WOMEN'S LIVES

1. See Oyarzun.

2. See Kathleen O'Quinn's article in Ahern and Vásquez, *Homenaje a Rosario Castellanos* for a detailed discussion of how Castellanos reworked the piece.

3. At the time the story was published, bars in Mexico had signs forbidding entry to women, but the laws have since changed.

4. "De esa clase, de esa familia, desertó Matilde para ir al encuentro de los desheredados, de los miserables, de los ignorantes. Pero una decisión tan insólita no logró sino multiplicar las trampas que le impidieran su realización" (81) [Matilde deserted that class, that family to go in search of the disinherited, the poverty-stricken, the uneducated. But such an unheard-of choice only succeeded in multiplying the traps that impeded her self-realization]. Matilde's description of the failures of her time living among the Indians she wanted to help (112–113) is a concise rendering of the critique contained in *Ciudad Real*.

8. PUBLIC WRITING, PUBLIC READING: ROSARIO CASTELLANOS AS ESSAYIST

1. The bibliography in Ahern and Vásquez, *Homenaje a Rosario Castellanos* mentions at least ninety other pieces that have not been anthologized. Until very recently, Castellanos' essays as a body did not receive the critical attention accorded the rest of

her work, although critics have focused on individual essays or specific themes. Two studies approach Castellanos' essays as a body: the section of Ahern's introductory essay to *A Rosario Castellanos Reader* called "Essays: Writing Her Self" (39–53) focuses primarily on themes and strategies of Castellanos' feminism in her essays; Claudia Schaeffer's "Rosario Castellanos and the Confessions of Literary Journalism," chap. 2 of *Textured Lives*, examines Castellanos' essay writing in its engagement with Mexican political discourses of the sixties and seventies. Castillo makes substantial use of the essays in her discussion of Latin American women writers.

2. For an overview of Latin American women's organizing in the nineteenth century and the importance of journalism in those efforts, see chap. 4 of Francesca Miller. For two studies that recontextualize the writing of two prominent Latin American women writers through a consideration of their journalism, see Kirkpatrick and Greenberg.

AFTERWORD

1. Fernando Ulloa, the only one to enunciate a discourse of social justice, is unable to comprehend the social realities to which he is witness, in terms of both ethnic and sexual relations.

Bibliography

WORKS BY ROSARIO CASTELLANOS

Album de familia. Mexico City: Joaquín Mortiz, 1971.

Al pie de la letra: Poemas. Xalapa: Universidad Veracruzana, 1959.

Apuntes para una declaración de fé. Mexico City: Ediciones de América, Revista Antológica, 1949.

Balún Canán. Mexico City: Fondo de Cultura Económica, 1957.

Ciudad Real. Xalapa: Universidad Veracruzana, 1960.

Los convidados de agosto. Mexico City: Ediciones Era, 1964.

De la vigilia estéril. Mexico City: Ediciones de América, Revista Antológica, 1950.

Dos poemas. Mexico City: Icaro, Impresora Económica, 1950.

El eterno femenino: Farsa. Mexico City: Fondo de Cultura Económica, 1975.

"Introducción del Teatro Petul." *Teatro Petul.* Mexico City: Instituto Nacional Indigenista, 1962. 1–8.

Juicios sumarios. Xalapa: Universidad Veracruzana, 1966.

Lívida luz: Poemas. Mexico City: Universidad Nacional Autónoma de México, 1960.

El mar y sus pescaditos. Mexico City: Secretaría de Educación Pública, 1975.

Materia memorable. Mexico City: Universidad Nacional Autónoma de México, 1969.

Mujer que sabe latín . . . Mexico City: Secretaría de Educación Pública, 1973.

"La novela mexicana contemporánea y su valor testimonial." *Hispania* 47 (May 1964): 223–230. Also in *Juicios sumarios,* 114–130. Rpt. *La novela mexicana contemporánea y su valor testimonial.* Mexico City: Cuadernos de la Juventud, 1972.

Oficio de tinieblas. Mexico City: Joaquín Mortiz, 1962.

Poemas (1953–1955). Mexico City: Colección Metáfora, 1957.

Poesía no eres tú: Obra poética: 1948–1971. Mexico City: Fondo de Cultura Económica, 1972.

Presentación al templo: Poemas. (Madrid, 1951). Mexico City: Ediciones de América, Revista Antológica, 1952.

El rescate del mundo. Mexico City: Ediciones de América, Revista Antológica, 1952.

Salomé y Judith: Poemas dramáticos. Mexico City: Editorial Jus, 1959.

Sobre cultura femenina. Mexico City: Ediciones de *América, Revista Antológica,* 1950.
"Tablero de damas: Pieza en un acto." *América, Revista Antológica* 68 (June 1952): 185–224.
"Teatro Petul." *Revista de la Universidad* (January 1965): 30.
Trayectoria del polvo. Mexico City: Costa-Amic, 1948.
El uso de la palabra. Mexico City: Editorial Excélsior, 1975.
Castellanos, Rosario, et al. *La corrupción.* Mexico City: Editorial Nuestro Tiempo, 1969.

WORKS CITED

Agosín, Marjorie. "Rosario Castellanos ante el espejo." *Cuadernos Americanos* 2, no. 253 (1984): 219–226.
Aguirre Beltrán, Gonzalo. "Integración regional." *Los centros coordinadores indigenistas: Edición conmemorativa en ocasión del XXXV Congreso Internacional de Americanistas.* Mexico City: Instituto Nacional Indigenista, 1962, pp. 7–49.
———. *Regiones de refugio.* Mexico City: Instituto Internacional Indigenista, 1967.
Ahern, Maureen, and Mary Seale Vásquez, eds. *Homenaje a Rosario Castellanos.* Valencia: Albatrós Ediciones Hispanófila, 1980.
———, ed. and trans. *A Rosario Castellanos Reader: An Anthology of Her Poetry, Short Fiction, Essays, and Drama.* Austin: University of Texas Press, 1988.
Althusser, Louis. "Ideology and Ideological State Apparatuses (Notes towards an Investigation)." *Lenin and Philosophy and Other Essays,* trans. Ben Brewster. London: New Left Books, 1971, pp. 121–173.
Anderson, Helene M. "Rosario Castellanos and the Structures of Power." *Contemporary Women Authors of Latin America: Introductory Essays.* Ed. Doris Meyer. New York: Brooklyn College Press, 1983, pp. 22–32.
Annis, Sheldon. *God and Production in a Guatemalan Town.* Austin: University of Texas Press, 1987.
Armanda Alegría, Juana. *Emancipación femenina en el subdesarrollo.* Mexico City: Editorial Diana, 1982.
Baker, Houston A. "Caliban's Triple Play." *Critical Inquiry* 13 (Autumn 1986): 182–196.
Bakhtin, Mikhail. *The Dialogic Imagination: Four Essays.* Ed. Michael J. Holquist. Austin: University of Texas Press, 1981.
———. "Discourse Typology in Prose." *Readings in Russian Poetics: Formalist and Structuralist Views.* Eds. Ladislav Mateja and Krystyna Pormorska. Cambridge: MIT Press, 1971, pp. 176–197.
Benedetti, Mario. "Rosario Castellanos y la incomunicación racial." *Letras del continente mestizo.* Montevideo: Arca, 1969, pp. 165–170.
Beverly, John, and Marc Zimmerman. *Literature and Politics in the Central American Revolutions.* Austin: University of Texas Press, 1990.
Blau du Plessis, Rachel. "For the Etruscans." *The New Feminist Criticism.* Ed. Elaine Showalter. New York: Pantheon, 1985, pp. 271–290.

Bonfil Batalla, Guillermo, et al. *América Latina: Etnodesarrollo y etnocidio*. San José, Costa Rica: Ediciones FLACSO, 1982.

Bonifaz, Oscar. *Rosario*. Mexico City: Presencia Latinoamericana, 1984.

Bricker, Victoria Reifler. *The Indian Christ, the Indian King: The Historical Substrate of Maya Myth and Ritual*. Austin: University of Texas Press, 1981.

Brown, Paul. "'This Thing of Darkness I Acknowledge Mine': *The Tempest* and the Discourse of Colonialism." *Political Shakespeare: New Essays in Cultural Materialism*. Eds. Jonathan Dollimore and Alan Sinfield. Ithaca, N.Y.: Cornell University Press, 1985, pp. 48–71.

Brushwood, John. *Mexico in Its Novel: A Nation's Search for Identity*. Austin: University of Texas Press, 1966.

———. *The Spanish-American Novel: A Twentieth Century Survey*. Austin: University of Texas Press, 1975.

Busia, Abena P. A. "Silencing Sycorax: On African Colonial Discourse and the Unvoiced Female." *Cultural Critique* 14 (Winter 1989–1990): 81–104.

Calderón, Germaine. *El universo poético de Rosario Castellanos*. Mexico City: Cuadernos UNAM, 1979.

Campos, Jorge. "Novelas e ideas de Rosario Castellanos." *Insula* 19, no. 211 (1964): 11.

Carballo, Emmanuel. *Diecinueve protagonistas de la literatura mexicana del siglo XX*. Mexico City: Empresas Editoriales, 1965.

———. "Rosario Castellanos: La historia de sus libros contada por ella misma." *Diecinueve protagonistas de la literatura mexicana del siglo XX*. Mexico City: Empresas Editoriales, 1965, pp. 411–424.

Caso, Alfonso. "Los ideales de la acción indigenista." *Los centros coordinadores indigenistas: Edición conmemorativa en ocasión del XXXV Congreso Internacional de Americanistas*. Mexico City: Instituto Nacional Indigenista, 1962, pp. 7–49.

———. *Indigenismo*. Mexico City: Instituto Nacional Indigenista, 1958.

———. "El indigenismo mexicano." *Cahiers d'histoire mondiale* 10 (1967): 438–444.

Castillo, Debra. *Talking Back: Toward a Latin American Feminist Literary Criticism*. Ithaca, N.Y.: Cornell University Press, 1992.

Castro, Dolores. "Reseña: *Balún-Canán*." *La Palabra y el Hombre* 7 (July–September 1958): 333–336.

Castro-Klarén, Sara, Silvia Molloy, and Beatriz Sarlo. *Latin American Women's Writing: An Anthology*. Boulder, Colo.: Westview, 1991.

Césaire, Aimé. *Discours sur le colonialisme*. Paris: Présence Africaine, 1955.

Cornejo Polar, Antonio. "El indigenismo y las literaturas heterogéneas: Su doble estatuto socio-cultural." *Revista de Crítica Literaria Latinoamericana* 7–8 (1978): 7–21.

———. "Sobre el 'neo-indigenismo' y las novelas de Manuel Scorza." *Revista Iberoamericana* 50, no. 127 (April–June 1984): 549–557.

Cosse, Rómulo. *Crítica latinoamericana: Propuestas y ejercicios. Horacio Quiroga, Ricardo Guiraldes, Rosario Castellanos, Fray Matías de Córdoba*. Xalapa: Universidad Veracruzana, 1982.

Cresta de Leguizamón, María Luisa. "En recuerdo de Rosario Castellanos." *La Palabra y el Hombre* 19 (1976): 3–18.

Crumley de Pérez, Laura Lee. "*Balún-Canán* and the Narrative Structure of an Indigenous View of the World: Mesoamerican Myth in Rosario Castellanos." *Revista Iberoamericana* 50, no. 127 (April–June 1984): 491–503.

Cypess, Sandra Messinger. "*Balún-Canán*: A Model Demonstration of Discourse as Power." *Revista de Estudios Hispánicos* 19, no. 3 (1985): 1–15.

———. *La Malinche in Mexican Literature: From History to Myth*. Austin: University of Texas Press, 1991.

de Beer, Gabriella. "Feminismo en la obra poética de Rosario Castellanos." *Revista de Crítica Literaria Latinoamericana* 7 (1981): 105–112.

de la Fuente, Julio. "Relaciones étnicas en los altos de Chiapas." *Relaciones interétnicas*. Mexico City: Instituto Nacional Indigenista, 1965, pp. 162–182.

———. "Resumen de la acción indigenista." *Los centros coordinadores indigenistas: Edición conmemorativa en ocasión del XXXV Congreso Internacional de Americanistas*. Mexico City: Instituto Nacional Indigenista, 1962, pp. 159–166.

de Lauretis, Teresa. *Alice Doesn't: Feminism, Semiotics, Cinema*. Bloomington: Indiana University Press, 1984.

Dorward, Frances R. "The Function of Interiorization in *Oficio de tinieblas*." *Neophilologus* 69, no. 3 (1985): 374–385.

Dybvig, Rhoda. *Rosario Castellanos, biografía y novelística*. Mexico City: N.p., 1965.

Fanon, Frantz. *Peau noire, masques blanches*. Paris: Seuil, 1952.

———. "The Pitfalls of National Consciousness." *The Wretched of the Earth*. New York: Grove, 1968, pp. 148–205.

Fernández Retamar, Roberto. *Calibán: Apuntes sobre la cultura en nuestra América*. Mexico City: Editorial Diógenes, 1972.

Ferrari, Américo. "El concepto de indio y la cuestión racial en el Perú en los 'Siete ensayos' de José Carlos Mariátegui." *Revista Iberoamericana* 50 (April–June 1984): 395–410.

Fetterly, Judith. *The Resisting Reader: A Feminist Approach to American Literature*. Bloomington: Indiana University Press, 1978.

Fiscal, María Rosa. "Identidad y lenguaje en los personajes femeninos de Rosario Castellanos." *Chasqui* 14, nos. 2–3 (1985): 25–35.

Foster, David William, and Virginia Ramos Foster. "Castellanos, Rosario (1925–). In *A Library of Literary Criticism: Modern Latin American Literature*. Vol. 1: A–L. New York: Ungar, 1975, pp. 240–246.

Franco, Jean. *A Literary History of Spain: Spanish American Literature since Independence*. New York: Barnes and Noble, 1973.

———. *The Modern Culture of Latin America*. London: Penguin, 1967.

———. *Plotting Women: Gender and Representation in Mexico*. New York: Columbia University Press, 1989.

Franco Leñero, María Estela. *Rosario Castellanos. Semblanza psicoanalítica: otro modo de ser humano y libre*. Mexico City: Plaza y Janes, 1985.

Fremantle, Anne, ed. *Latin American Literature Today*. New York: Mentor, 1977.

Friedlander, Judith. *Being Indian in Hueyapan: A Study of Forced Indian Identity in Contemporary Mexico*. New York: St. Martin's Press, 1975.

Frischmann, Donald H. "El sistema patriarcal y las relaciones heterosexuales en *Balún-Canán* de Rosario Castellanos." *Revista Iberoamericana* 51 (1985): 665–678.

Furnival, Chloe. "Confronting Myths of Oppression: The Short Stories of Rosario Castellanos." *Knives and Angels: Women Writers in Latin America.* Ed. Susan Bassnett. London: Zed Books, 1990, pp. 52–73.

Gamio, Manuel. *Forjando patria.* Mexico City: Porrúa Hnos., 1916.

García Flores, Margarita. "Adelina Zendejas: la lucha de las mujeres mexicanas." *fem: Diez años de periodismo feminista.* Ed. Carmen Ramos Escandón. Mexico City: Grupo Editorial Planeta, 1988.

Gates, Henry Louis, Jr. "The Blackness of Blackness: A Critique of the Sign and the Signifying Monkey." *Black Literature and Literary Theory.* Ed. H. L. Gates, Jr. New York: Methuen, 1984, pp. 285–381.

———. "'What's Love Got to Do with It?': Critical Theory, Integrity, and the Black Idiom." *New Literary History* 18 (Winter 1987): 347–348.

Godoy, Emma. "Rosario Castellanos." *Abside* 39 (1975): 350–354.

González, Alfonso. "Lenguaje y protesta en *Oficio de Tinieblas.*" *Revista de Estudios Hispánicos* 9 (October 1975): 441–450.

———. "La soledad y los patrones de dominio en la cuentística de Rosario Castellanos." Ed. Maureen Ahern and Mary Seale Vásquez. Valencia: Albatrós Ediciones Hispanófila, 1980, pp. 107–113.

González Navarro, Moisés. "'Mestizaje' in Mexico during the National Period." *Race and Class in Latin America.* Ed. M. Mörner. New York: Columbia University Press, 1970, pp. 145–169.

Gordimer, Nadine. *The Essential Gesture: Writing, Politics and Places.* New York: Knopf, 1988.

Gordon, Samuel. "Cuando el pasado maneja la pluma con ira." *Revista de la Universidad Hebrea de Jerusalén* (1973): 34–40.

Gramsci, Antonio. *Selections from the Prison Notebooks of Antonio Gramsci.* Ed. and trans. Quintin Hoare and Geoffrey Nowell Smith. New York: International Publishers, 1971.

Greenberg, Janet. "A Question of Blood: The Conflict of Sex and Class in the *Autobiografía* of Victoria Ocampo." *Women, Culture, and Politics in Latin America.* Seminar on Feminism and Culture in Latin America. Berkeley and Los Angeles: University of California Press, 1990, pp. 130–150.

Harlow, Barbara. *Resistance Literature.* New York: Methuen,1987.

Harrison-MacDonald, Regina. "Rosario Castellanos: On Language." *Homenaje a Rosario Castellanos.* Ed. Maureen Ahern and Mary Seale Vásquez. Valencia: Albatrós Ediciones Hispanófila, 1980, pp. 41–64.

Heath, Shirley Brice. *Telling Tongues: Language Problems in Mexico, Colony to Nation.* New York: Columbia University Press, 1972.

Hendrickson, Margarita D. "Rosario Castellanos: Origen y búsqueda en su poesía temprana." *Letras femeninas* 13, nos. 1–2 (1987): 21–27.

Hewitt de Alcántara, Cynthia. *Anthropological Perspectives on Rural Mexico.* New York: Routledge, 1984.

Homans, Margaret. "Her Very Own Howl: The Ambiguities of Representation in Recent Women's Fiction." *Signs* 9, no. 2 (1983): 186–205.

hooks, bell, and Cornel West. *Breaking Bread: Insurgent Black Intellectual Life.* Boston: South End Press, 1991.

Hull, Gloria T., Patricia Bell Scott, and Barbara Smith, eds. *All the Women Are White, All the Blacks Are Men, but Some of Us Are Brave: Black Women's Studies.* Old Westbury, N.Y.: Feminist Press, 1982.

Irigaray, Luce. *Ce sexe qui n'en est pas un.* Paris: Editions de Minuit, 1970.

———. *This Sex Which Is Not One.* Trans. Catherine Porter with Carolyn Burke. Ithaca, N.Y.: Cornell University Press, 1985.

Jacobus, Mary. "Is There a Woman in This Text?" *New Literary History* 14 (Autumn 1982): 117–141.

JanMohamed, Abdul R. *Manichean Aesthetics: The Politics of Literature in Colonial Africa.* Amherst: University of Massachussets Press, 1983.

Jehlen, Myra. "Archimedes and the Paradox of Feminist Criticism." *The Signs Reader.* Ed. E. Abel and E. Abel. Chicago: University of Chicago Press, 1983, pp. 69–95.

Kaminsky, Amy. *Reading the Body Politic: Feminist Criticism and Latin American Women Writers.* Minneapolis: University of Minnesota Press, 1993.

Keller, Evelyn Fox. *Reflections on Gender and Science.* New Haven, Conn.: Yale University Press, 1985.

Kirkpatrick, Gwen. "The Journalism of Alfonsina Storni: A New Approach to Women's History in Argentina." *Women, Culture, and Politics in Latin America.* Seminar on Feminism and Culture in Latin America. Berkeley and Los Angeles: University of California Press, 1990, pp. 105–129.

Lagos Pope, María Inés. "En busca de una identidad: Individuo y sociedad: *Balún-Canán* de Rosario Castellanos." *Revista/Review Interamericana* 25, nos. 1–4 (Spring–Winter 1985): 79–90.

Lamming, George. *The Pleasures of Exile.* London: M. Joseph, 1960.

Langford, Walter M. *The Mexican Novel Comes of Age.* Notre Dame, Ind.: Notre Dame University Press, 1971.

Lau Jaiven, Ana. *La nueva ola del feminismo en México.* Mexico City: Grupo Editorial Planeta, 1987.

Leal, Luis. *Breve historia de la literatura hispanoamericana.* New York: Knopf, 1971.

———. *Panorama de la literatura mexicana actual.* Washington: Organization of American States, 1968.

León-Portilla, Miguel. "La palabra antigua y nueva del hombre de Mesoamérica." *Revista Iberoamericana* 50, no. 127 (April–June 1984): 345–366.

Lienhard, Martin. "Las huellas de las culturas indígenas o mestizo-arcáicas en la literatura escrita de Hispanoamérica." *Hispamérica* 37 (April 1984): 3–13.

———. "The Legitimation of Native-Americans in Two Central American Novels (*Hombres de Maíz* and *Balún-Canán*)." *Cuadernos Hispanoamericanos* 414 (December 1984): 110–120.

Lindstrom, Naomi. "Women's Expression and Narrative Technique in Rosario Castellanos' *In Darkness*." *Modern Language Studies* 13, no. 3 (Summer 1983): 71–80.

Macías, Ana. *Against All Odds.* Westport, Conn.: Greenwood Press, 1982.

McLeod, Murdo J., and Robert Wasserstrom, eds. *Spaniards and Indians in Southeast Mesoamerica: Essays on the History of Ethnic Relations*. Lincoln: University of Nebraska Press, 1983.

Maíz, Magdalena. "Tres escritoras: Garro/Castellanos/Mendoza." *Plural* 12, no. 142 (July 1983): 62–65.

Mandlove, Nancy. "Toward the Ransom of Eve: Myth and History in the Poetry of Rosario Castellanos." *In Retrospect: Essays on Latin American Literature (In Memory of Willis Knapp Jones)*. Ed. Elizabeth S. Rogers and Timothy J. Rogers. York, S.C.: Spanish Literature Publications Company, 1987, pp. 68–84.

Mannoni, Octave. *Psychologie de la colonisation*. Paris: Seuil, 1950.

Mariátegui, José Carlos. *Siete ensayos de interpretación de la realidad peruana*. 1928. Lima: Biblioteca Amauta, 1973.

Marks, Elaine, and Isabelle de Courtivron, eds. *New French Feminisms: An Anthology*. New York: Schocken Books, 1981.

Martínez, José Luis. *De la naturaleza y carácter de la literatura mexicana*. Mexico City: Tezontle, 1960.

Materne, Yves, ed. *The Indian Awakening in Latin America*. New York: Friendship Press, 1980.

Megged, Nahum. *Rosario Castellanos: Un largo camino a la ironía*. Mexico City: Colegio de México, 1982.

Mejías Alonso, Almudena. "La narrativa de Rosario Castellanos y el indigenismo." *Cuadernos Americanos* 260, no. 3 (1985): 204–217.

Meléndez, Concha. *La novela indianista en Hispanoamérica*. Río Piedras: University of Puerto Rico, 1961.

Mignolo, Walter D. "La historia de la escritura y la escritura de la historia." *De la crónica a la nueva narrativa mexicana*. Eds. Merlin H. Forster and Julio Ortega. Mexico City: Editorial Oasis, 1986, pp. 13–28.

Millán, María del Carmen. "En torno a *Oficio de tinieblas*." *Anuario de Letras* 3 (1963): 287–299.

———. *Literatura mexicana*. Mexico City: Esfinge, 1962.

Miller, Beth. *Rosario Castellanos: Una conciencia feminista en México*. Mexico City: Colección Maciel, UNACH, 1983.

———. "Rosario Castellanos' *Guests in August*: Critical Realism and the Provincial Middle Class." *Latin American Literary Review* 7 (1979): 5–19.

Miller, Francesca. *Latin American Women and the Search for Social Justice*. Hanover, N.H.: University Press of New England, 1991.

Miller, Martha LaFollette. "A Semiotic Analysis of Three Poems by Rosario Castellanos." *Revista/Review Interamericana* 12, no. 1 (1982): 77–86.

Miller, Nancy K. "Emphasis Added: Plots and Plausibilities in Women's Fiction." *PMLA* 96 (January 1981): 36–48.

Miller, Yvette. "El temario poético de Rosario Castellanos." *Hispamérica* 10, no. 29 (1981): 107–115.

Molina, Cristóbal. *War of the Castes: Indian Uprisings in Chiapas, 1867–70*. Trans. Ernest Noyes and Dolores Morgandanes. Middle American Series, Pamphlet 5, no. 8. New Orleans: Tulane University Press, 1934.

Mörner, Magnus. "Historical Research on Race Relations in Latin America during the National Period." *Race and Class in Latin America*. Ed. M. Mörner. New York: Columbia University Press, 1970, pp. 199–229.

Morris, Walter F., Jr. *Living Maya*. New York: Henry N. Abrams, 1987.

Muñoz, Braulio. *Sons of the Wind: The Search for Identity in Spanish American Indian Literature*. New Brunswick, N.J.: Rutgers University Press, 1982.

Muñoz, Willy. "*Los convidados de agosto*: Acercamiento a un texto posible." *Letras femeninas* 16, nos. 1–2 (1990): 51–58.

Nixon, Rob. "Caribbean and African Appropriations of *The Tempest*." *Critical Inquiry* 13 (Spring 1987): 557–578.

Nolasco Armas, Margarita. "La antropología aplicada en México y su destino final: el indigenismo." *De eso que llaman antropología mexicana*. Ed. Arturo Warman et al. Mexico City: Editorial Nuestro Tiempo, 1970, pp. 66–93.

Ocampo, Aurora. "Rosario Castellanos and the Mexican Woman." *La Palabra y el Hombre* 53 (1985): 101–108.

Ocampo, Aurora M., and Ernesto Pardo Velázquez, eds. *Diccionario de escritores mexicanos*. Mexico City: Universidad de México, 1967.

O'Gorman, Edmundo. *La invención de América*. Bloomington: Indiana University Press, 1961.

Oyarzun, Kemy. "Beyond Hysteria: 'Haute Cuisine' and 'Cooking Lesson': Writing as Production." *Splintering Darkness: Latin American Writers in Search of Themselves*. Ed. Lucia Guerra Cunningham. Pittsburgh: Latin American Literary Review Press, 1990, pp. 87–110.

Pescatello, Ann, ed. *Female and Male in Latin America: Essays*. Pittsburgh: University of Pittsburgh Press, 1973.

Pineda, Vicente. *Historia de las sublevaciones habidas en el estado de Chiapas*. Chiapas: Tip. del Gobierno, 1888.

Poniatowska, Elena. *¡Ay vida, no me mereces! Carlos Fuentes, Rosario Castellanos, Juan Rulfo, la literatura de la onda*. Mexico City: Joaquín Mortiz, 1985.

———. "Prologue." *Meditación en el umbral: Antología poética. Rosario Castellanos*. Comp. Julian Palley. Mexico City: Fondo de Cultura Económica, 1985, pp. 21–22.

Portal, Marta. "Narrativa indigenista mexicana de mediados de siglo." *Cuadernos Hispanoamericanos* 298 (1975): 196–207.

———. *Proceso narrativo de la Revolución Mexicana*. Madrid: Ediciones Cultura Hispánica, 1977.

Pozas, Ricardo. *Chamula: Un pueblo indio de los altos de Chiapas*. Mexico City: Instituto Nacional Indigenista, 1959.

———. *Juan Pérez Jolote: Biografía de un Tzotzil*. Mexico City: Fondo de Cultura Económica, 1952.

Pratt, Mary Louise. "Women, Literature, and National Brotherhood." *Women, Culture, and Politics in Latin America*. Seminar on Feminism and Culture in Latin America. Berkeley and Los Angeles: University of California Press, 1990, pp. 48–73.

Rama, Angel. *Transculturación narrativa en América Latina*. Mexico City: Siglo XXI, 1982.

Reed, Nelson. *The Caste War of Yucatán*. Palo Alto, Calif.: Stanford University Press, 1964.

Reina, Leticia. *Las rebeliones campesinas en México, 1819–1906*. Mexico City: Siglo XXI, 1980.

Reyes Nevares, Beatriz, and Salvador Reyes Nevares. "Quien era y cómo era Rosario Castellanos." *¡Siempre!* (August 21, 1974): 14–15.

Rich, Adrienne. "Disloyal to Civilization: Feminism, Racism, Gynephobia." *On Lies, Secrets, and Silence: Selected Prose, 1966–78*. New York: Norton, 1979.

———. "When We Dead Awaken: Writing as Re-Vision." *On Lies, Secrets, and Silence: Selected Prose, 1966–78*. New York: Norton, 1979.

Riefkohl, Roman. "Note: Polysemous Structure in 'Lecturas tempranas.'" *Romance Notes* 23, no. 2 (1982): 115–118.

Rivero, Eliana. "Paradigma de la poética femenina hispanoamericana y su evolución: Rosario Castellanos." *De la crónica a la nueva narrativa mexicana: Coloquio sobre literatura mexicana*. Ed. Merlin H. Forster and Julio Ortega. Mexico City: Editorial Oasis, 1986, 391–406.

———. "Visión social y feminista en la obra poética de Rosario Castellanos." Ed. Maureen Ahern and Mary Seale Vásquez. Valencia: Albatrós Ediciones Hispanófila, 1980, pp. 85–97.

Robles, Martha. *La sombra fugitiva: Escritoras en la cultura nacional*. Mexico City: Universidad Nacional Autónoma de México, 1987, vol. 2: 147–191.

Rodríguez-Luis, Julio. *Hermenéutica y praxis del indigenismo: la novela indigenista de Clorinda Matto a José María Arguedas*. Mexico City: Fondo de Cultura Económica, 1980.

Rodríguez Peralta, Phyllis. "Images of Women in Rosario Castellanos' Prose." *Latin American Literary Review* 6 (1977): 68–80.

Rojas, Lourdes. "La indagación desmitificadora en la poesía de Rosario Castellanos." *Revista/Review Interamericana* 12, no. 1 (1982): 65–76.

Rosser, Harry C. *Conflict and Tradition in Rural Mexico: The Fiction of Social Realism*. Westham, Mass.: Crossroads Press, 1980.

Rus, Jan. "Whose Caste War? Indians, Ladinos, and the Chiapas 'Caste War' of 1869." *Spaniards and Indians in Southeast Mesoamerica: Essays on the History of Ethnic Relations*. Ed. Murdo McLeod and Robert Wasserstrom. Lincoln: University of Nebraska Press, 1983, pp. 127–168.

Said, Edward W. *Orientalism*. New York: Vintage Books, 1979.

Sarfati-Arnaud, Monique. "Los 'buenos' y los 'malos' en 'Modesta Gómez': Lectura ideológica de un cuento de Rosario Castellanos." *Actas del IX Congreso de la Asociación Internacional de Hispanistas: 18–26 de agosta 1986, Berlín*. Frankfurt: Sebastian Neumeister, 1989, pp. 703–709.

Schaeffer, Claudia. *Textured Lives: Women, Art, and Representation in Modern Mexico*. Tucson: University of Arizona Press, 1992.

Schlau, Stacey. "Conformity and Resistance to Enclosure: Female Voices in Rosario Castellanos' *Oficio de Tinieblas*." *Latin American Literary Review* 7, no. 24 (Spring–Summer 1984): 45–57.

Schwartz, Perla. *Rosario Castellanos: Mujer que supo latín*. Mexico City: Editorial Katún, 1984.

Schweickart, Patrocinio. "Reading Ourselves: Toward a Feminist Theory of Reading." *Gender and Reading: Essays on Readers, Texts, and Contexts.* Ed. Elizabeth A. Flynn and Patrocinio Schweickart. Baltimore, Md.: Johns Hopkins University Press, 1986, pp. 31–62.

Sedgwick, Eve Kosofsky. *Between Men: English Literature and Male Homosocial Desire.* New York: Columbia University Press, 1985.

Seminar on Feminism and Culture in Latin America. *Women, Culture, and Politics in Latin America.* Berkeley and Los Angeles: University of California Press, 1990.

Shakespeare, William. *A New Variorum Edition of The Tempest.* Ed. Horace Howard Furness. 10th ed. Philadelphia: Lippincott, 1892.

———. *The Oxford Shakespeare: The Tempest.* Ed. Stephen Orgel. Oxford: Clarendon Press, 1987.

Showalter, Elaine. "Feminist Criticism in the Wilderness." *Writing and Sexual Difference.* Ed. Elizabeth Abel. Chicago: University of Chicago Press, 1982, pp. 9–36.

Slocum, Marianna C. "The Origin of Corn and Other Tzeltal Myths." *Tlalocan* 1 (1965): 1–7.

Solana, Rafael, et al. *Los narradores ante el público.* Mexico City: Joaquín Mortiz, 1966.

Sommers, Joseph. *After the Storm.* Albuquerque: University of New Mexico Press, 1968.

———. "The Changing View of the Indian in Mexican Literature." *Hispania* 48 (March 1964): 47–55.

———. "El ciclo de Chiapas: Nueva corriente literaria." *Cuadernos Americanos* 133 (1964): 246–261.

———. "Forma e ideología en *Oficio de tinieblas* de Rosario Castellanos." *Revista de Crítica Literaria Latinoamericana* 7–8 (1978): 73–91.

———. "Literatura e historia: Las contradicciones de la ficción indigenista." *Revista de Crítica Literaria* 10 (1979): 9–39.

———. "Rosario Castellanos: Nuevo enfoque del indio mexicano." *La Palabra y el Hombre* 8 (1964): 83–88.

Soto, Shirlene. *Emergence of the Modern Mexican Woman: Her Participation in Revolution and Struggle for Equality, 1910–1940.* Denver, Colo.: Arden Press, 1990.

Spivak, Gayatri. "Three Women's Texts and a Critique of Imperialism." *Critical Inquiry* 12 (Autumn 1985): 243–261.

Steele, Cynthia. *Narrativa indigenista en los Estados Unidos y México.* Mexico City: Instituto Nacional Indigenista, 1985.

———. "The Other Within: Class and Ethnicity as Difference in Mexican Women's Literature." *Cultural and Historical Grounding for Hispanic and Luso-Brazilian Feminist Literary Criticism.* Ed. Hernán Vidal. Minneapolis, Minn.: Institute for the Study of Ideologies and Literature, 1989, pp. 297–328.

Stoll, A. K. "Arthur Smith salva su alma": Rosario Castellanos and Social Protest." *Crítica Hispánica* 7, no. 2 (1985): 141–147.

Sweet, David G., and Gary B. Nash. *Struggle and Survival in Colonial America.* Berkeley and Los Angeles: University of California Press, 1981.

Tedlock, Dennis, trans. *Popol Vuh: The Mayan Book of Life.* New York: Simon and Schuster, 1985.

Tron de Bouchony, Claire. "Women in the Work of Rosario Castellanos: A Struggle for Identity." *Culture* 8, no. 3 (1982): 66–82.

Turner, Victor. "Social Dramas and Stories about Them." *On Narrative.* Ed. W. J. T. Mitchell. Chicago: University of Chicago Press, 1981, pp. 137–164.

Urbano, Victoria. "La justicia femenina en Rosario Castellanos." *Letras Femeninas* 1, no. 2 (Fall 1975): 9–20.

Van Zantwijk, R. A. M. "Indigenisimo: A Philosophy and a Method of Guided Development of the Aboriginal Minorities in Mexico: Historical Background and Actual Orientations." *Plural Societies* 7 (1976): 95–103.

Vásquez, Mary Seale. "Rosario Castellanos: Image and Idea." Ed. Maureen Ahern and Mary Seale Vásquez. Valencia: Albatrós Ediciones Hispanófila, 1980, pp. 15–40.

Villa Rojas, Alfonso. "El centro coordinador Tzeltal-Tzotzil." *Los centros coordinadores indigenistas: Edición conmemorativa en ocasión del XXXV Congreso Internacional de Americanistas.* Mexico City: Instituto Nacional Indigenista, 1962, pp. 51–78.

Villoro, Luis. *Los grandes momentos del indigenismo en México.* Mexico City: Colegio de México, 1950.

Vogt, Evon A. *The Zinacantecos of Mexico: A Modern Maya Way of Life.* New York: Holt, Rinehart and Winston, 1970.

Wade, Gerald E., and William H. Archer. "The Indigenista Novel since 1889." *Hispania* 33 (August 1950): 211–220.

Wallace, Anthony F. C. "Revitalization Movements." *American Anthropologist* 58 (1956): 264–281.

Warman, Arturo, et al. *De eso que llaman antropología mexicana.* Mexico City: Editorial Nuestro Tiempo, 1970.

Wasserstrom, Robert. "Spaniards and Indians in Colonial Chiapas, 1528–1790." *Spaniards and Indians in Southeast Mesoamerica: Essays on the History of Ethnic Relations.* Ed. Murdo McLeod and Robert Wasserstrom. Lincoln: University of Nebraska Press, 1983, pp. 92–125.

Welch, Sharon D. *Communities of Resistance and Solidarity: A Feminist Theology of Liberation.* Maryknoll, N.Y.: Orbis Books, 1985.

Williams, Raymond. *Keywords: A Vocabulary of Culture and Society.* Rev. ed. New York: Oxford University Press, 1983.

———. *Marxism and Literature.* Oxford: Oxford University Press, 1977.

Wolf, Eric. *Sons of the Shaking Earth.* Chicago: University of Chicago Press, 1959.

Woolf, Virginia. *A Room of One's Own.* New York: Harcourt, 1929.

Wynters, Sylvia. "Afterword: Beyond Miranda's Meanings: Un/silencing the 'Demonic Ground' of Caliban's 'Woman.'" *Out of the Kumbla: Caribbean Women and Literature.* Ed. Carole Boyce Davies and Elaine Savory Fido. Trenton, N.J.: Africa World Press, 1990, 355–372.

Index

M8202-TX
62